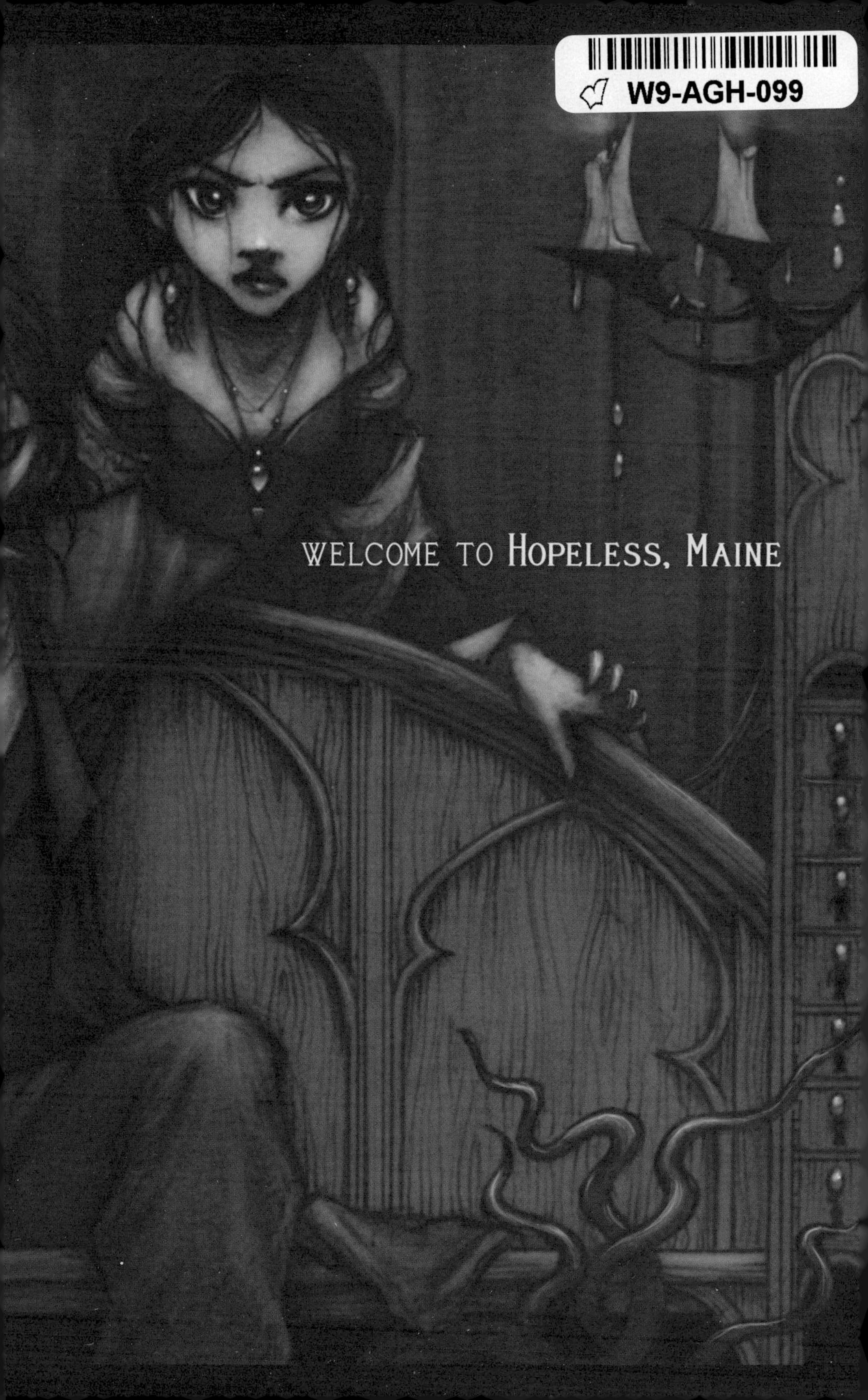
WELCOME TO HOPELESS, MAINE

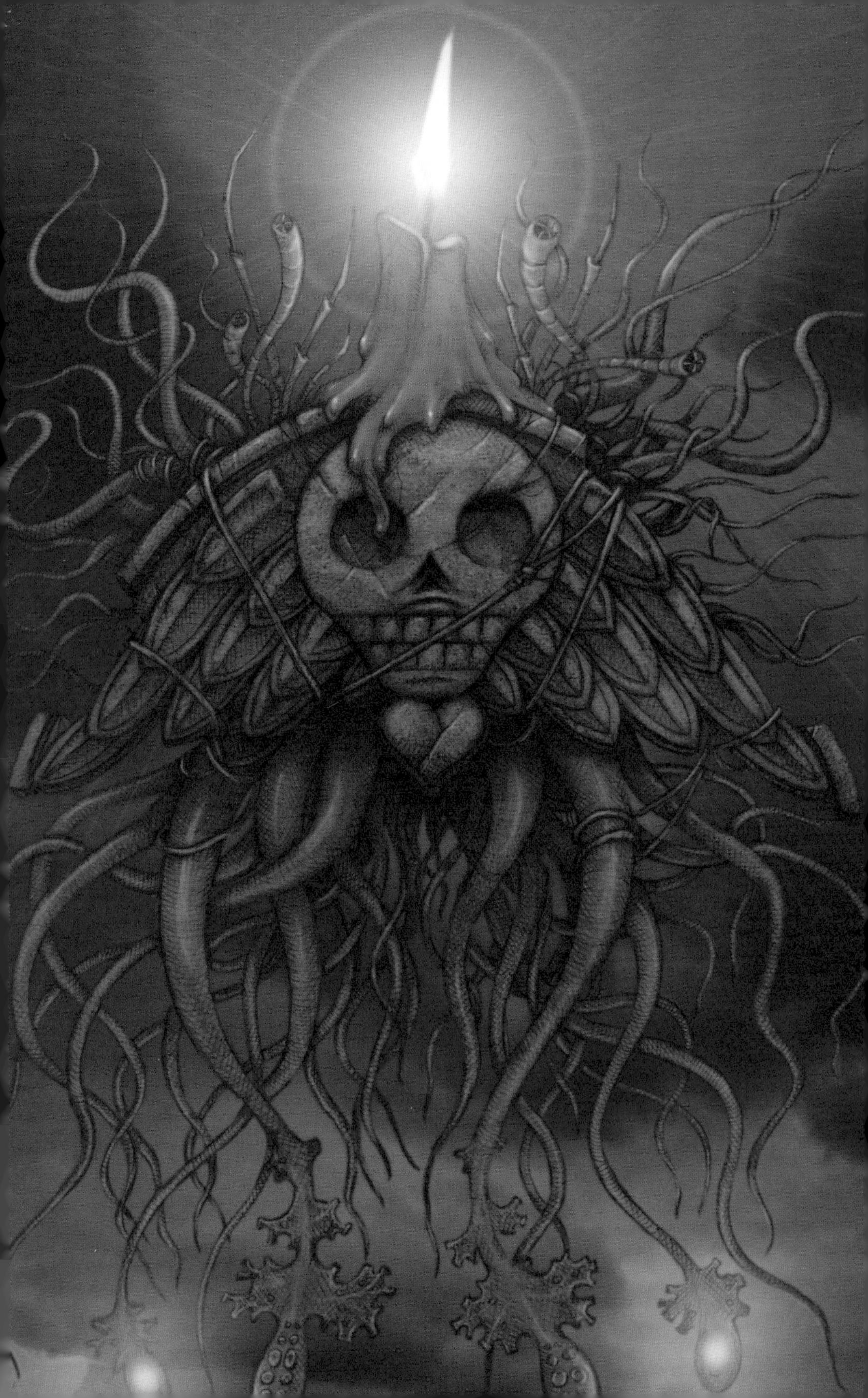

HOPELESS, MAINE
+PERSONAL DEMONS+ ™

TOM & NIMUE BROWN

ARCHAIA ENTERTAINMENT LLC
WWW.ARCHAIA.COM

HOPELESS, MAINE
+PERSONAL DEMONS+

CREATED BY
TOM & NIMUE BROWN

WRITTEN BY
TOM & NIMUE BROWN

ILLUSTRATED BY
TOM BROWN

Deron Bennett, *Lettering*
Paul Morrissey, *Editor*
Scott Newman, *Production Manager*

Archaia Entertainment LLC

PJ Bickett, *CEO*
Mark Smylie, *CCO*
Mike Kennedy, *Publisher*
Stephen Christy, *Editor-in-Chief*

Published by **Archaia**

Archaia Entertainment LLC
1680 Vine Street, Suite 1010
Los Angeles, California, 90028, USA
www.archaia.com

ARCHAIA
NEW STORIES. NEW WORLDS.

HOPELESS, MAINE Volume One PERSONAL DEMONS Original Graphic Novel Hardcover. April 2012. FIRST PRINTING.

10 9 8 7 6 5 4 3 2 1

ISBN: 1-936393-57-3
ISBN 13: 978-1-936393-57-2

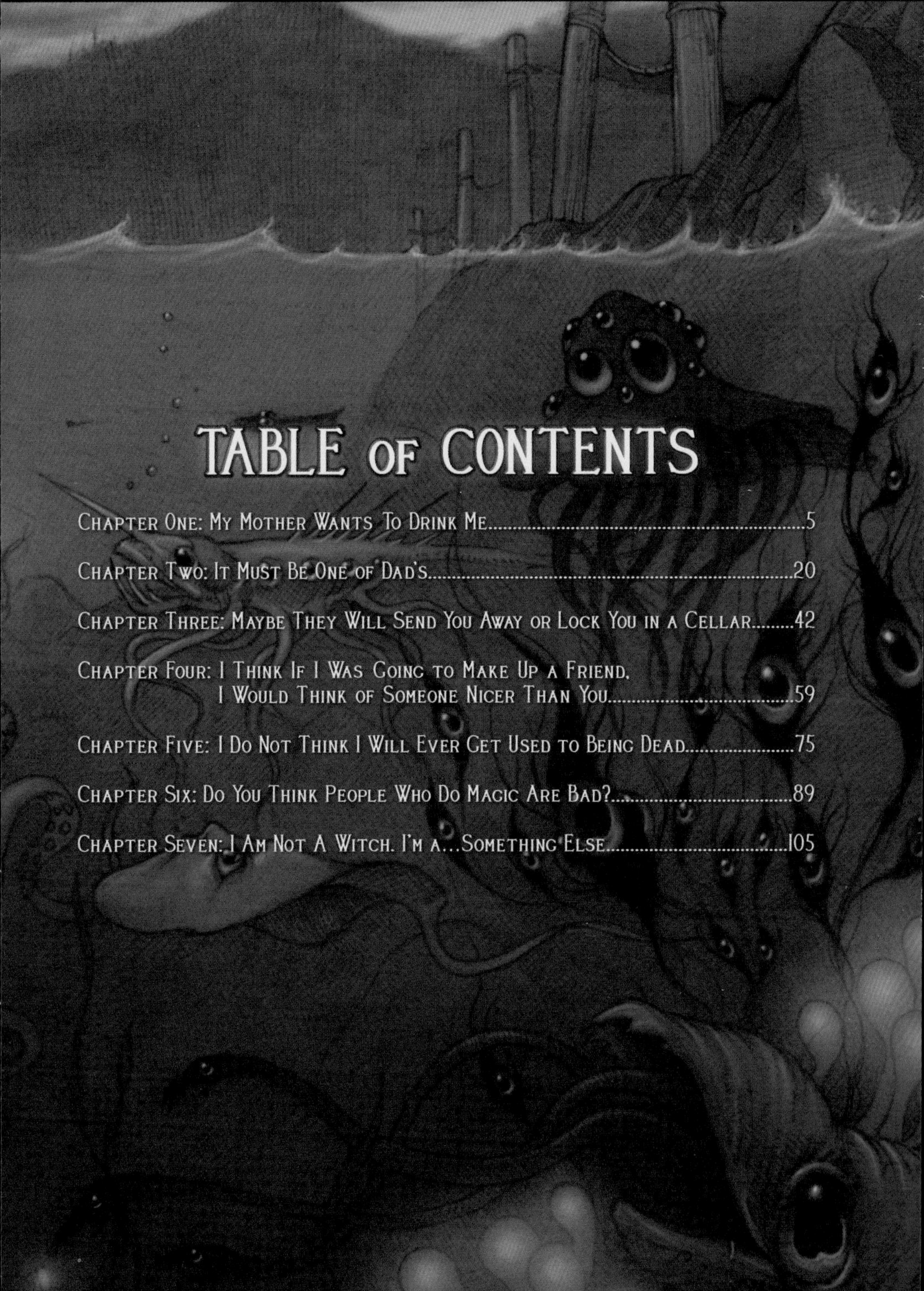

TABLE of CONTENTS

DEDICATION

THIS ONE IS FOR OUR BOYS,
CORMAC AND JAMES.

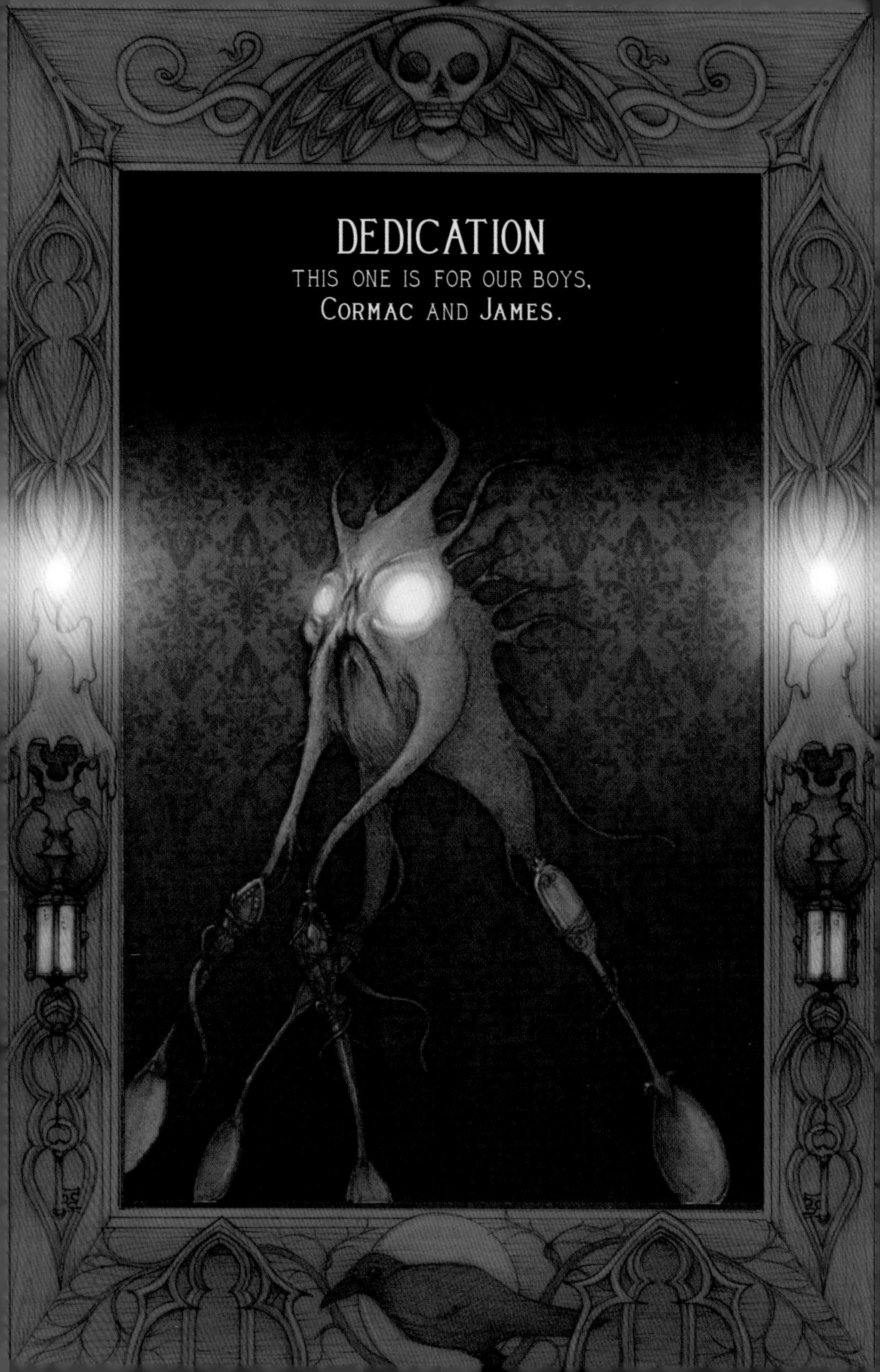

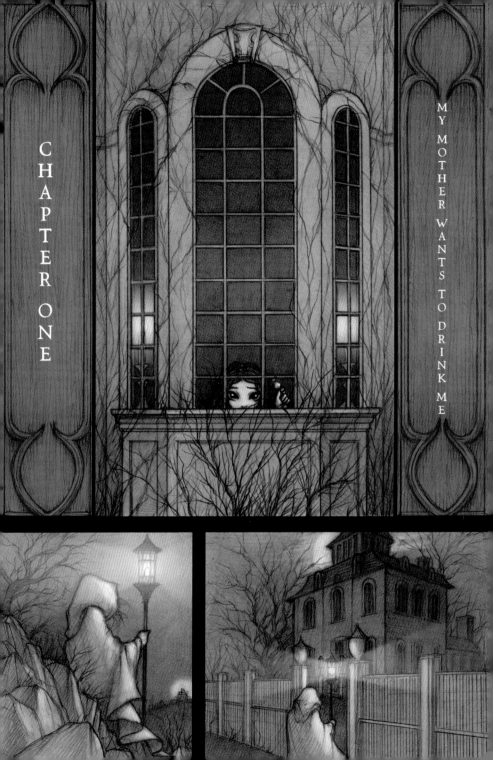

CHAPTER ONE

MY MOTHER WANTS TO DRINK ME

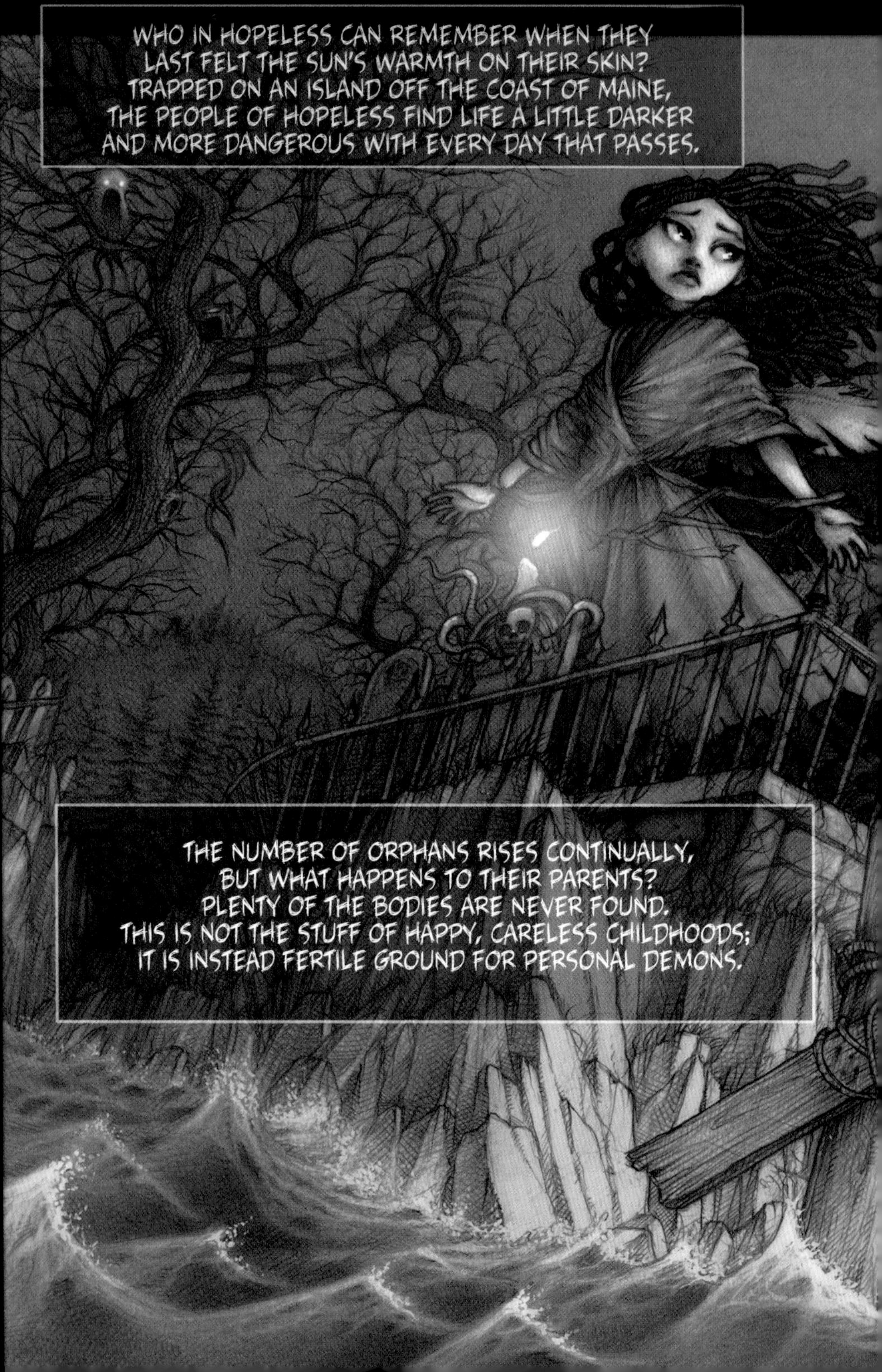
WHO IN HOPELESS CAN REMEMBER WHEN THEY LAST FELT THE SUN'S WARMTH ON THEIR SKIN? TRAPPED ON AN ISLAND OFF THE COAST OF MAINE, THE PEOPLE OF HOPELESS FIND LIFE A LITTLE DARKER AND MORE DANGEROUS WITH EVERY DAY THAT PASSES.
THE NUMBER OF ORPHANS RISES CONTINUALLY, BUT WHAT HAPPENS TO THEIR PARENTS? PLENTY OF THE BODIES ARE NEVER FOUND. THIS IS NOT THE STUFF OF HAPPY, CARELESS CHILDHOODS; IT IS INSTEAD FERTILE GROUND FOR PERSONAL DEMONS.

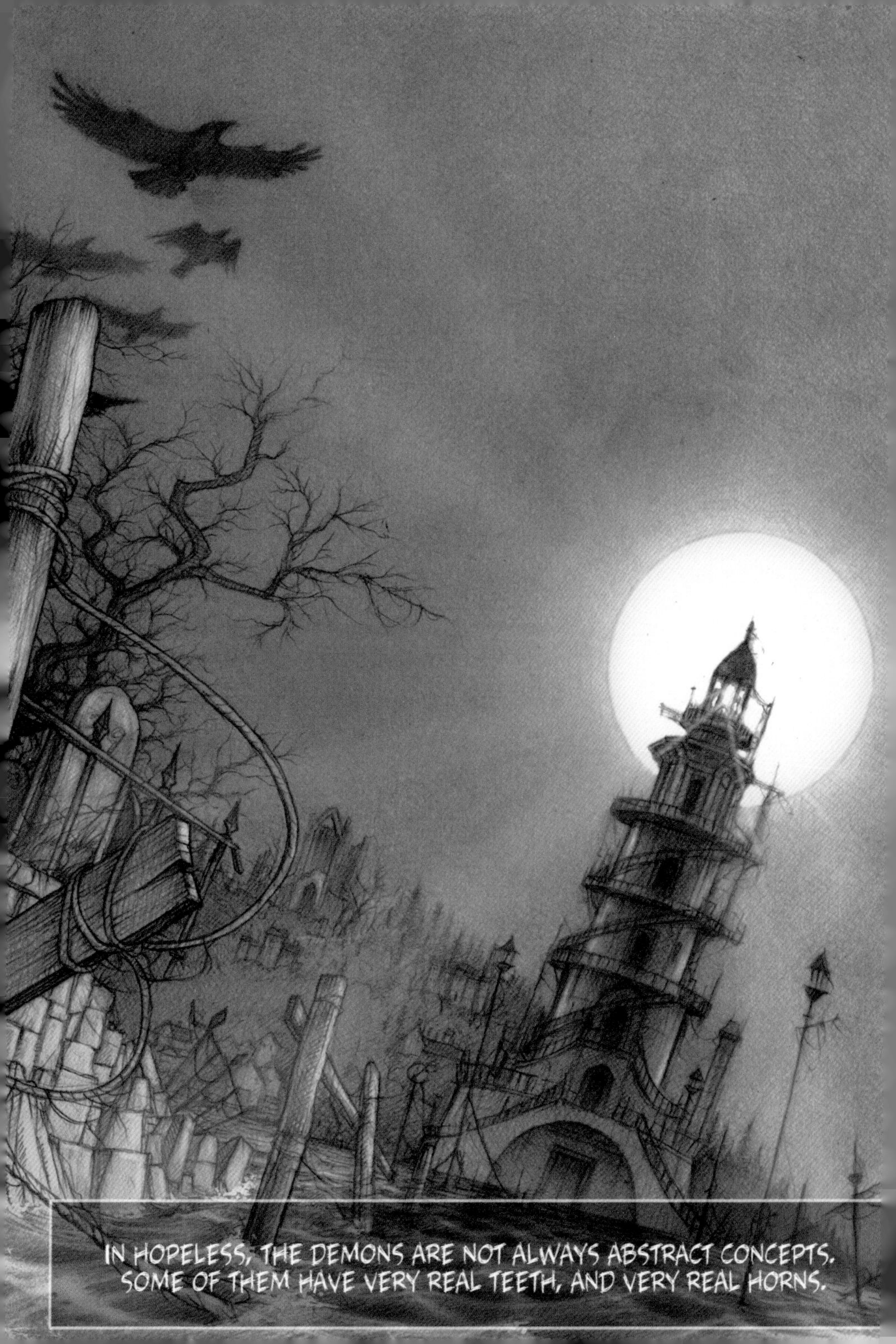
IN HOPELESS, THE DEMONS ARE NOT ALWAYS ABSTRACT CONCEPTS.
SOME OF THEM HAVE VERY REAL TEETH, AND VERY REAL HORNS.

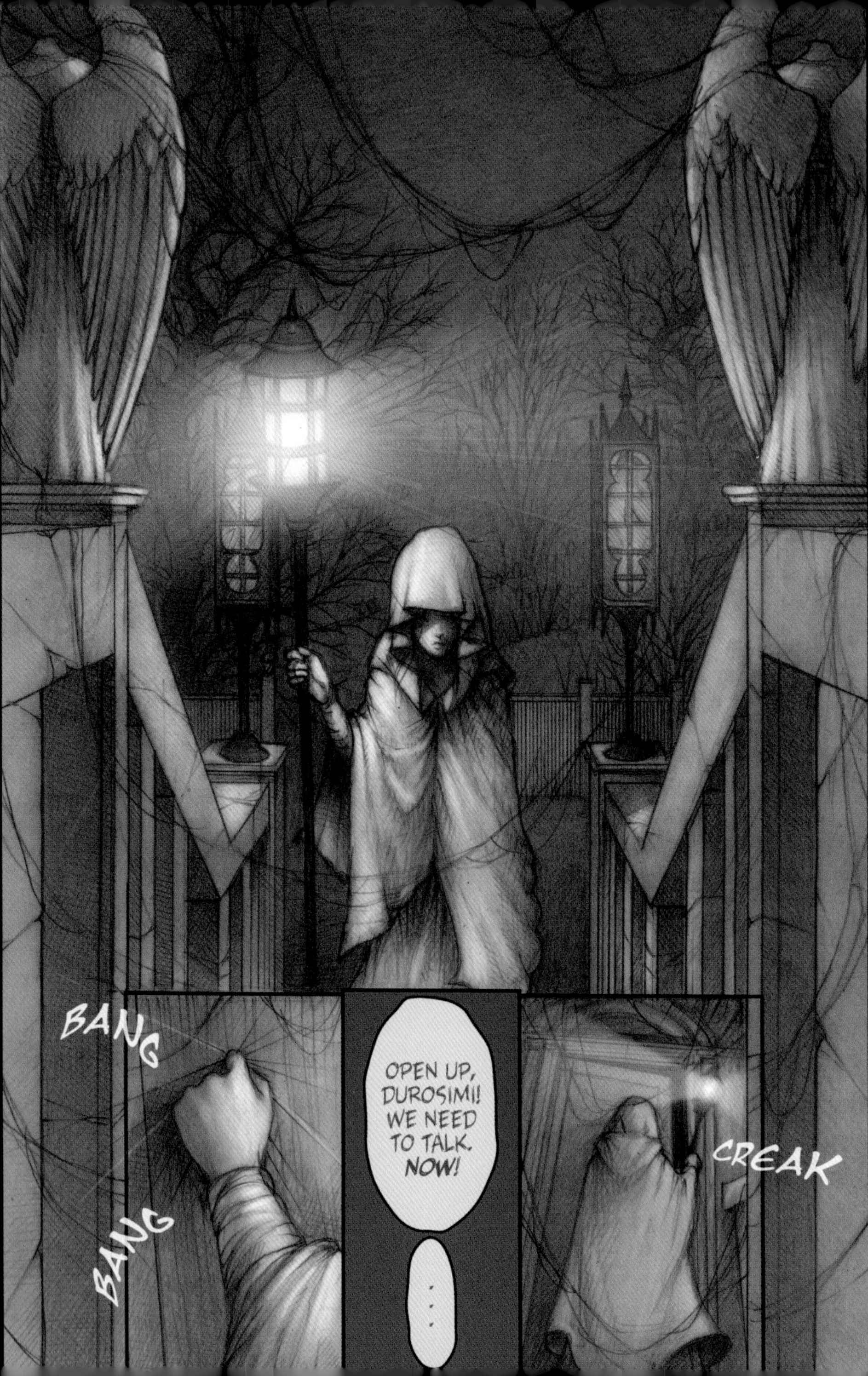
BANG
BANG
OPEN UP, DUROSIMI! WE NEED TO TALK. NOW!
...
CREAK

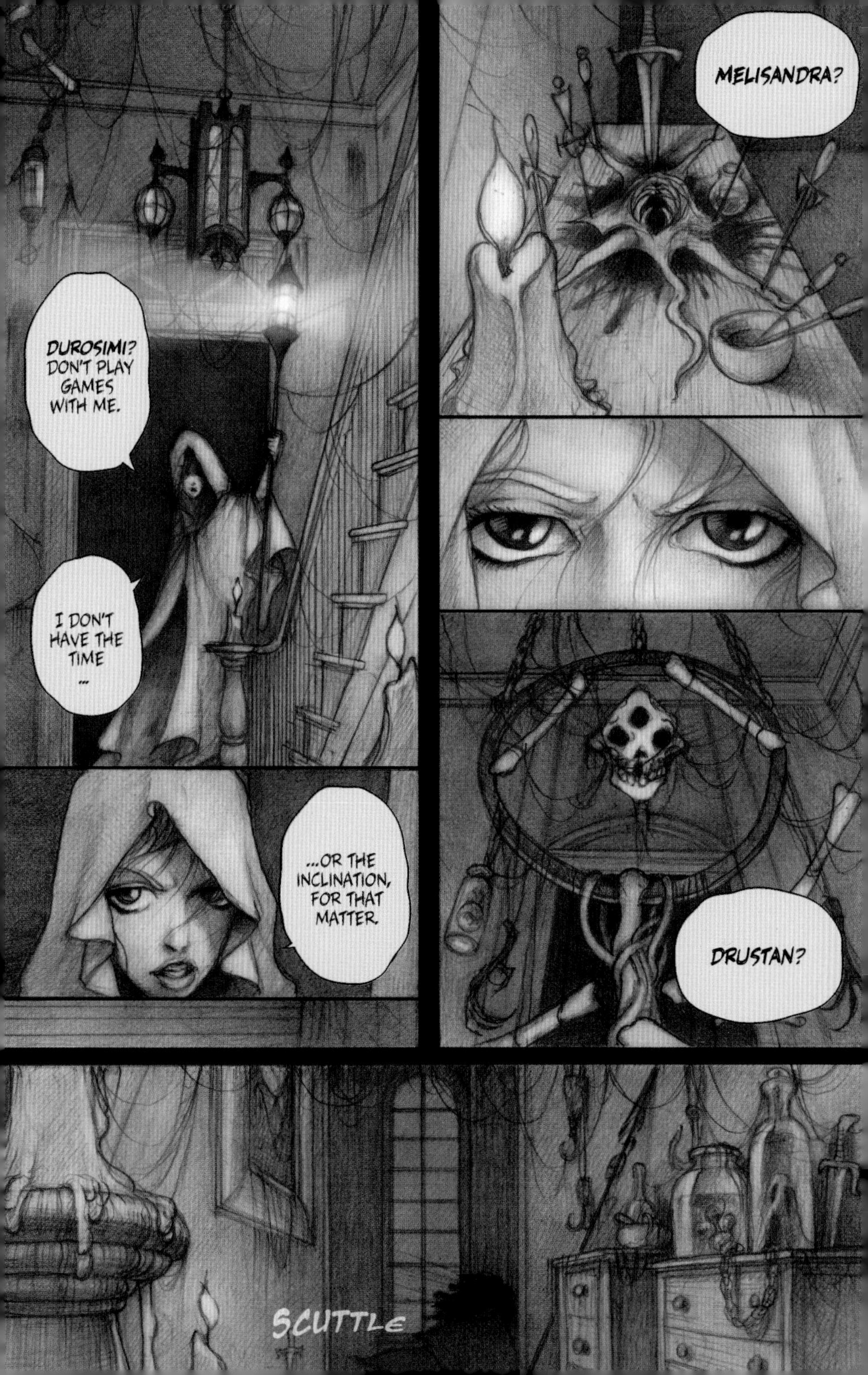
DUROSIMI? DON'T PLAY GAMES WITH ME.
I DON'T HAVE THE TIME ...
...OR THE INCLINATION, FOR THAT MATTER.
MELISANDRA?
DRUSTAN?
SCUTTLE

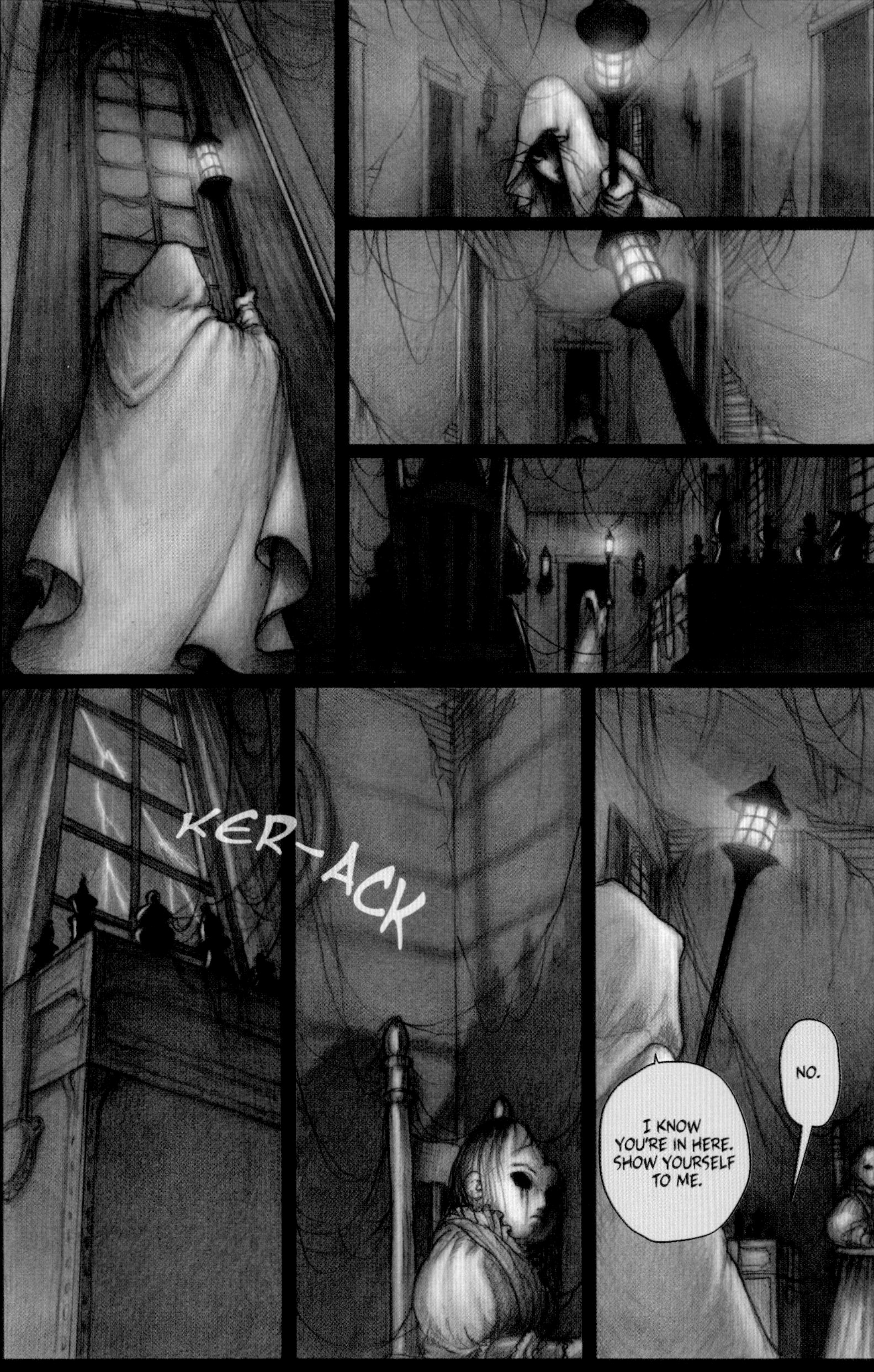
KER-ACK
I KNOW YOU'RE IN HERE. SHOW YOURSELF TO ME.
NO.

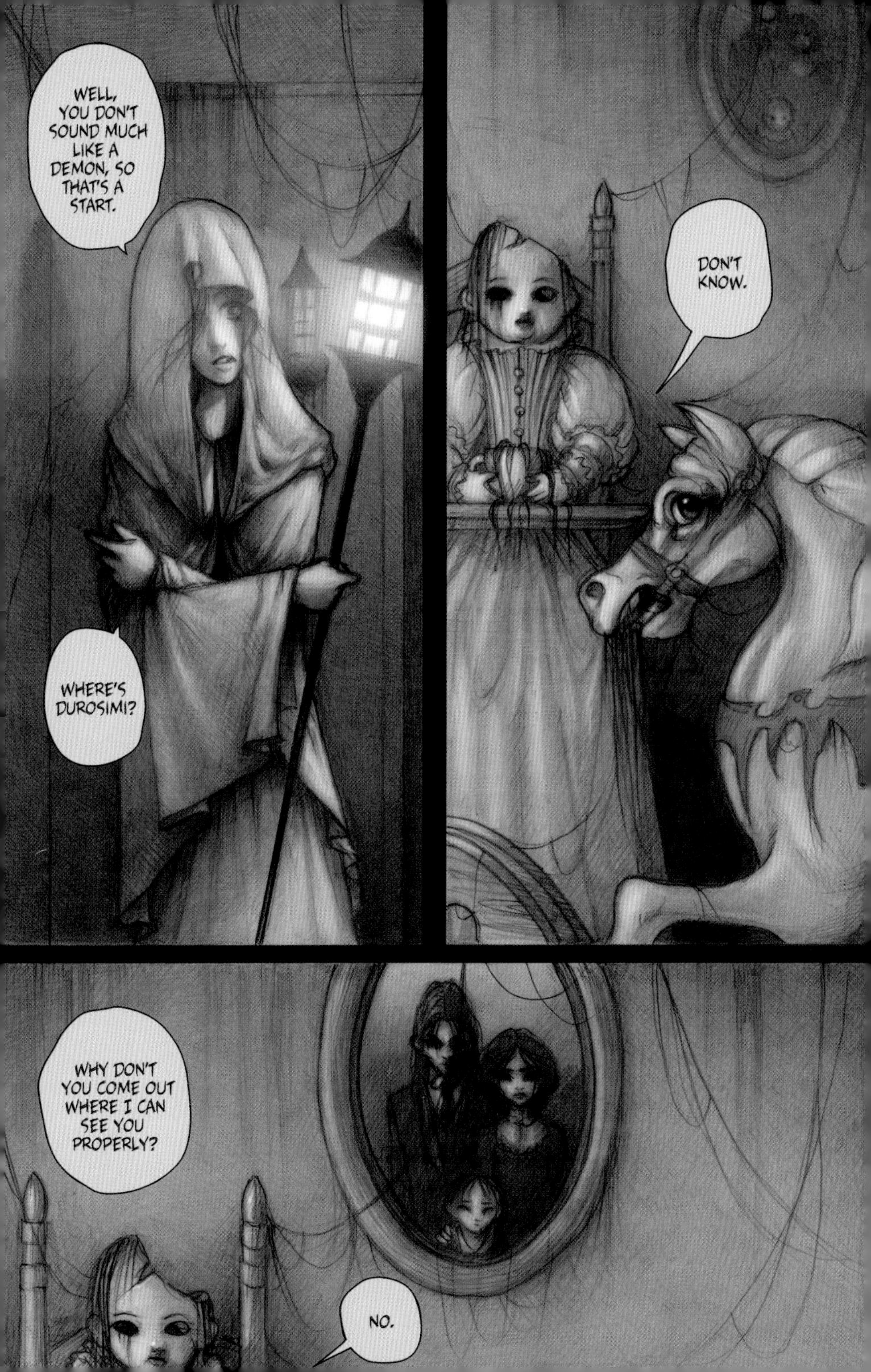
WELL, YOU DON'T SOUND MUCH LIKE A DEMON, SO THAT'S A START.
WHERE'S DUROSIMI?
DON'T KNOW.
WHY DON'T YOU COME OUT WHERE I CAN SEE YOU PROPERLY?
NO.

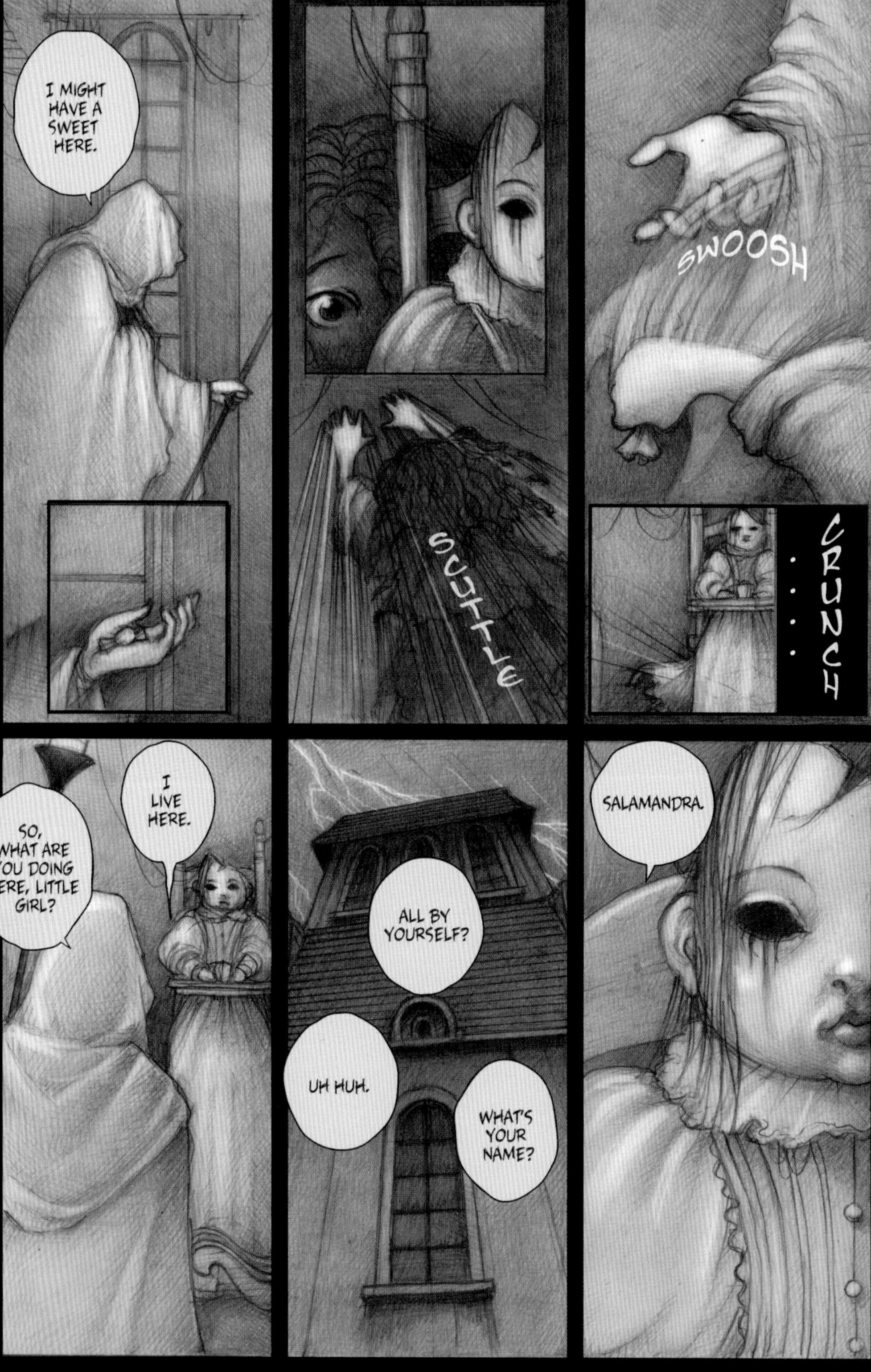

I MIGHT HAVE A SWEET HERE.
SWOOSH
SCUTTLE
. . . . CRUNCH
SO, WHAT ARE YOU DOING HERE, LITTLE GIRL?
I LIVE HERE.
ALL BY YOURSELF?
UH HUH.
WHAT'S YOUR NAME?
SALAMANDRA.

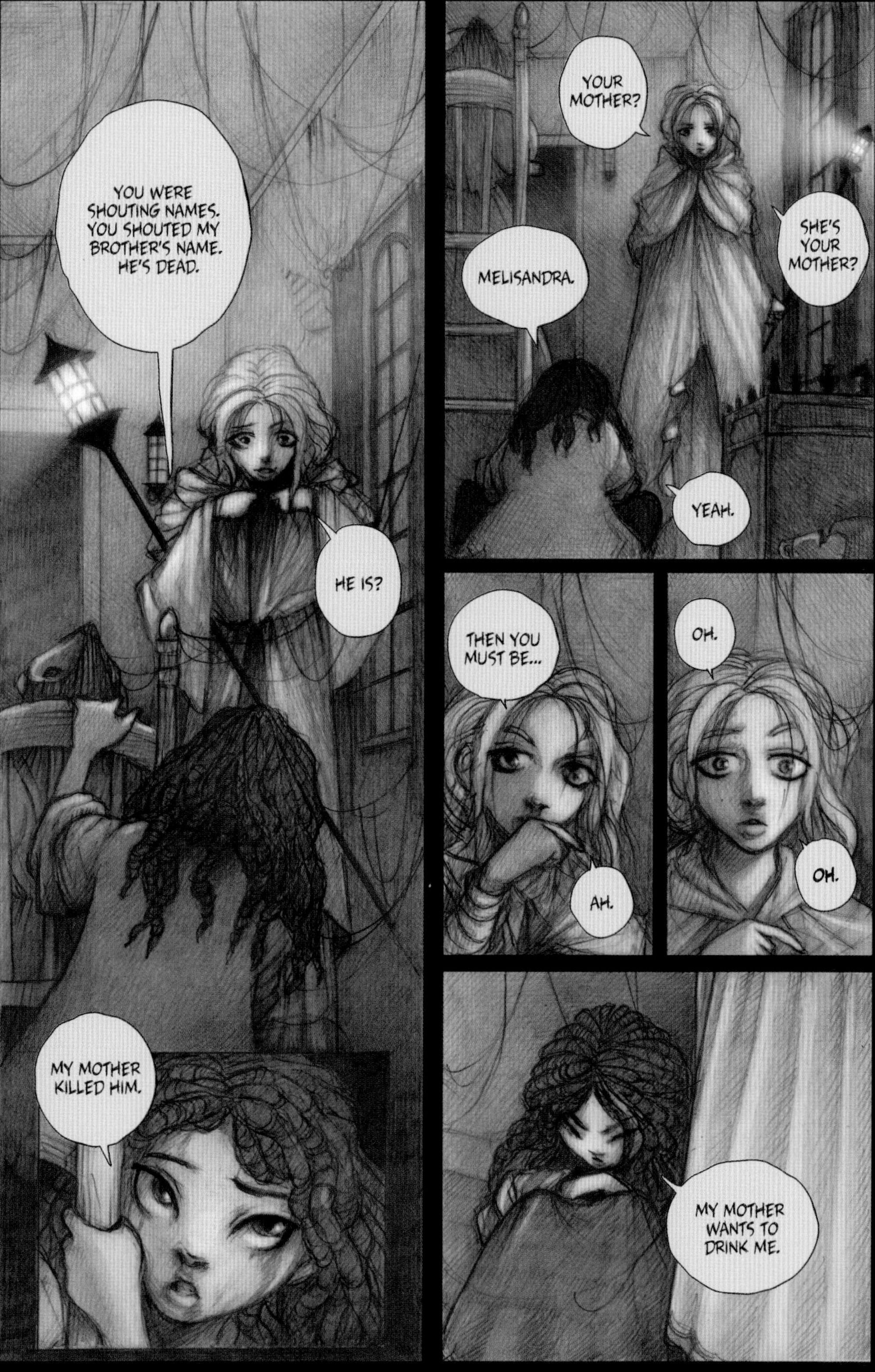
YOU WERE SHOUTING NAMES. YOU SHOUTED MY BROTHER'S NAME. HE'S DEAD.
HE IS?
MY MOTHER KILLED HIM.
YOUR MOTHER?
MELISANDRA.
SHE'S YOUR MOTHER?
YEAH.
THEN YOU MUST BE...
AH.
OH.
OH.
MY MOTHER WANTS TO DRINK ME.

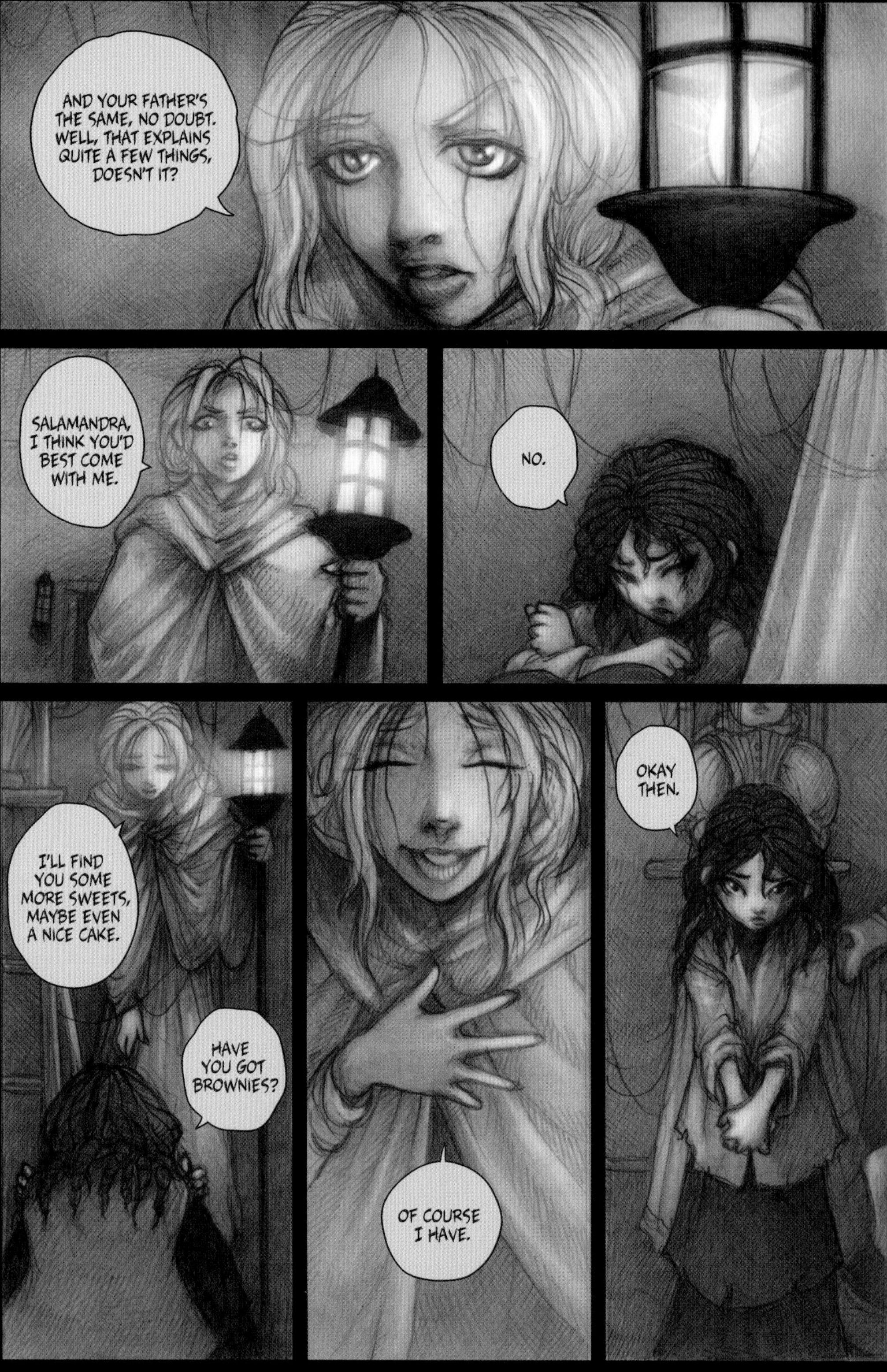
AND YOUR FATHER'S THE SAME, NO DOUBT. WELL, THAT EXPLAINS QUITE A FEW THINGS, DOESN'T IT?
SALAMANDRA, I THINK YOU'D BEST COME WITH ME.
NO.
I'LL FIND YOU SOME MORE SWEETS, MAYBE EVEN A NICE CAKE.
HAVE YOU GOT BROWNIES?
OF COURSE I HAVE.
OKAY THEN.

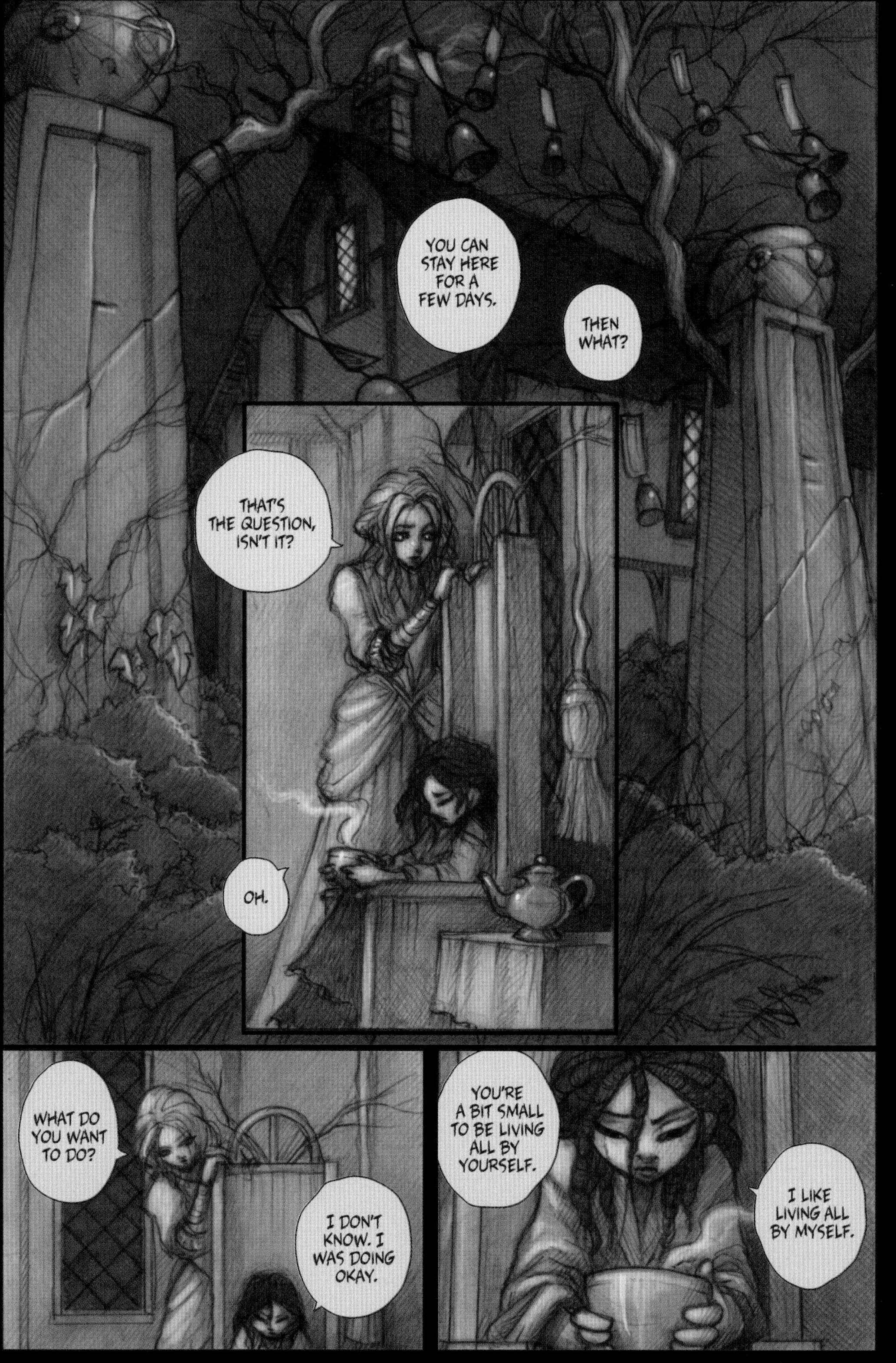
YOU CAN STAY HERE FOR A FEW DAYS.
THEN WHAT?
THAT'S THE QUESTION, ISN'T IT?
OH.
WHAT DO YOU WANT TO DO?
I DON'T KNOW. I WAS DOING OKAY.
YOU'RE A BIT SMALL TO BE LIVING ALL BY YOURSELF.
I LIKE LIVING ALL BY MYSELF.

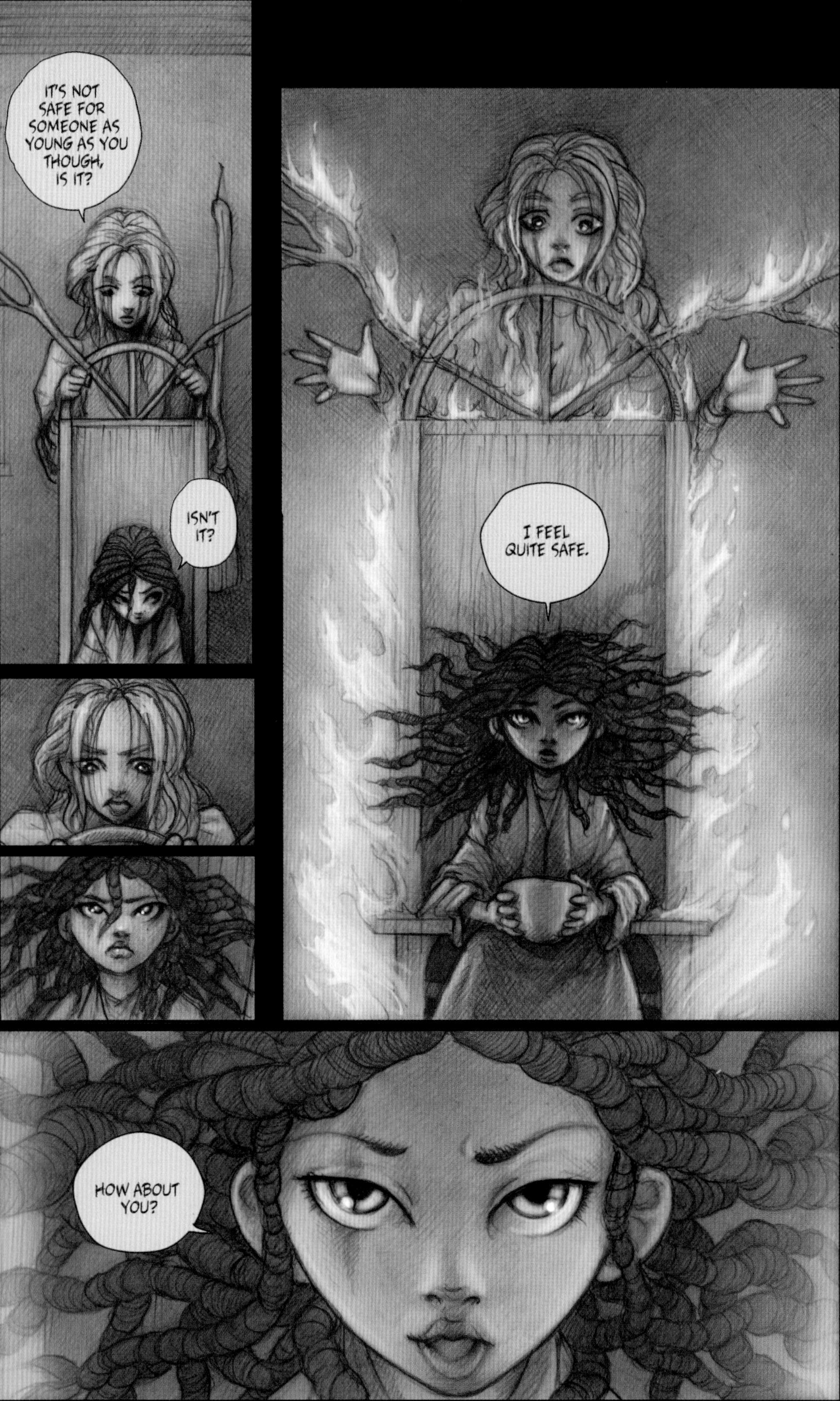
IT'S NOT SAFE FOR SOMEONE AS YOUNG AS YOU THOUGH, IS IT?
ISN'T IT?
I FEEL QUITE SAFE.
HOW ABOUT YOU?

I THINK WE NEED TO FIND YOU SOMEWHERE TO LIVE, SALAMANDRA.
BUT NOT HERE.
DEFINITELY NOT HERE.
OH.

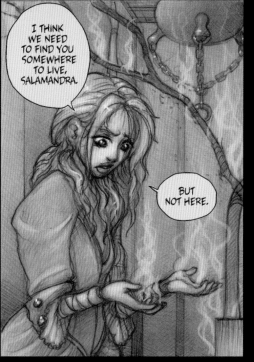

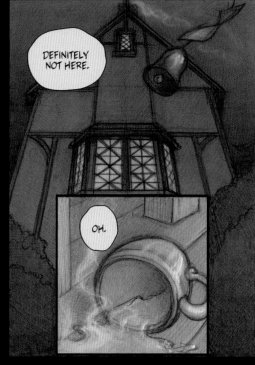

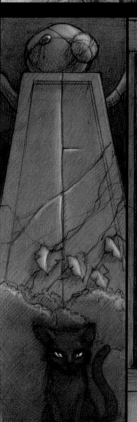

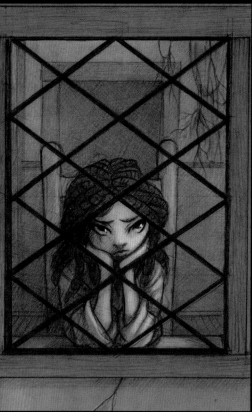

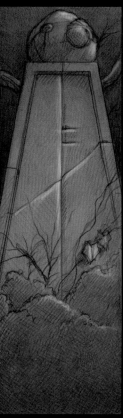

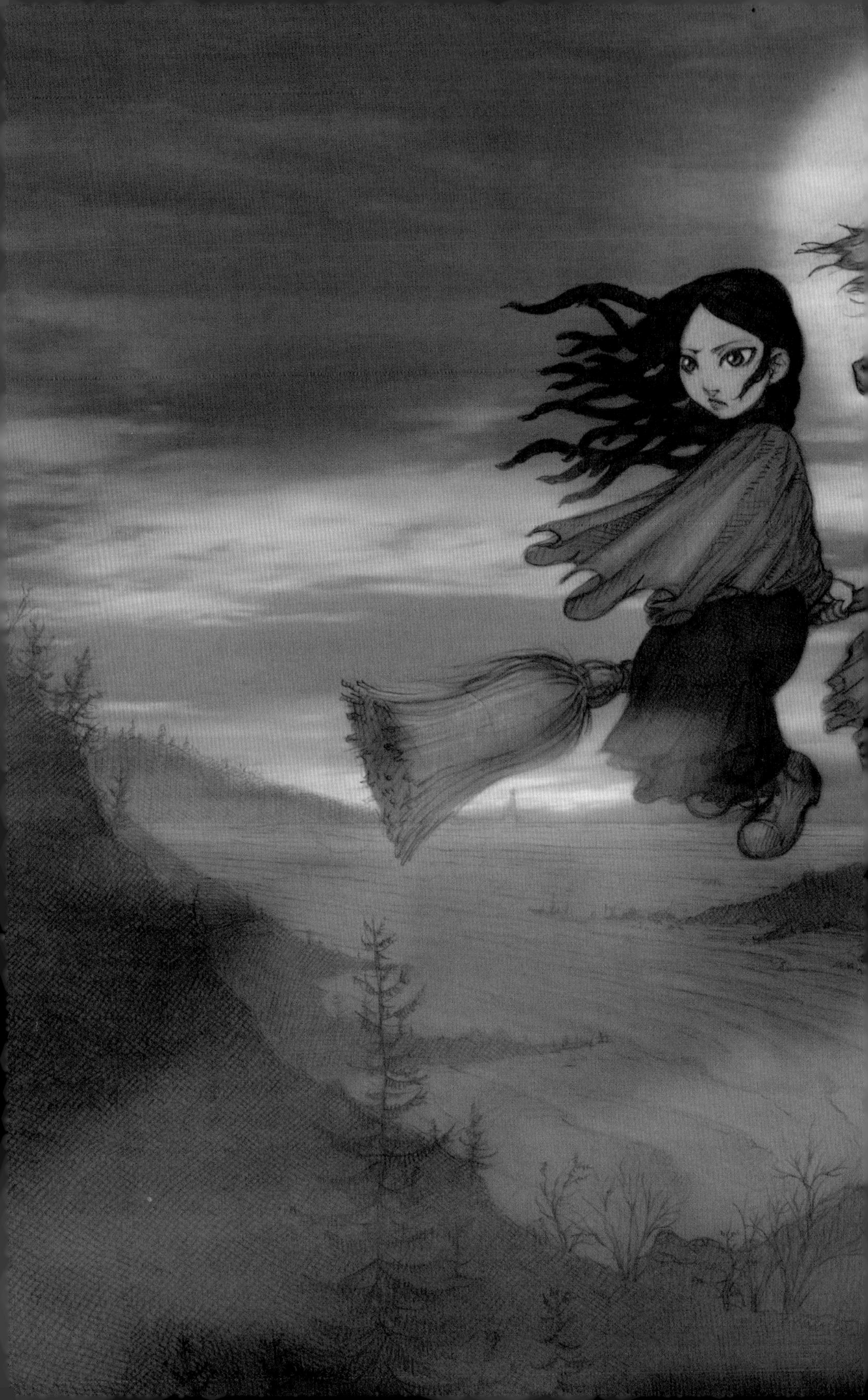

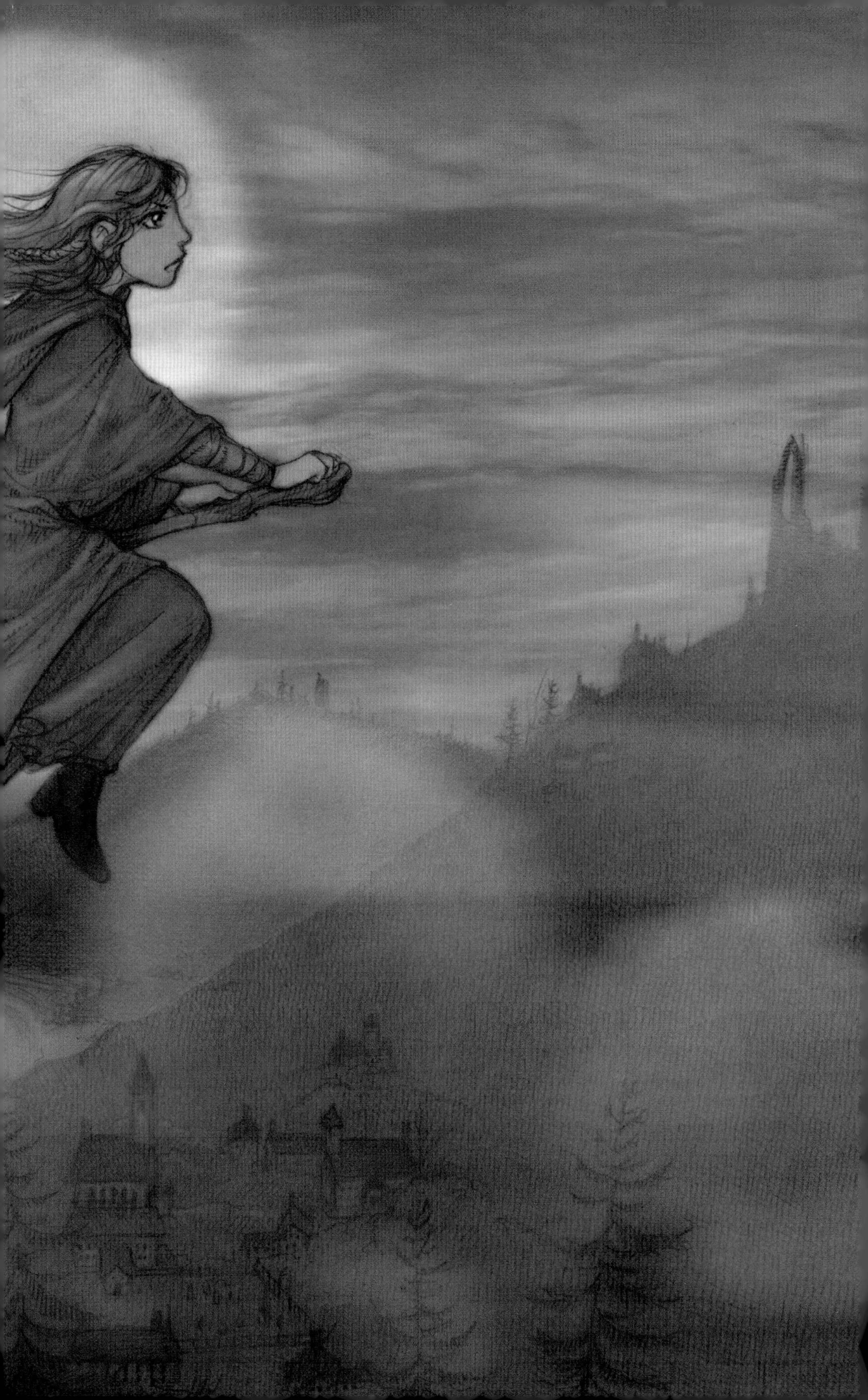

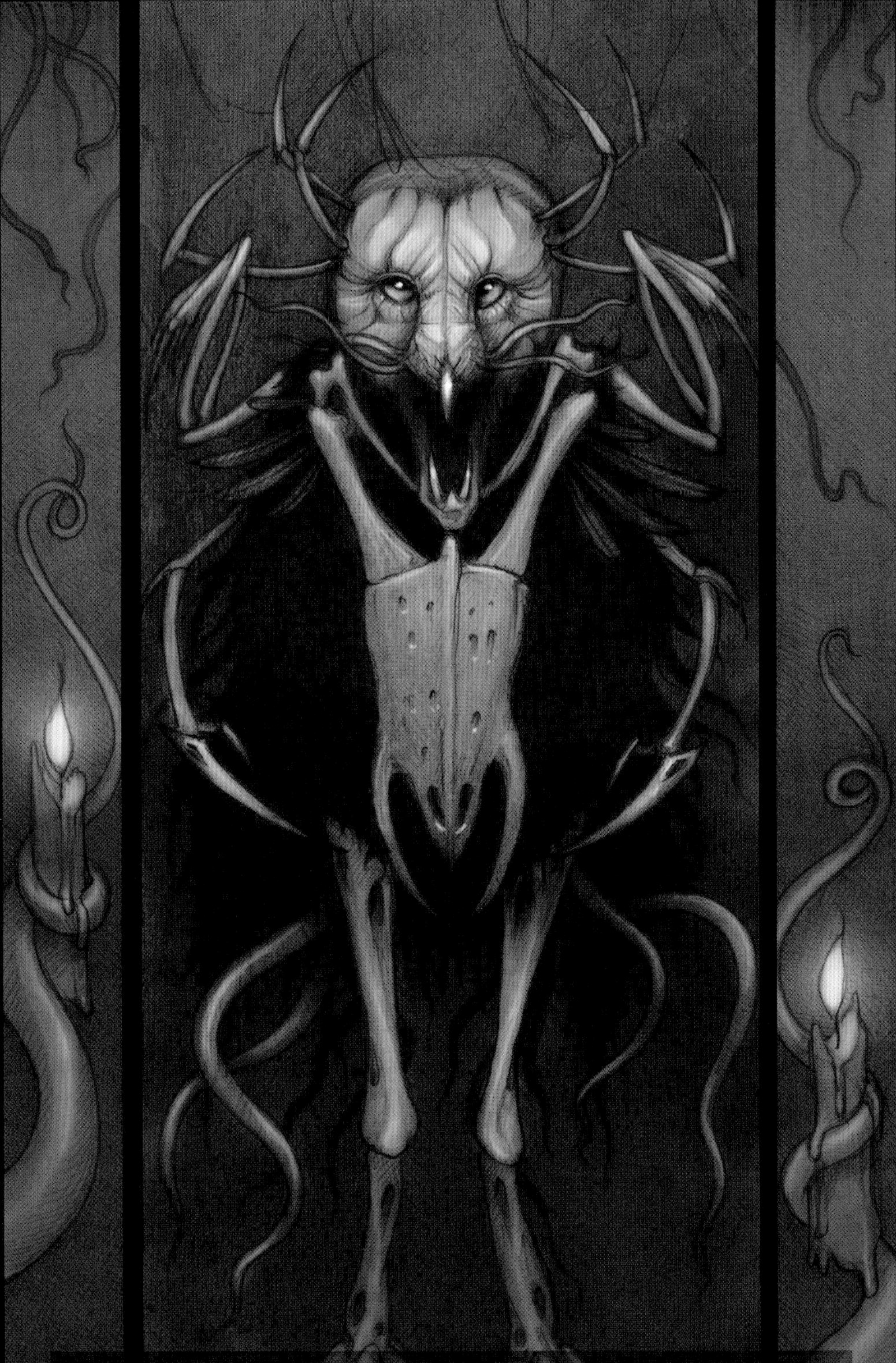

IT MUST BE ONE OF DAD'S

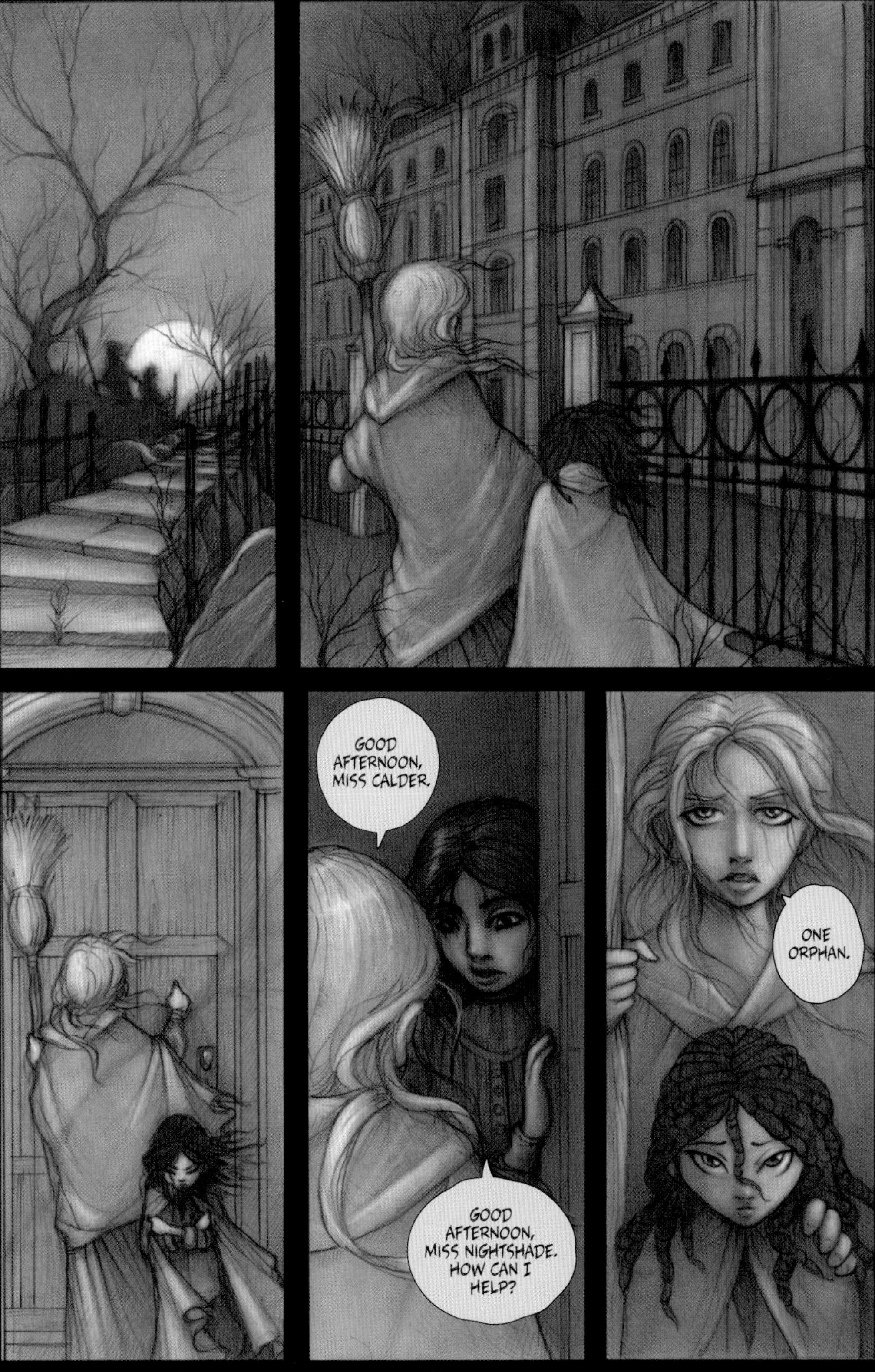
GOOD AFTERNOON, MISS CALDER.
GOOD AFTERNOON, MISS NIGHTSHADE. HOW CAN I HELP?
ONE ORPHAN.

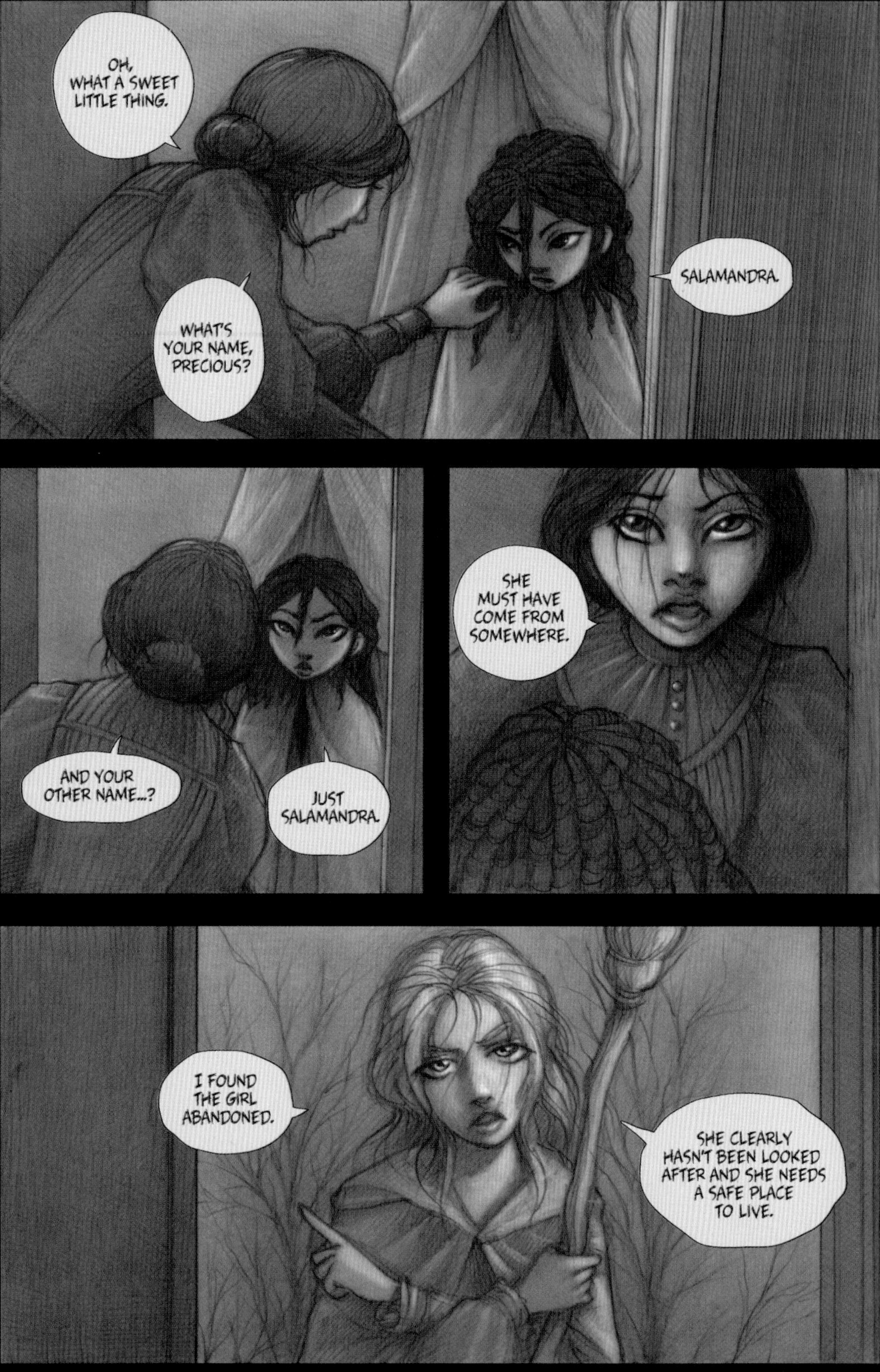
OH, WHAT A SWEET LITTLE THING.
WHAT'S YOUR NAME, PRECIOUS?
SALAMANDRA.
AND YOUR OTHER NAME...?
JUST SALAMANDRA.
SHE MUST HAVE COME FROM SOMEWHERE.
I FOUND THE GIRL ABANDONED.
SHE CLEARLY HASN'T BEEN LOOKED AFTER AND SHE NEEDS A SAFE PLACE TO LIVE.

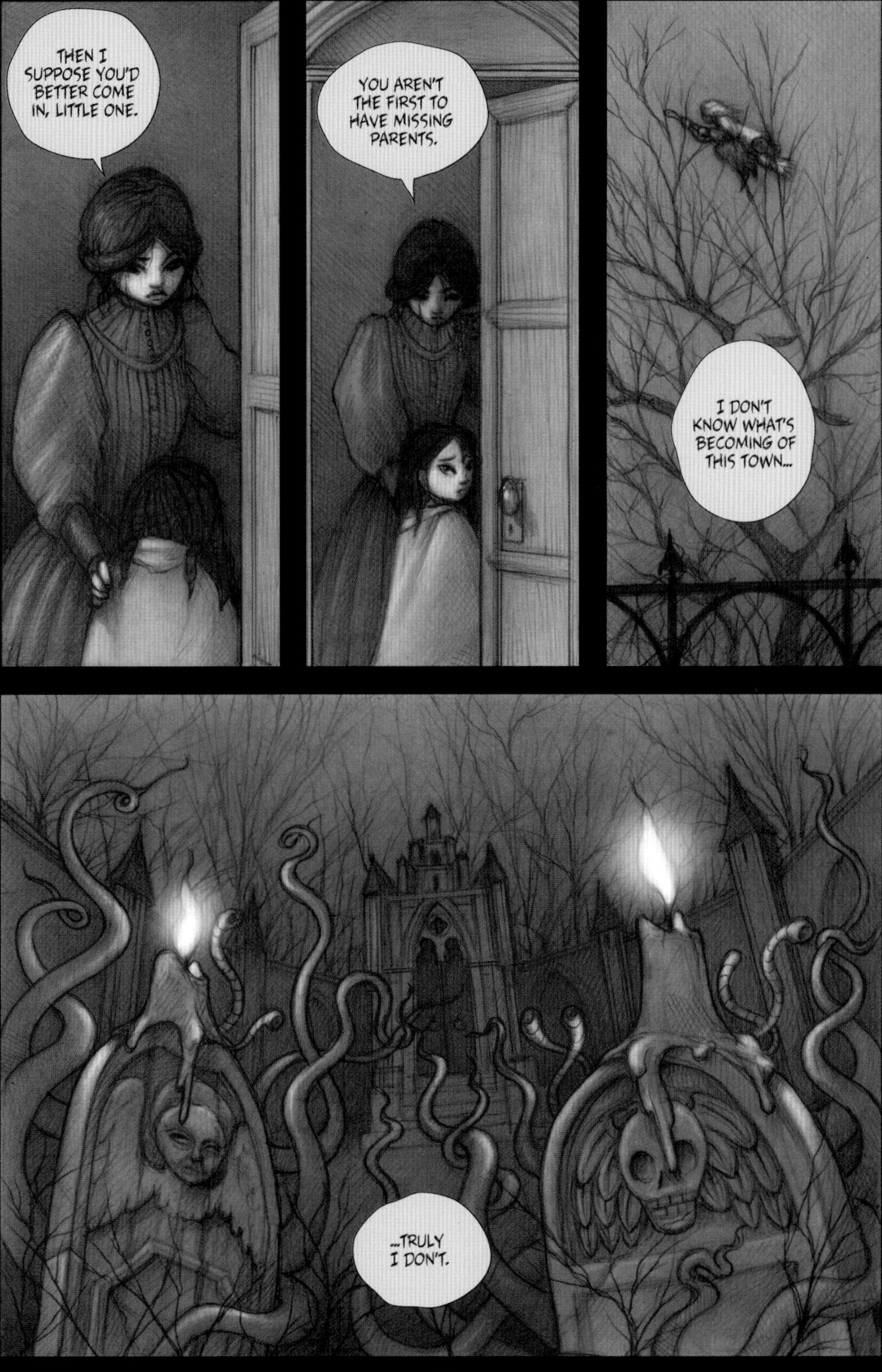
THEN I SUPPOSE YOU'D BETTER COME IN, LITTLE ONE.
YOU AREN'T THE FIRST TO HAVE MISSING PARENTS.
I DON'T KNOW WHAT'S BECOMING OF THIS TOWN...
...TRULY I DON'T.

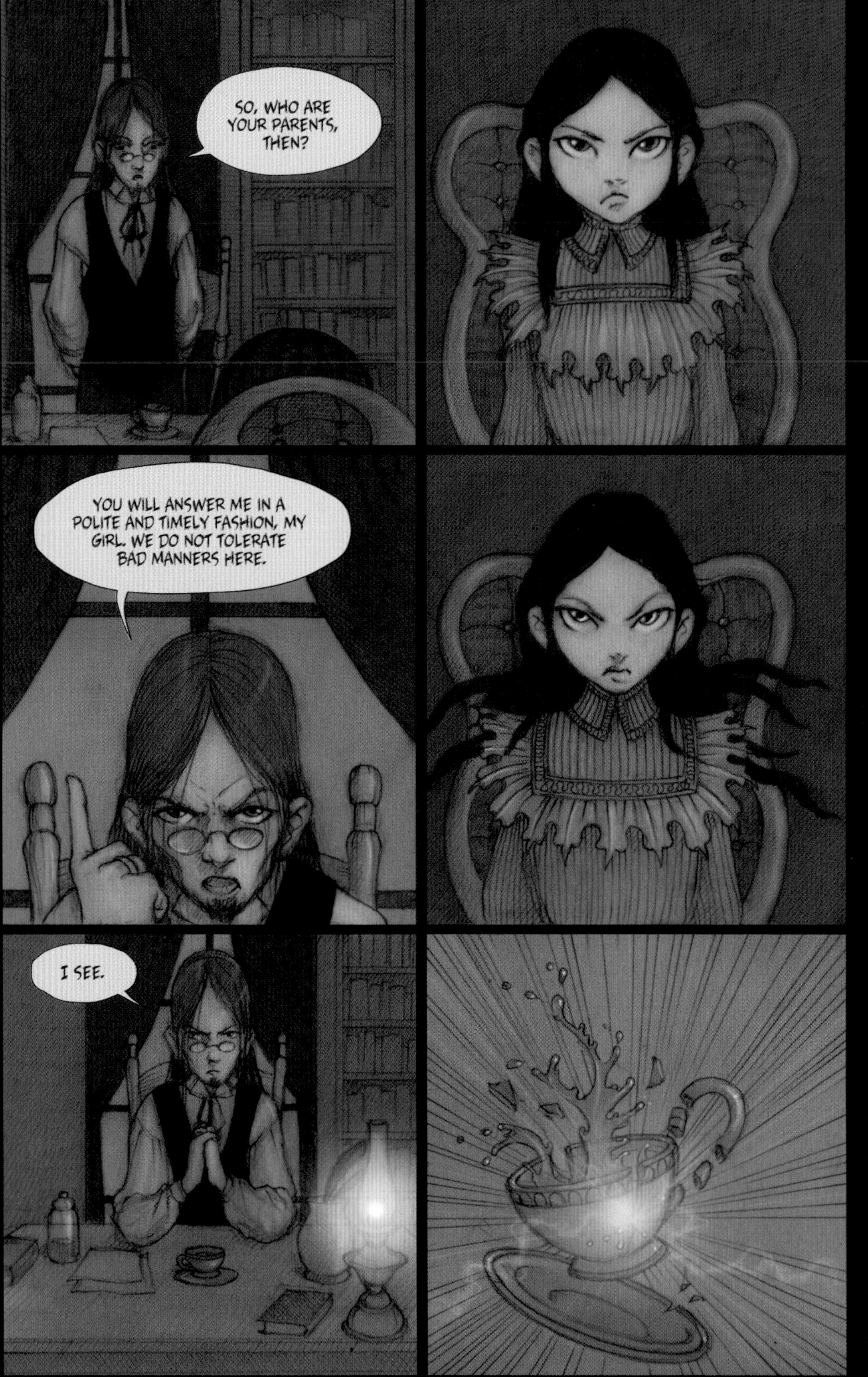
SO, WHO ARE YOUR PARENTS, THEN?
YOU WILL ANSWER ME IN A POLITE AND TIMELY FASHION, MY GIRL. WE DO NOT TOLERATE BAD MANNERS HERE.
I SEE.

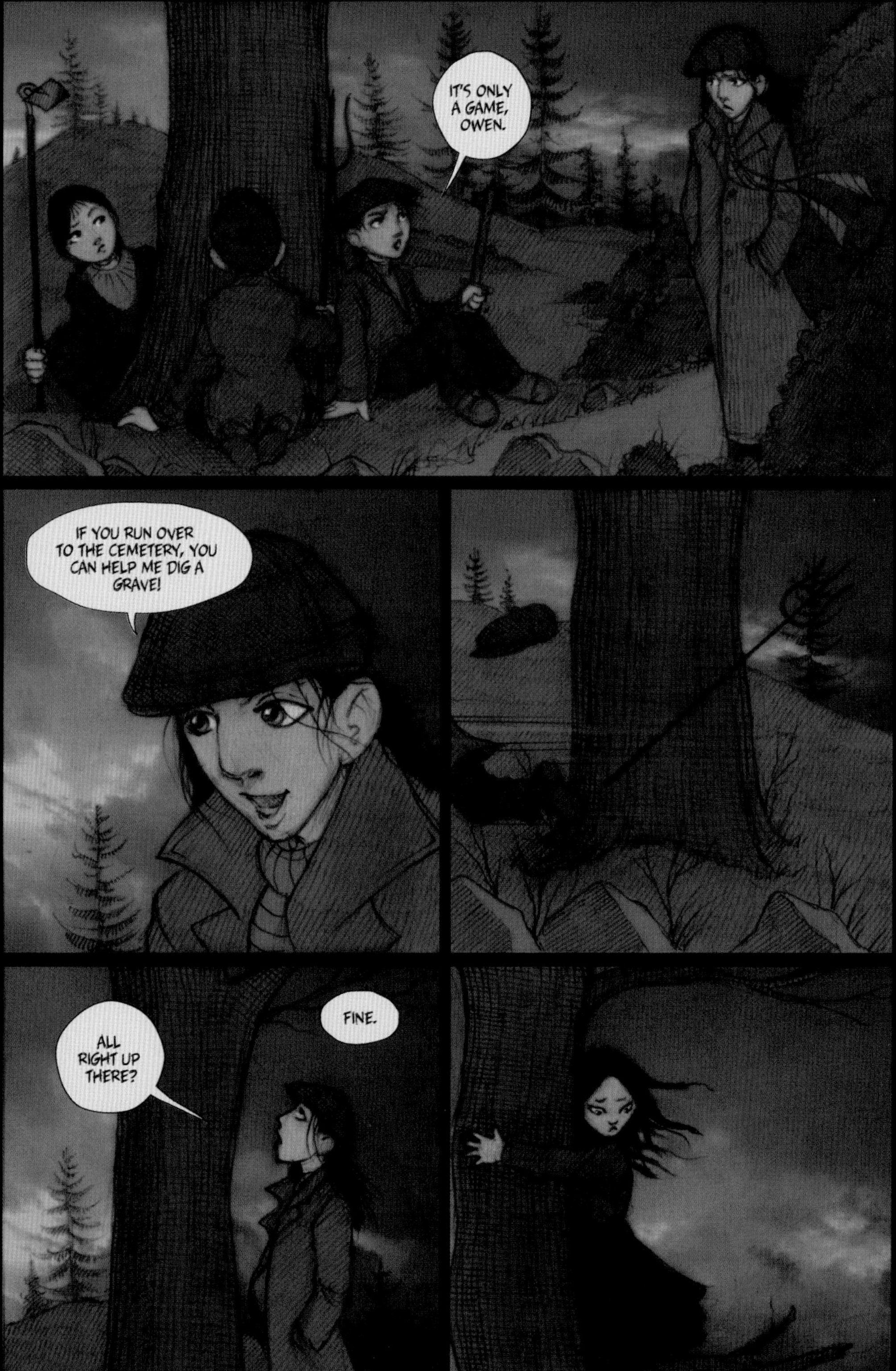
IT'S ONLY A GAME, OWEN.
IF YOU RUN OVER TO THE CEMETERY, YOU CAN HELP ME DIG A GRAVE!
ALL RIGHT UP THERE?
FINE.

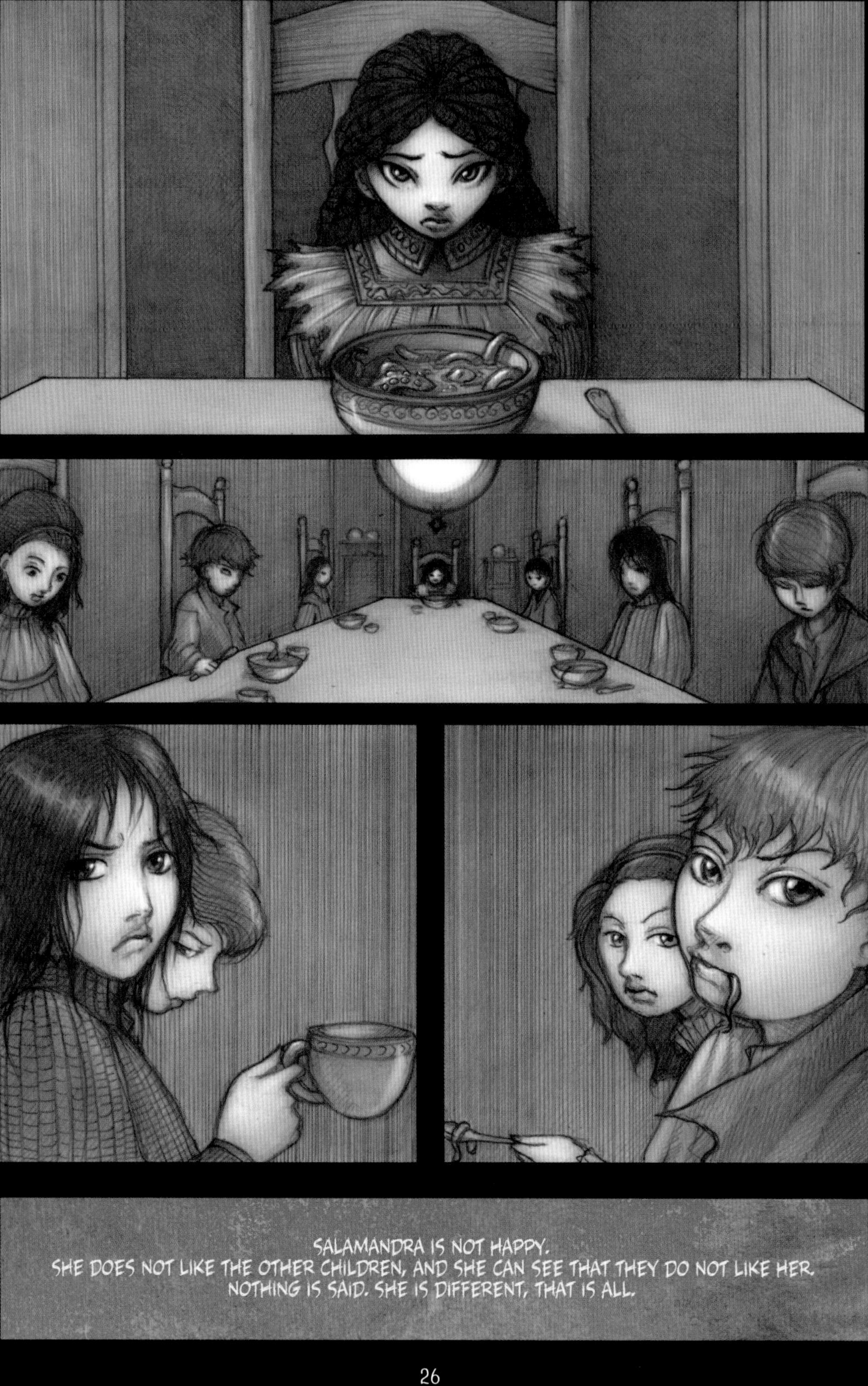

SALAMANDRA IS NOT HAPPY.
SHE DOES NOT LIKE THE OTHER CHILDREN, AND SHE CAN SEE THAT THEY DO NOT LIKE HER.
NOTHING IS SAID. SHE IS DIFFERENT, THAT IS ALL.

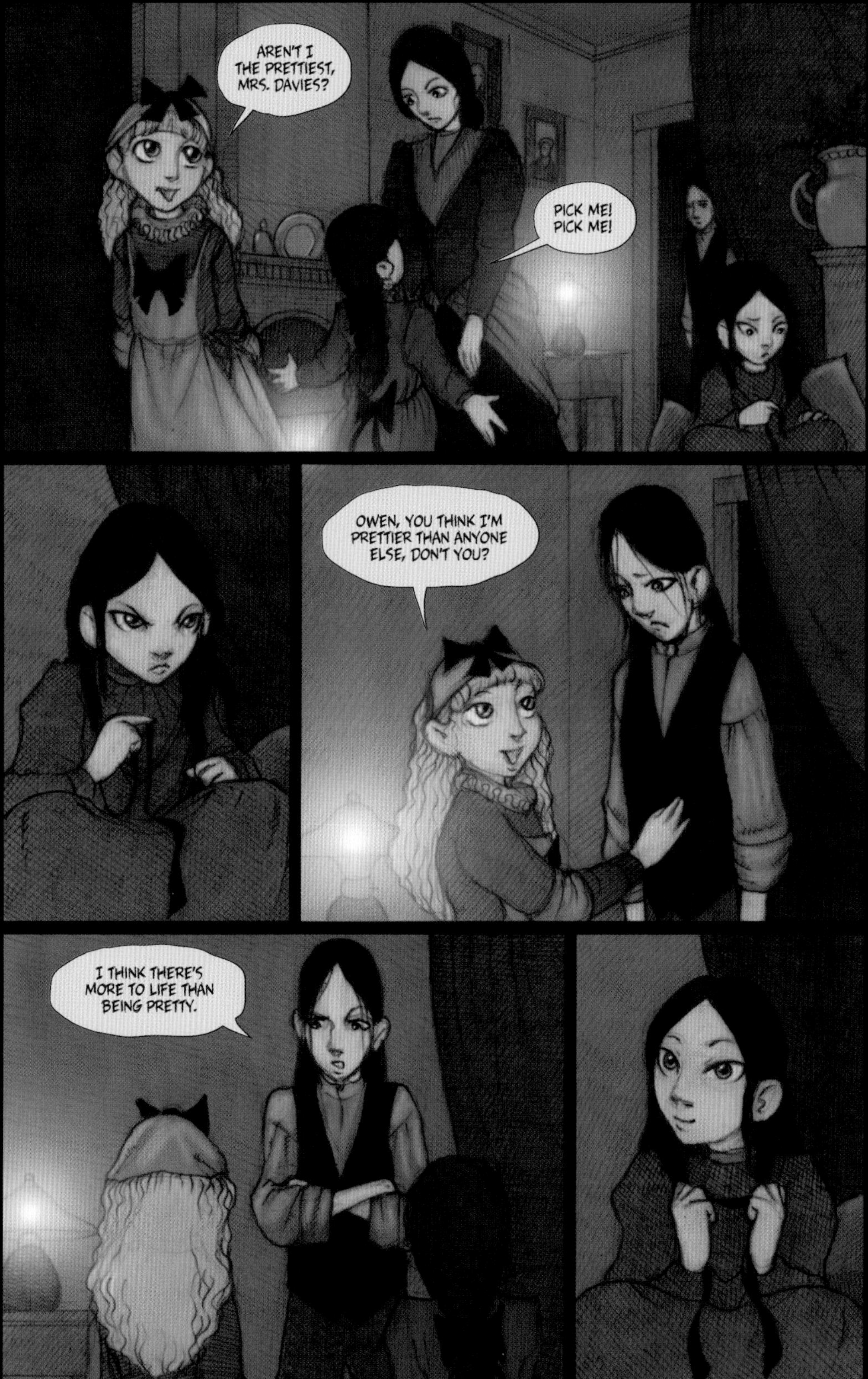

AREN'T I THE PRETTIEST, MRS. DAVIES?
PICK ME! PICK ME!
OWEN, YOU THINK I'M PRETTIER THAN ANYONE ELSE, DON'T YOU?
I THINK THERE'S MORE TO LIFE THAN BEING PRETTY.

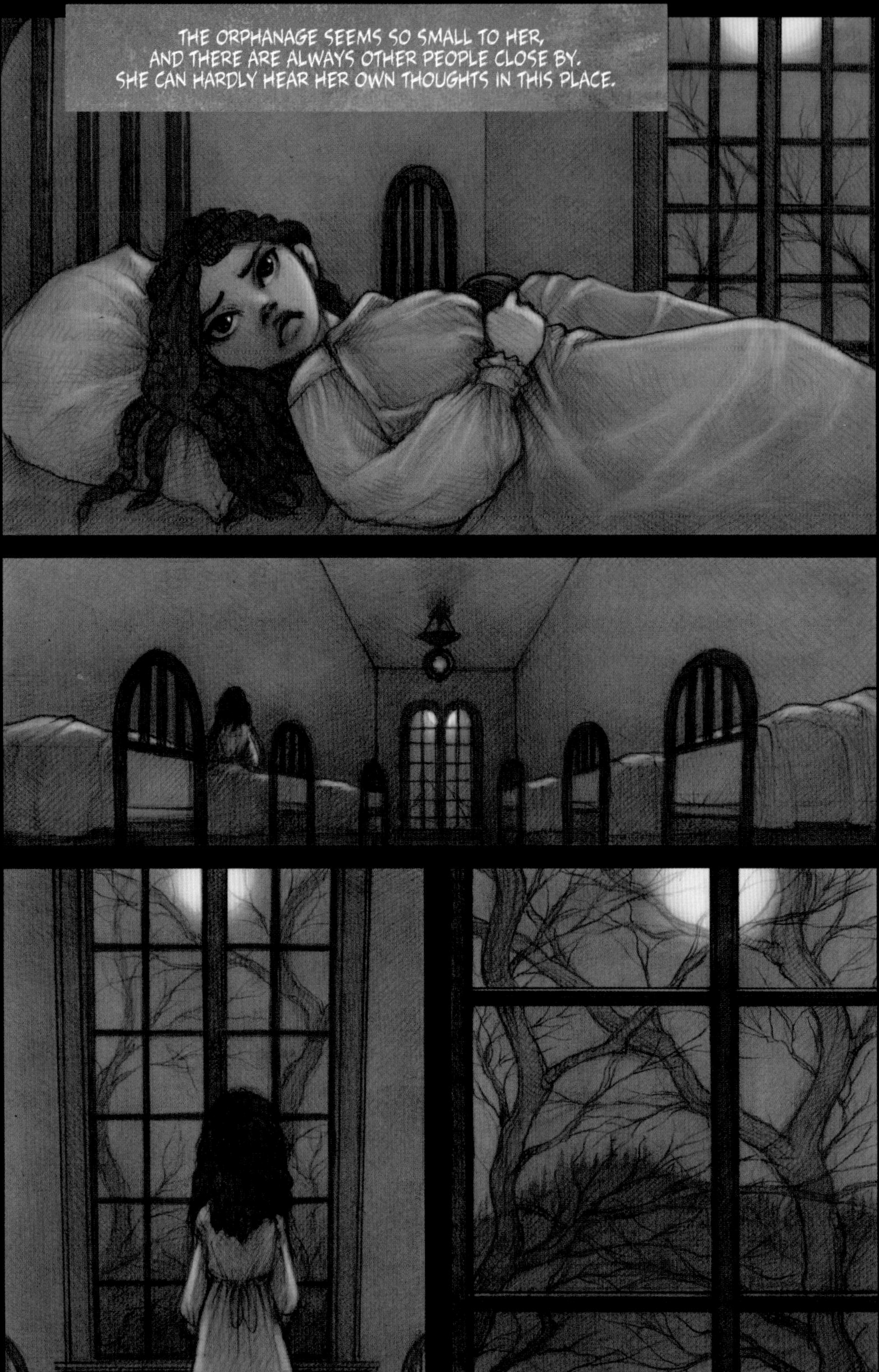
THE ORPHANAGE SEEMS SO SMALL TO HER, AND THERE ARE ALWAYS OTHER PEOPLE CLOSE BY. SHE CAN HARDLY HEAR HER OWN THOUGHTS IN THIS PLACE.

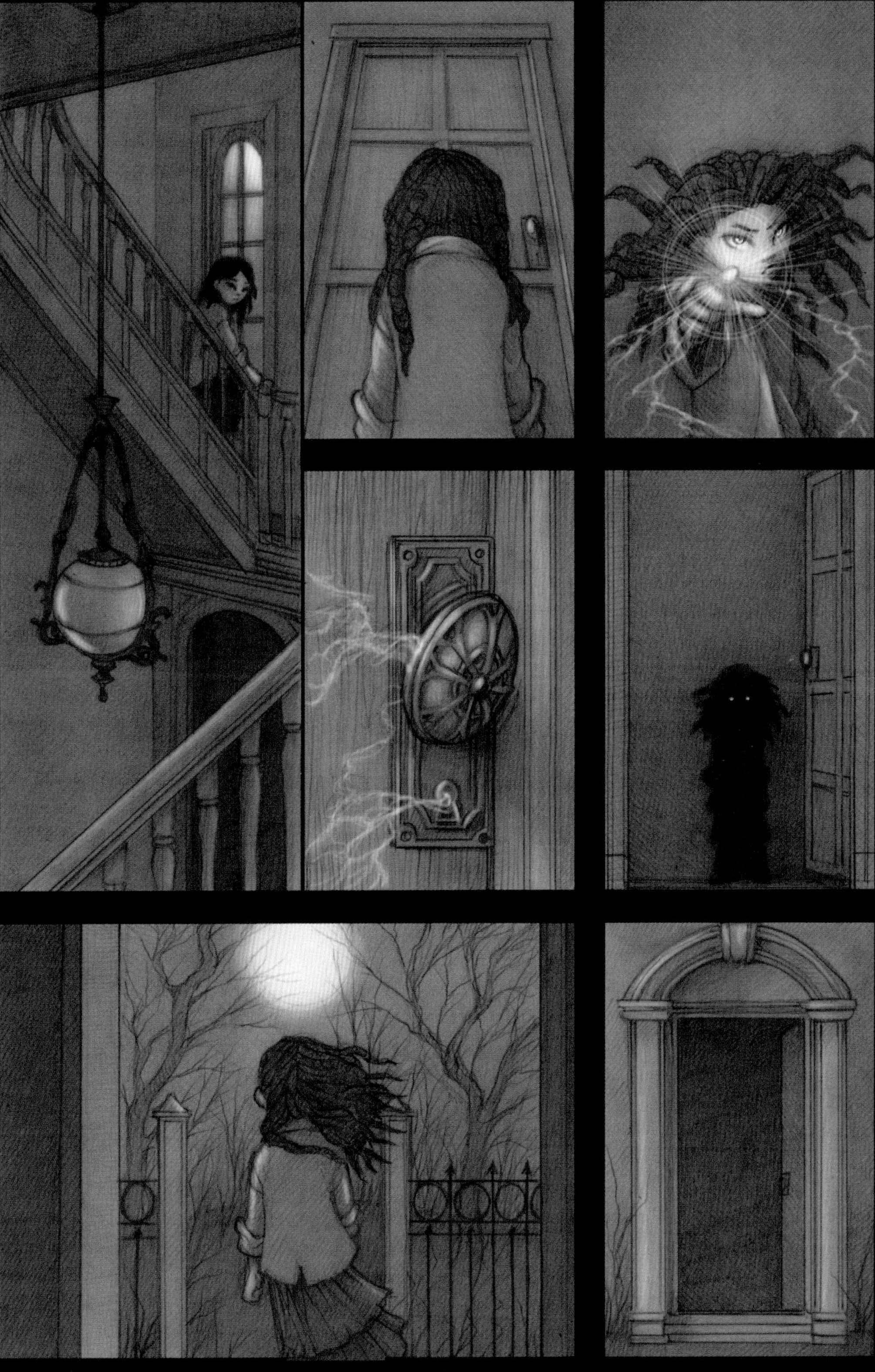

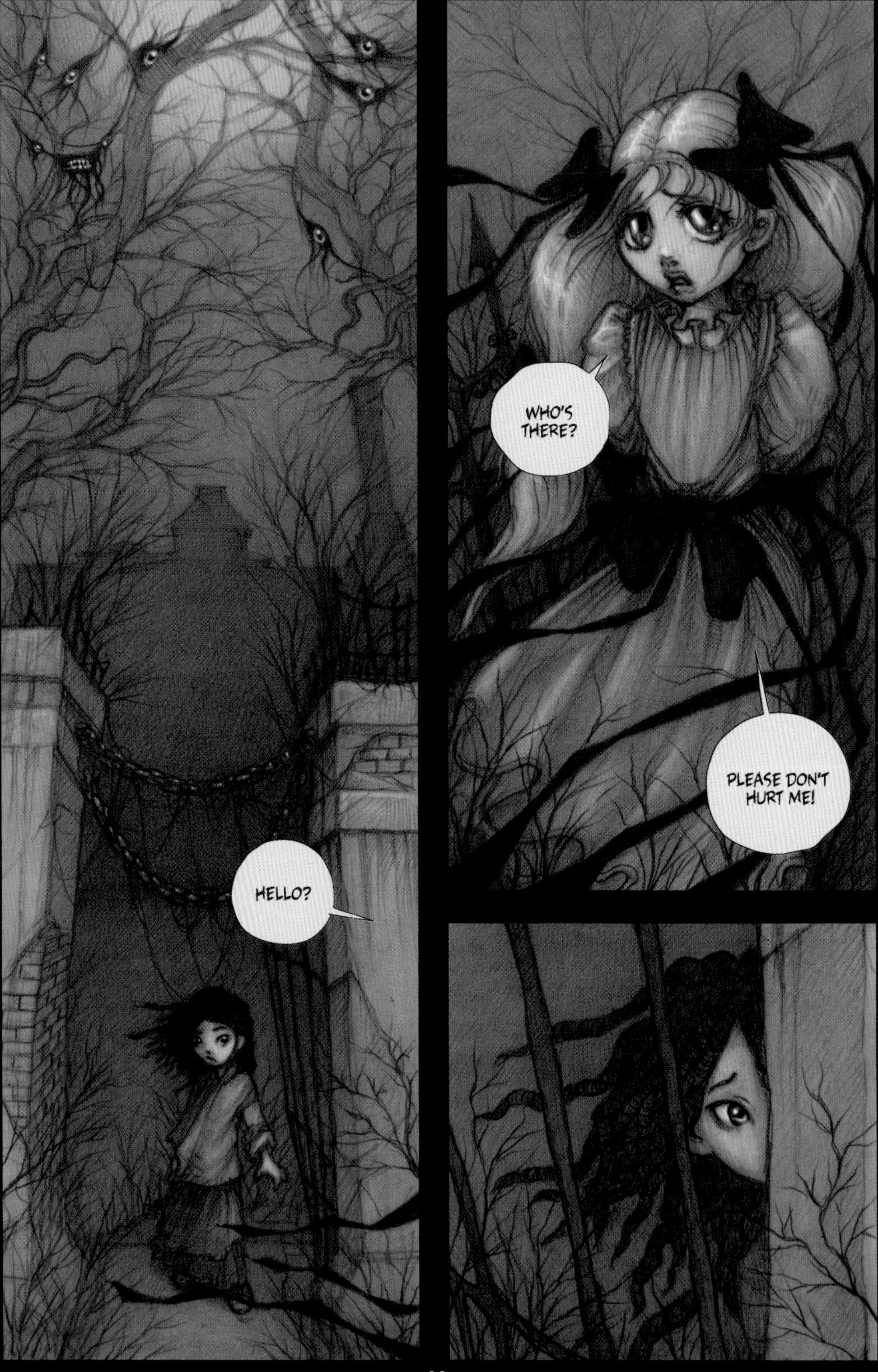
HELLO?
WHO'S THERE?
PLEASE DON'T HURT ME!

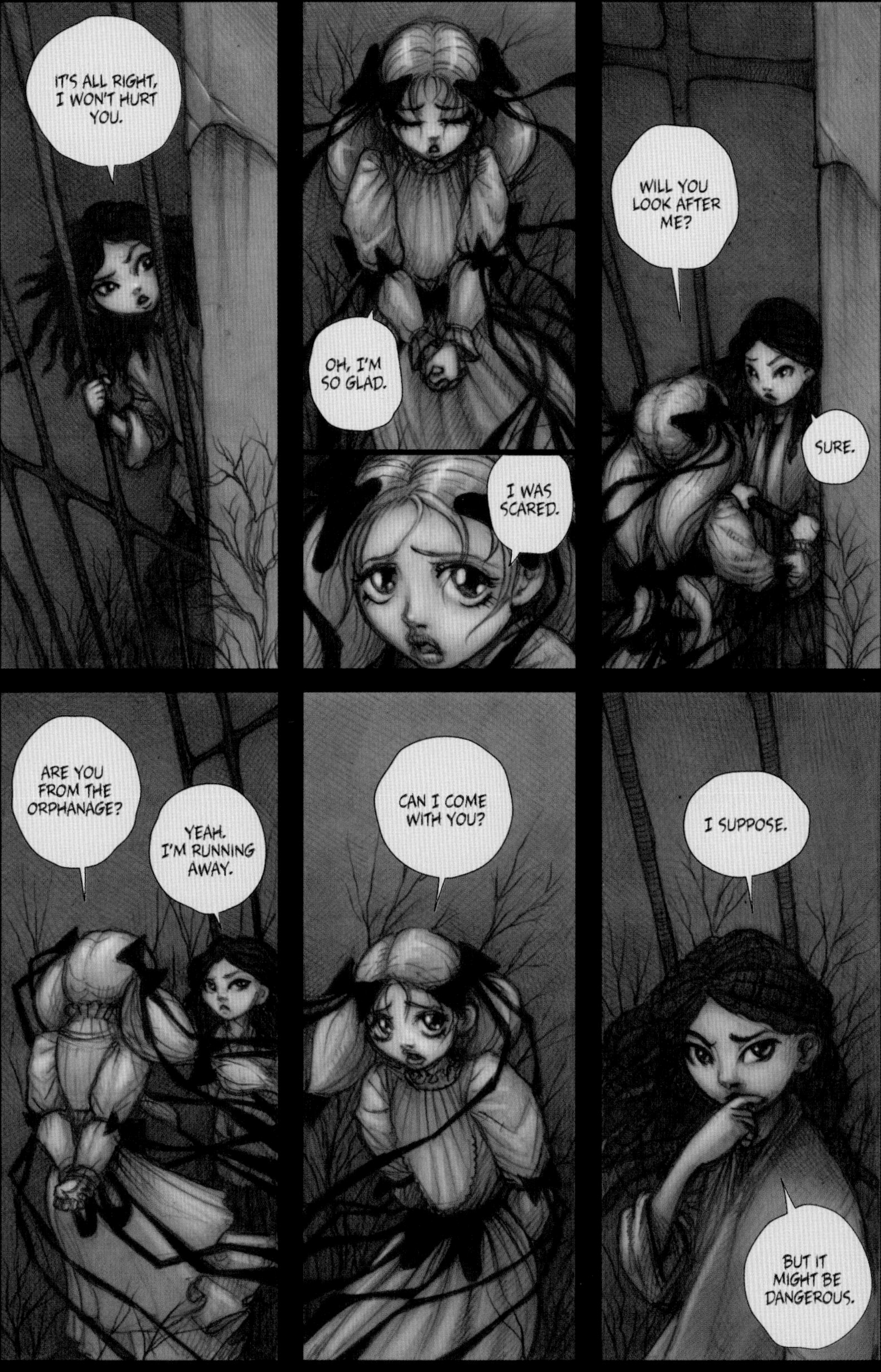
IT'S ALL RIGHT, I WON'T HURT YOU.
OH, I'M SO GLAD.
I WAS SCARED.
WILL YOU LOOK AFTER ME?
SURE.
ARE YOU FROM THE ORPHANAGE?
YEAH. I'M RUNNING AWAY.
CAN I COME WITH YOU?
I SUPPOSE.
BUT IT MIGHT BE DANGEROUS.

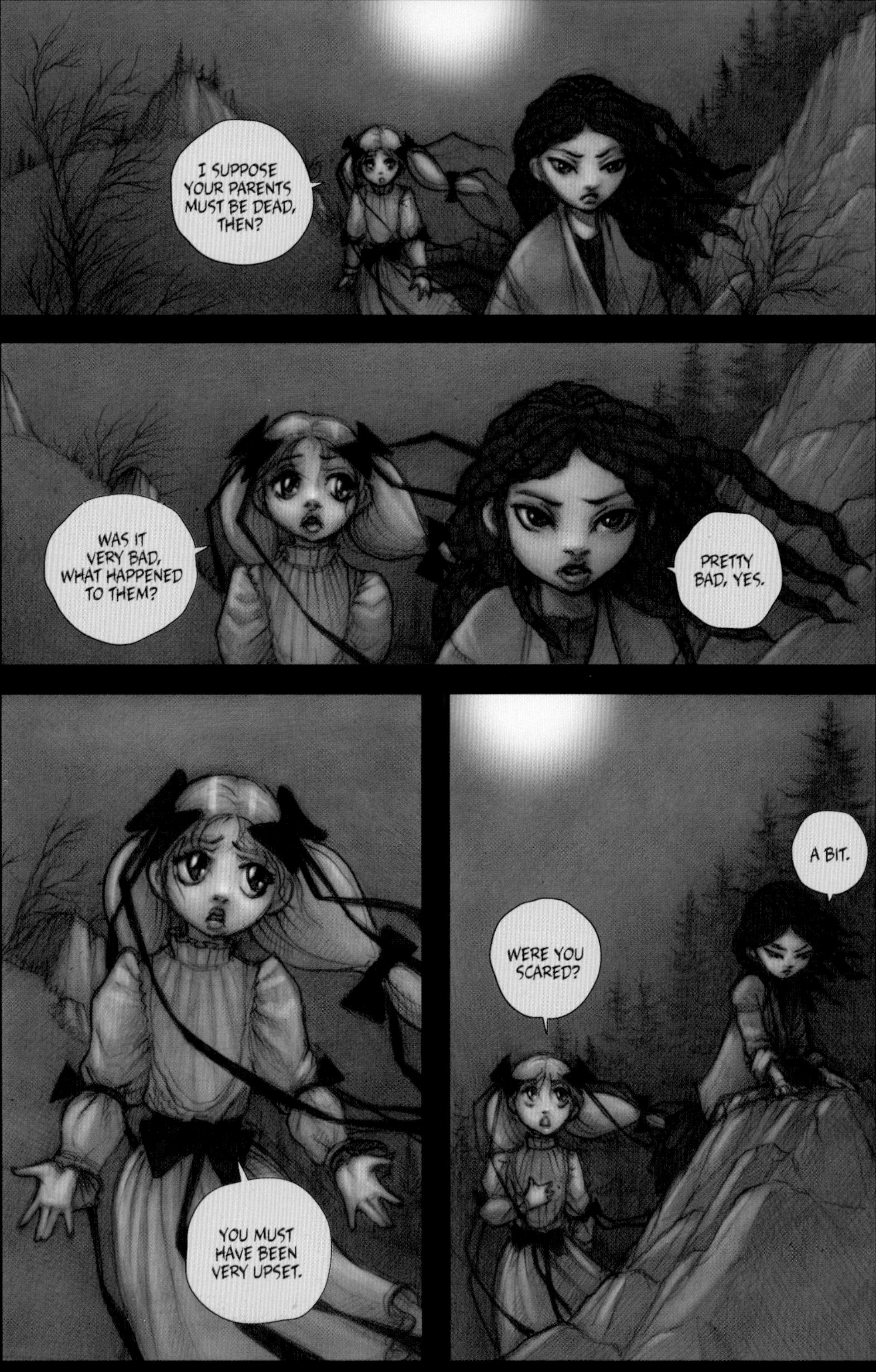
I SUPPOSE YOUR PARENTS MUST BE DEAD, THEN?
WAS IT VERY BAD, WHAT HAPPENED TO THEM?
PRETTY BAD, YES.
YOU MUST HAVE BEEN VERY UPSET.
WERE YOU SCARED?
A BIT.

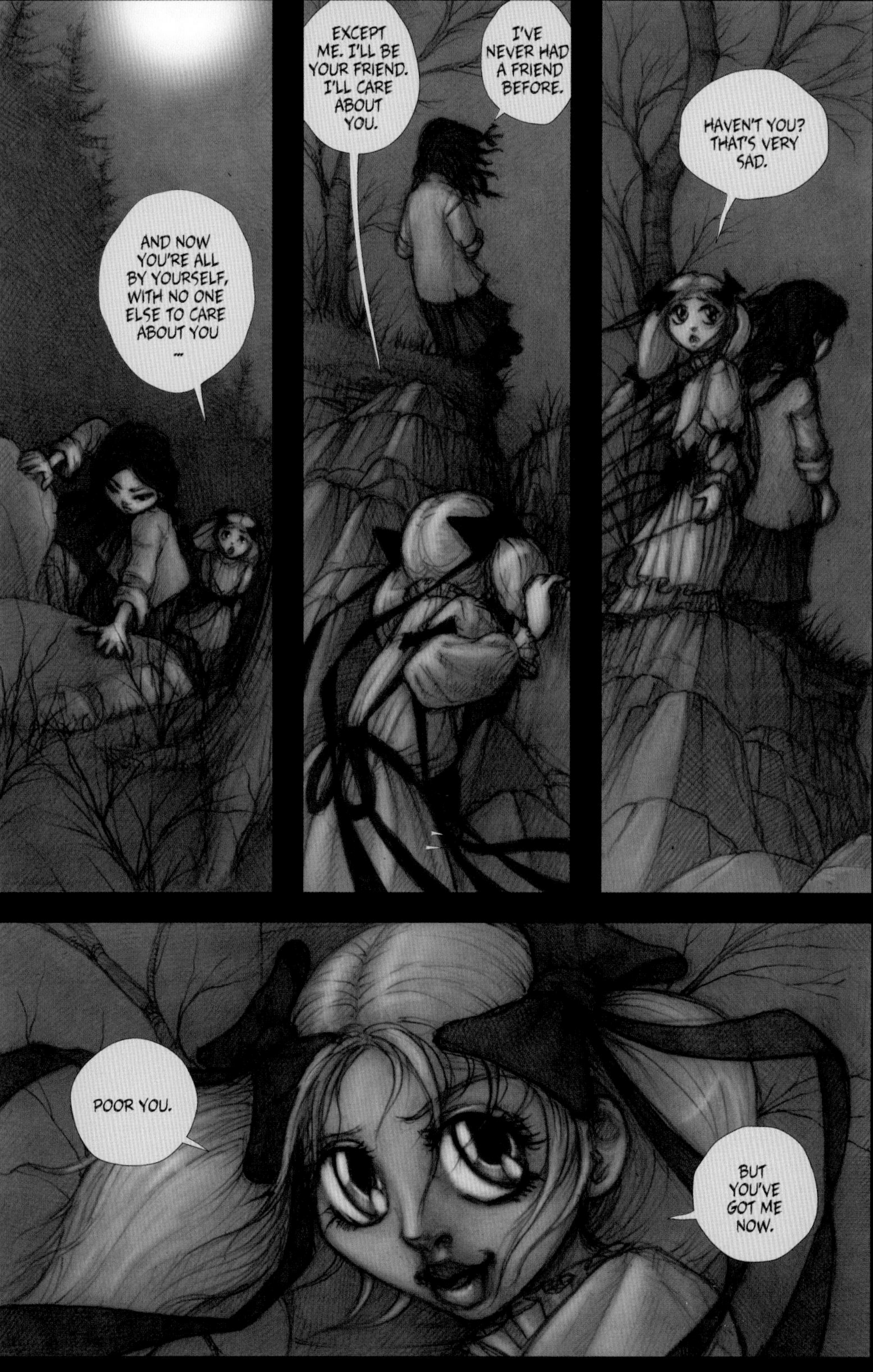
AND NOW YOU'RE ALL BY YOURSELF, WITH NO ONE ELSE TO CARE ABOUT YOU ...
I'VE NEVER HAD A FRIEND BEFORE.
EXCEPT ME. I'LL BE YOUR FRIEND. I'LL CARE ABOUT YOU.
HAVEN'T YOU? THAT'S VERY SAD.
POOR YOU.
BUT YOU'VE GOT ME NOW.

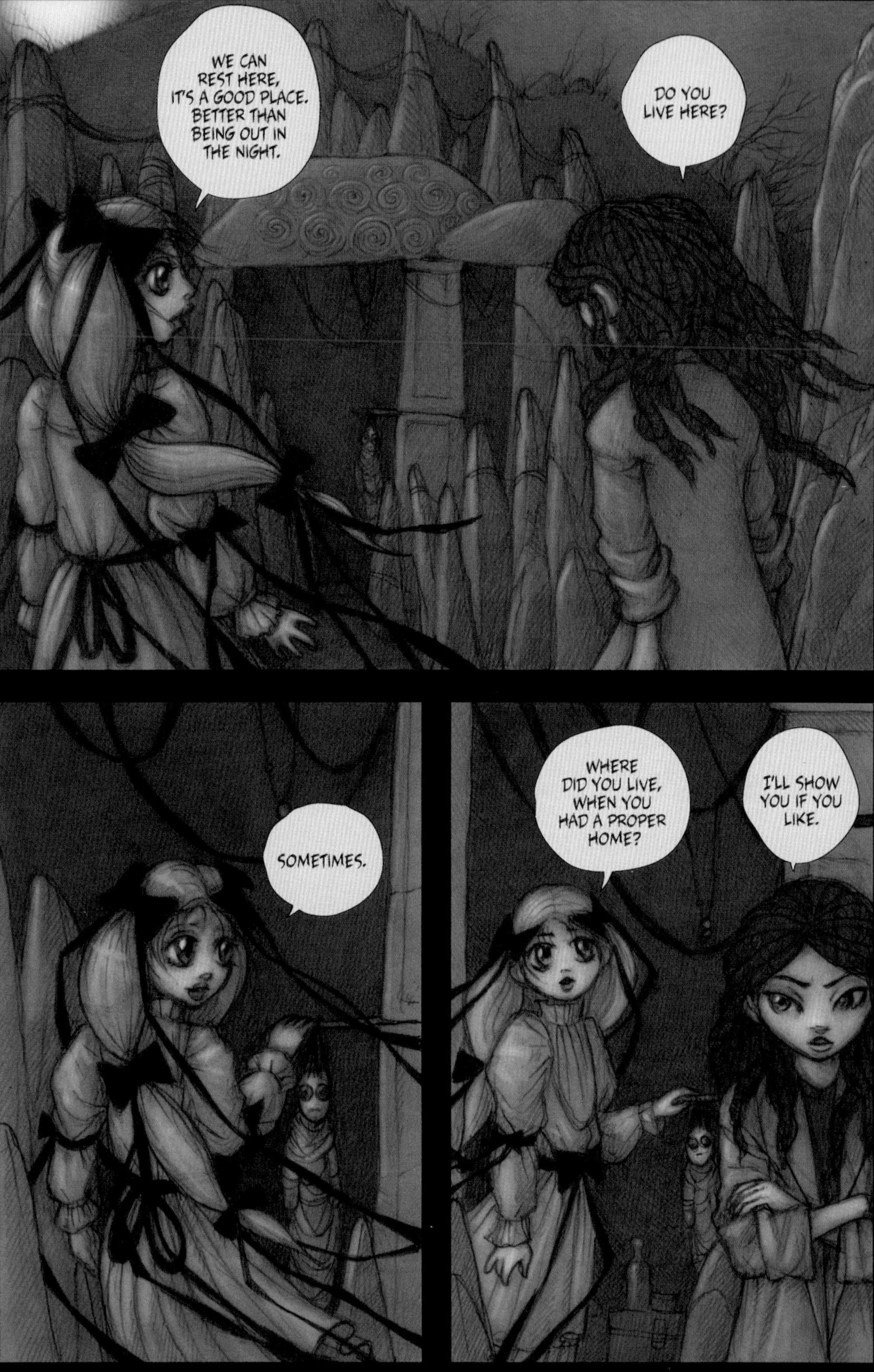
WE CAN REST HERE, IT'S A GOOD PLACE. BETTER THAN BEING OUT IN THE NIGHT.
DO YOU LIVE HERE?
SOMETIMES.
WHERE DID YOU LIVE, WHEN YOU HAD A PROPER HOME?
I'LL SHOW YOU IF YOU LIKE.

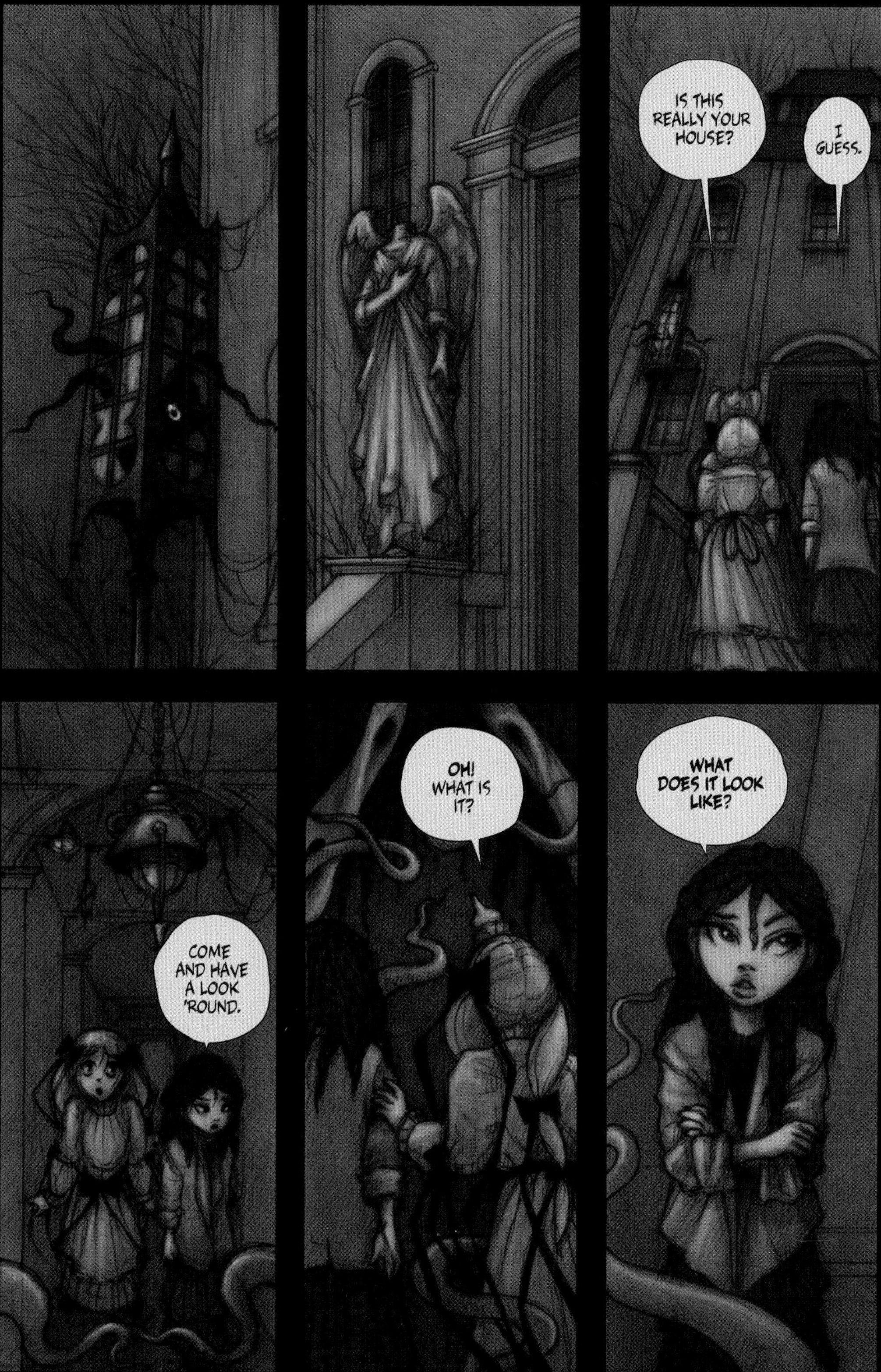
IS THIS REALLY YOUR HOUSE?
I GUESS.
COME AND HAVE A LOOK 'ROUND.
OH! WHAT IS IT?
WHAT DOES IT LOOK LIKE?

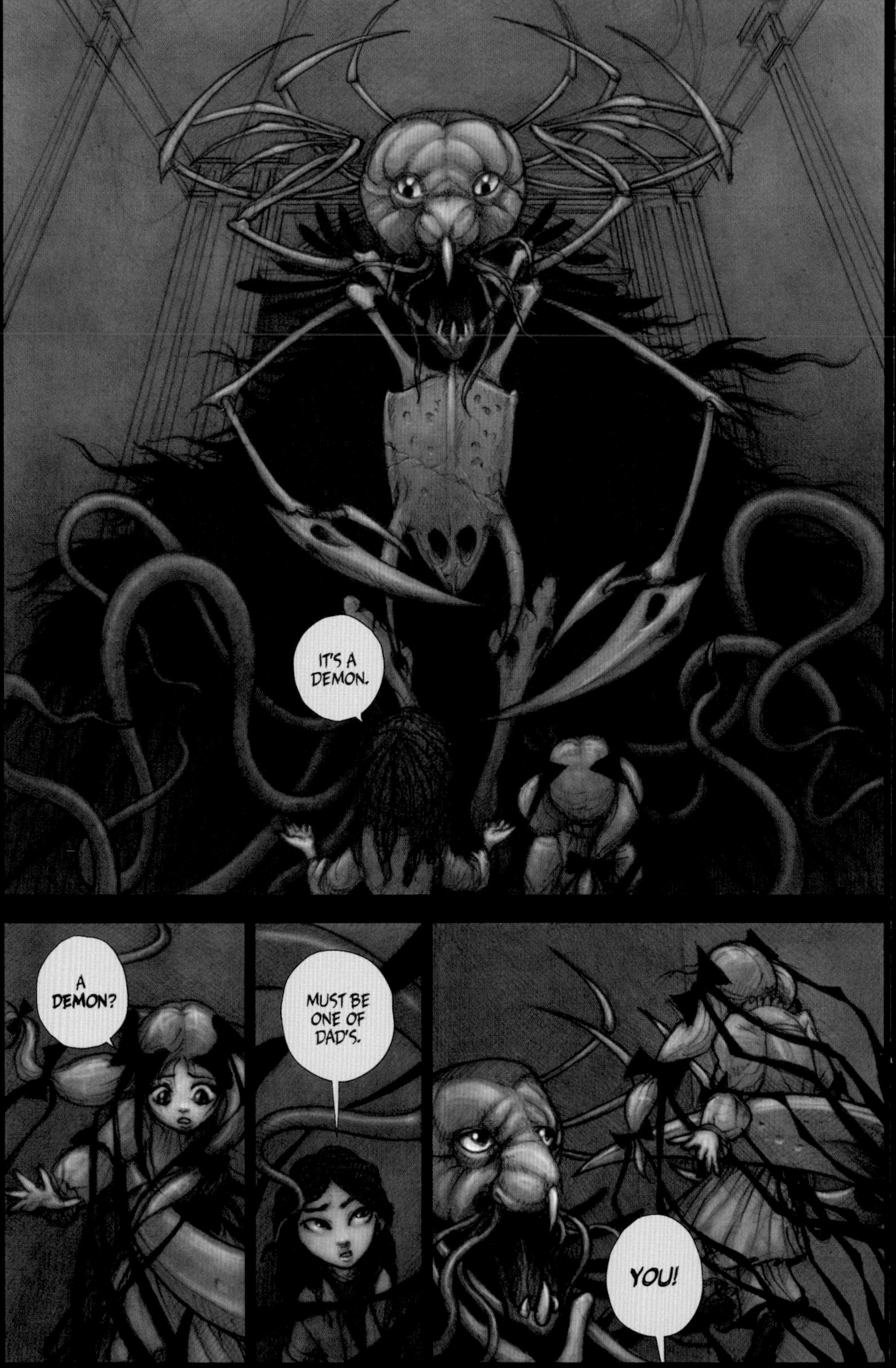
IT'S A DEMON.
A DEMON?
MUST BE ONE OF DAD'S.
YOU!

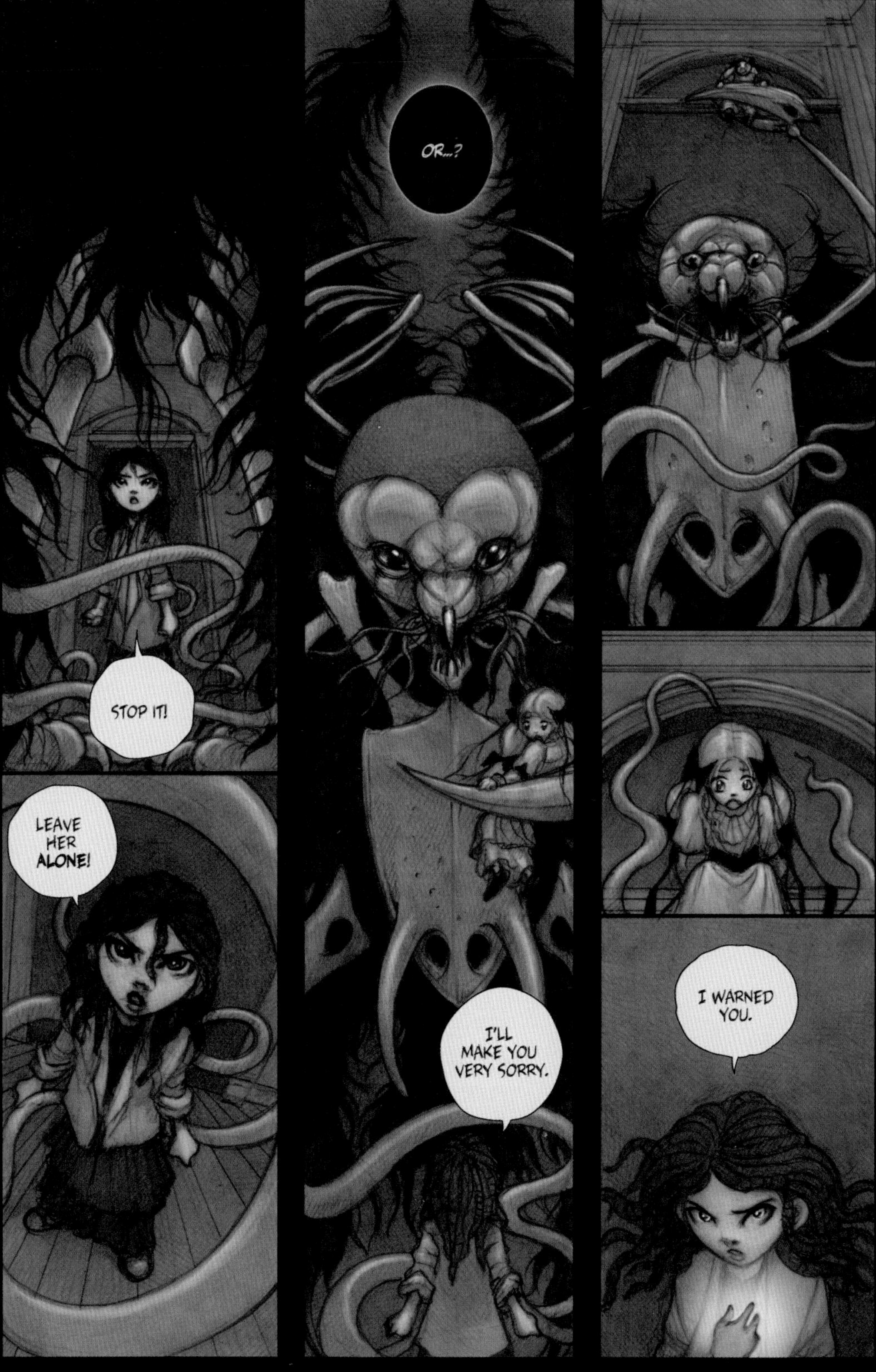
STOP IT!
LEAVE HER ALONE!
OR...?
I'LL MAKE YOU VERY SORRY.
I WARNED YOU.

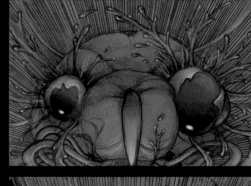

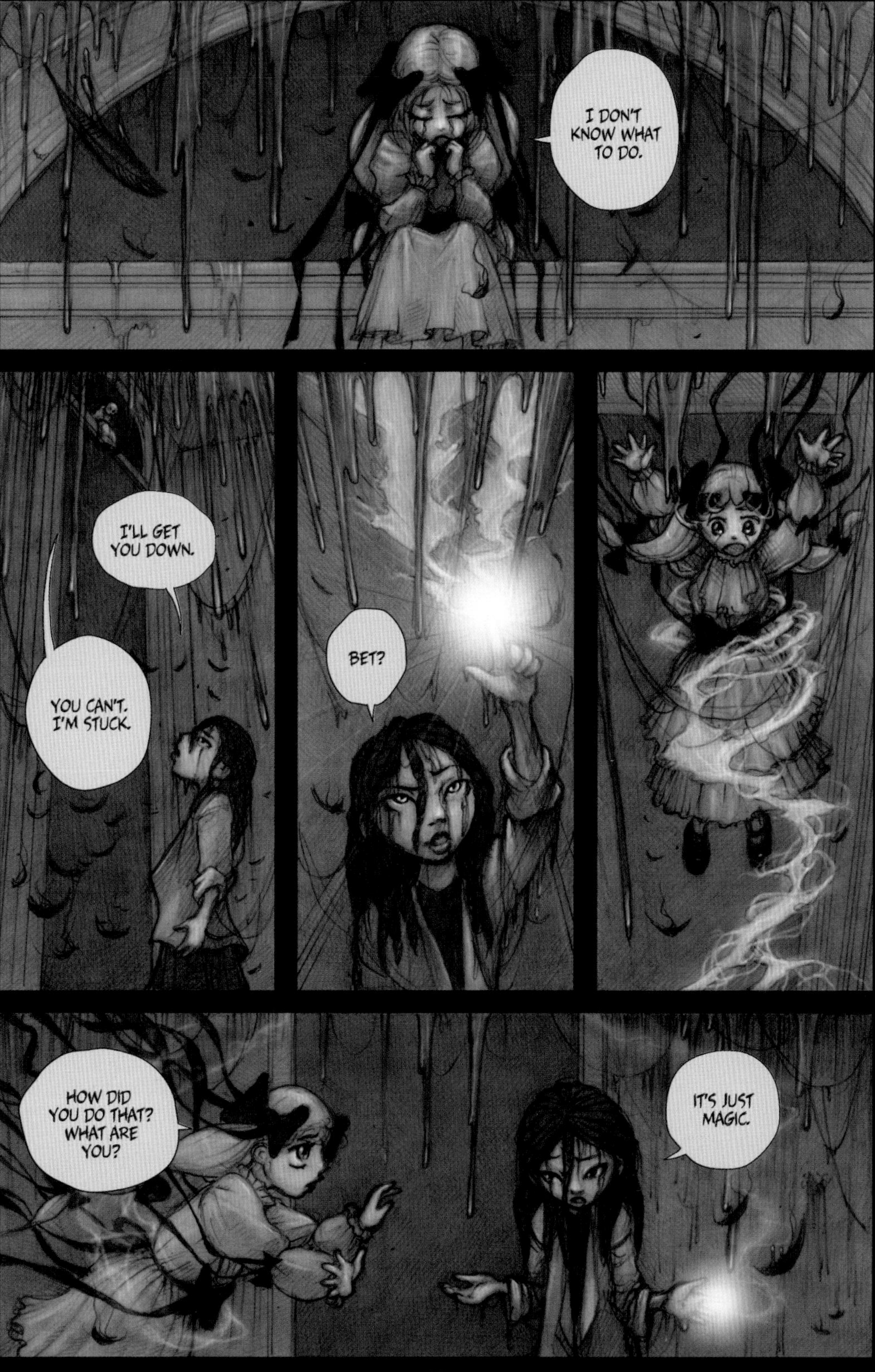
I DON'T KNOW WHAT TO DO.
I'LL GET YOU DOWN.
YOU CAN'T. I'M STUCK.
BET?
HOW DID YOU DO THAT? WHAT ARE YOU?
IT'S JUST MAGIC.

YOU DO MAGIC?

A BIT, YEAH.

SHOW ME SOME MORE! PLEASE. MAKE ME FLOAT AGAIN OR SOMETHING.

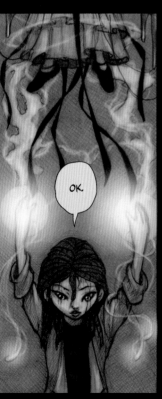

OK.

SO WHAT ELSE CAN YOU DO?

I CAN MAKE FIRE...

...WATCH!

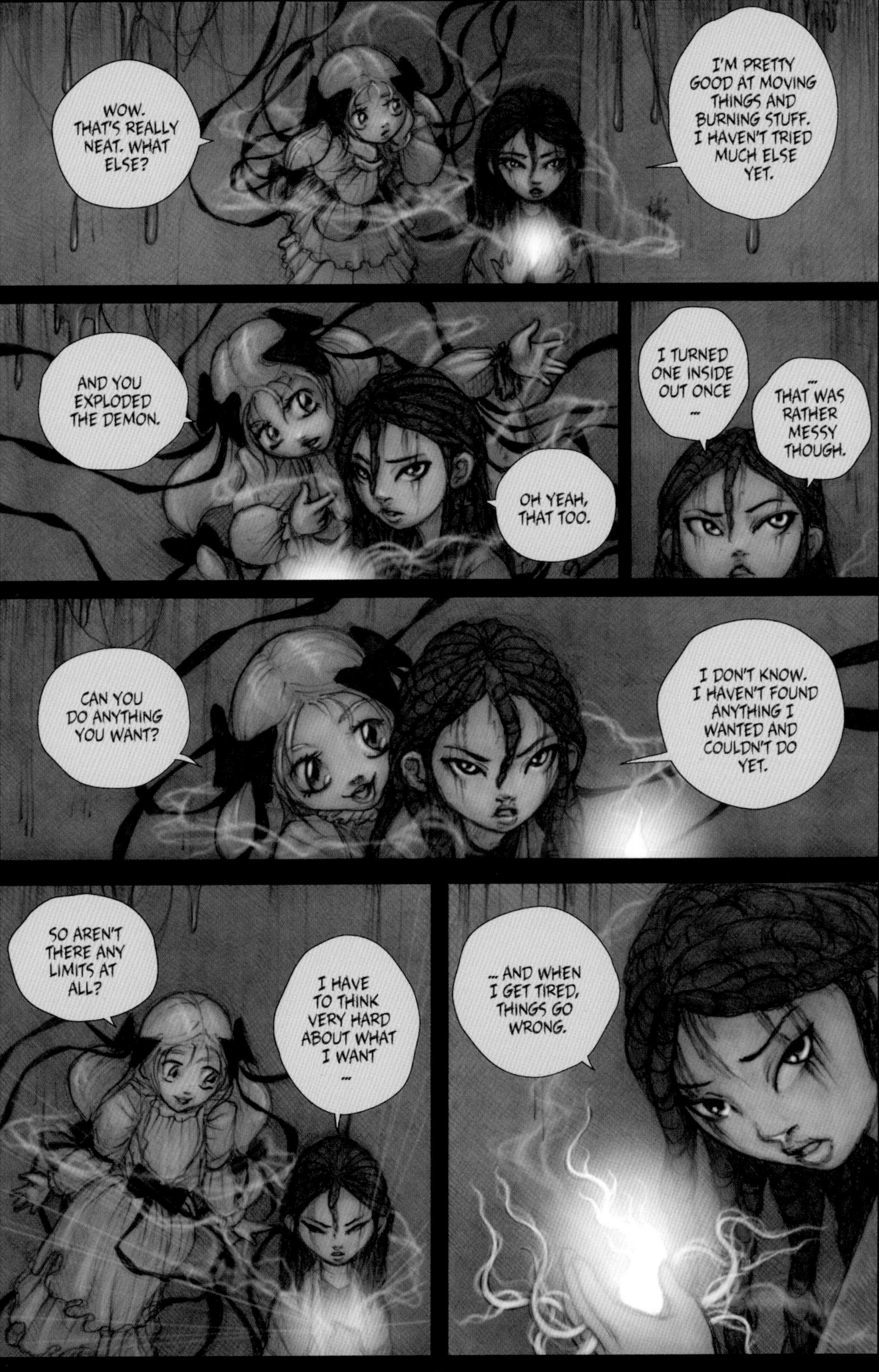
WOW. THAT'S REALLY NEAT. WHAT ELSE?
I'M PRETTY GOOD AT MOVING THINGS AND BURNING STUFF. I HAVEN'T TRIED MUCH ELSE YET.
AND YOU EXPLODED THE DEMON.
OH YEAH, THAT TOO.
I TURNED ONE INSIDE OUT ONCE ...
... THAT WAS RATHER MESSY THOUGH.
CAN YOU DO ANYTHING YOU WANT?
I DON'T KNOW. I HAVEN'T FOUND ANYTHING I WANTED AND COULDN'T DO YET.
SO AREN'T THERE ANY LIMITS AT ALL?
I HAVE TO THINK VERY HARD ABOUT WHAT I WANT ...
... AND WHEN I GET TIRED, THINGS GO WRONG.

CHAPTER THREE

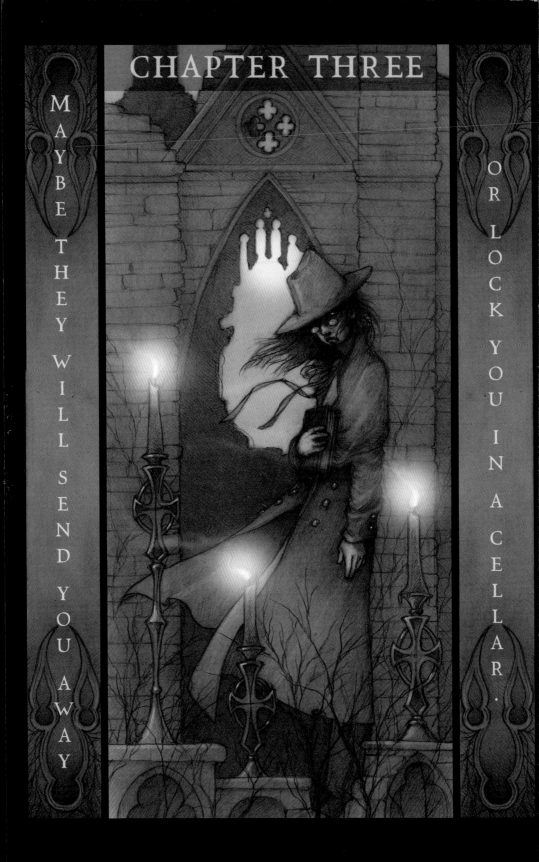

MAYBE THEY WILL SEND YOU AWAY

OR LOCK YOU IN A CELLAR.

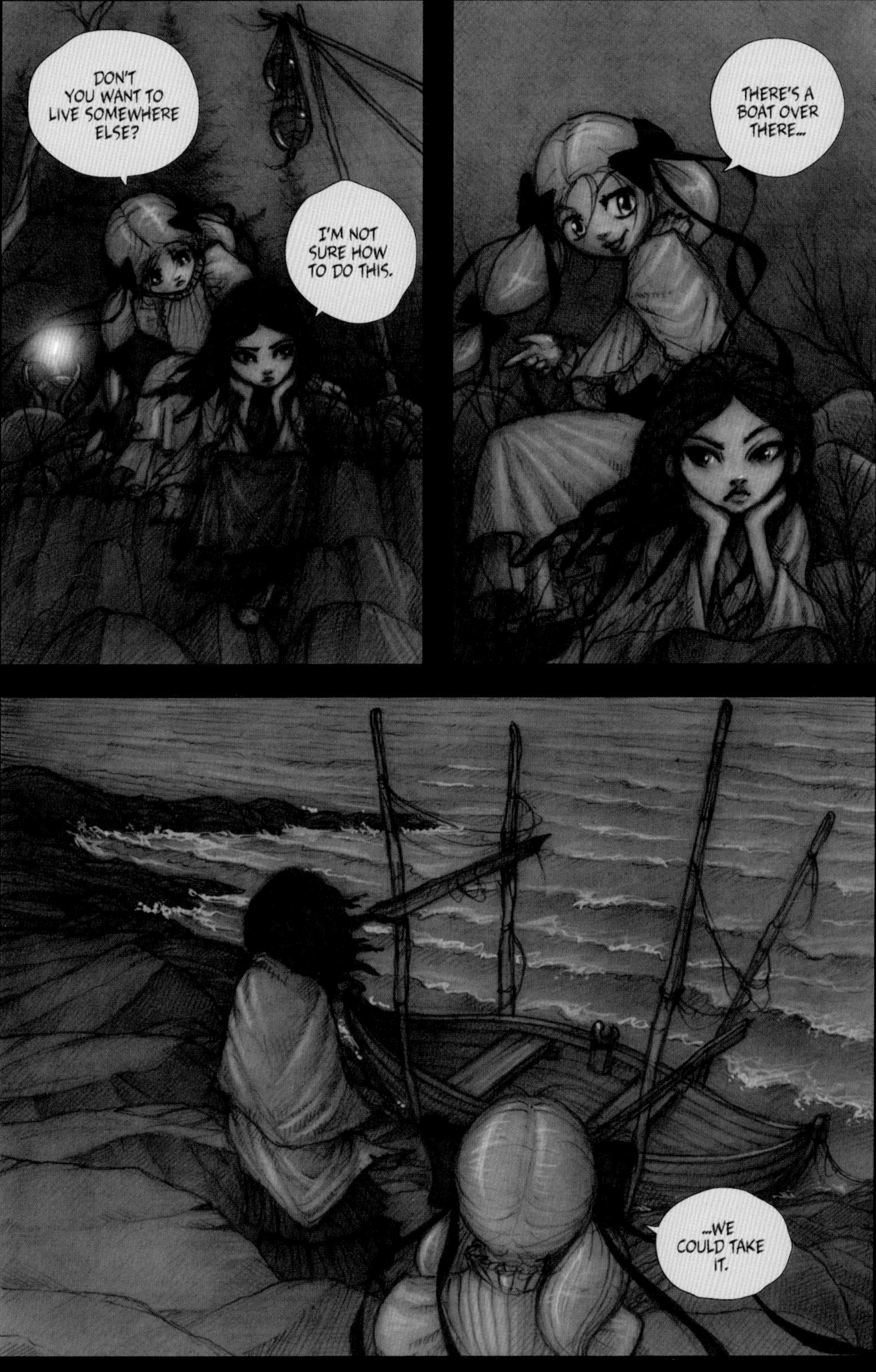
DON'T YOU WANT TO LIVE SOMEWHERE ELSE?
I'M NOT SURE HOW TO DO THIS.
THERE'S A BOAT OVER THERE...
...WE COULD TAKE IT.

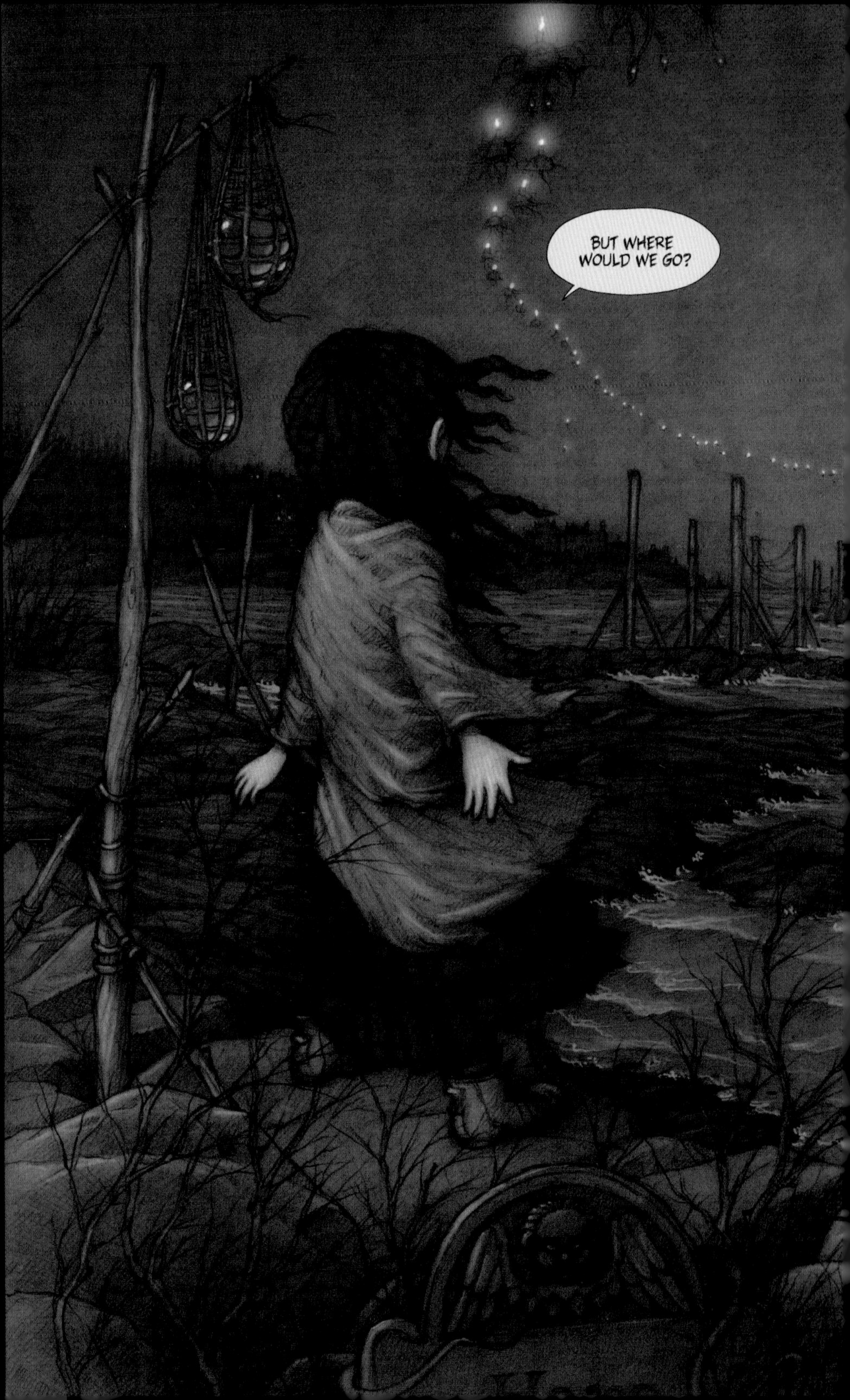
BUT WHERE WOULD WE GO?

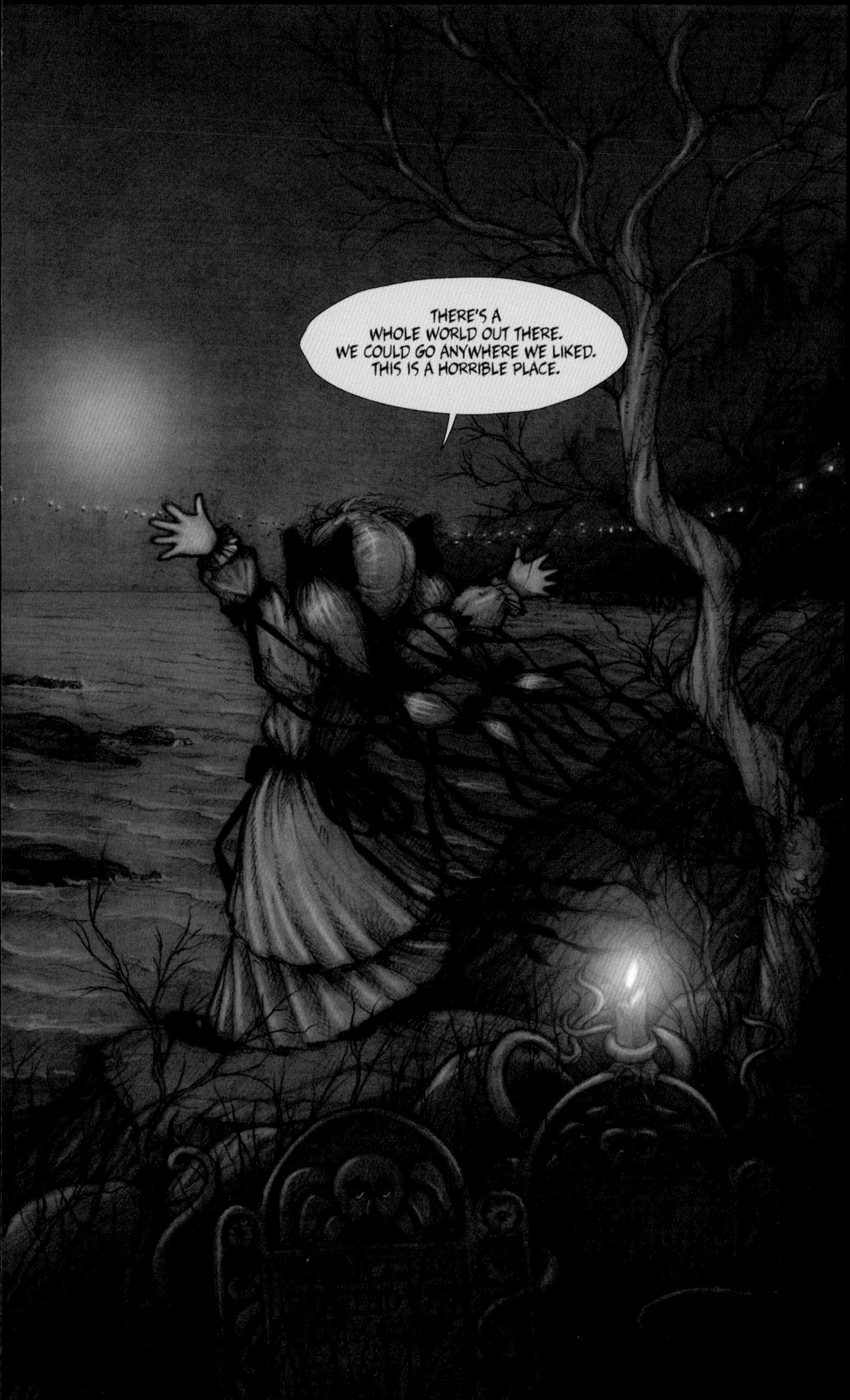
THERE'S A WHOLE WORLD OUT THERE. WE COULD GO ANYWHERE WE LIKED. THIS IS A HORRIBLE PLACE.

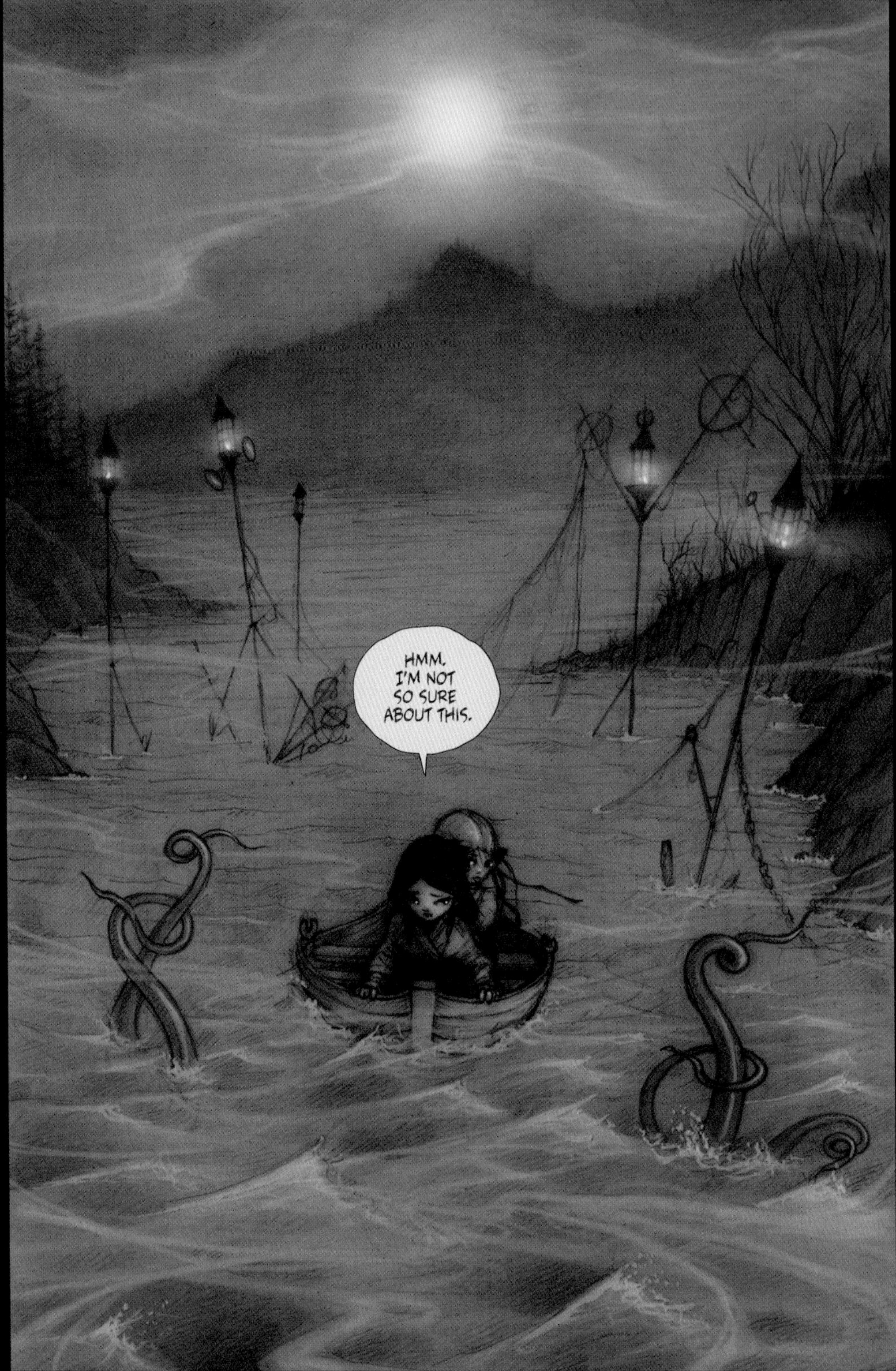
HMM. I'M NOT SO SURE ABOUT THIS.

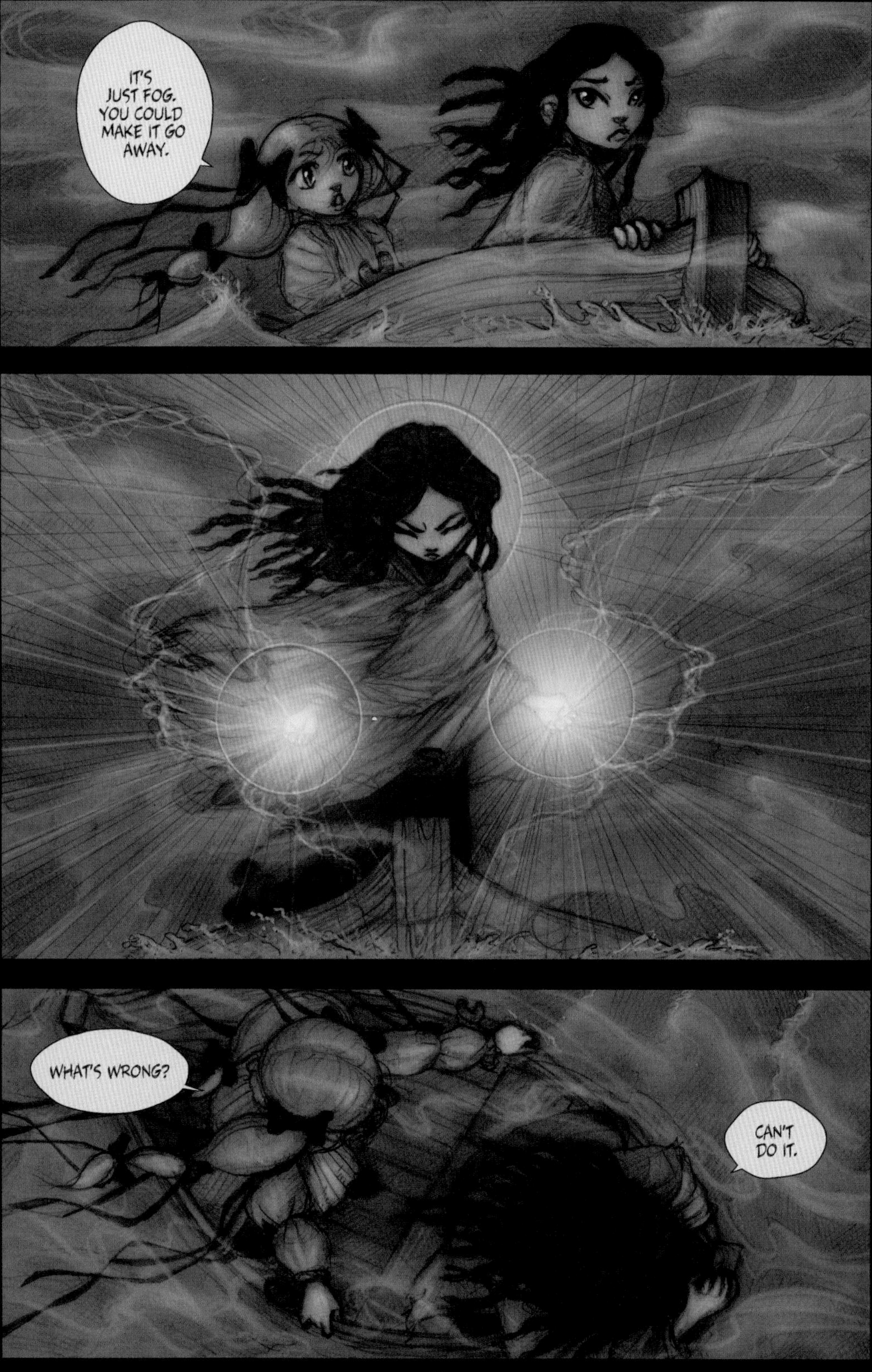
IT'S JUST FOG. YOU COULD MAKE IT GO AWAY.
WHAT'S WRONG?
CAN'T DO IT.

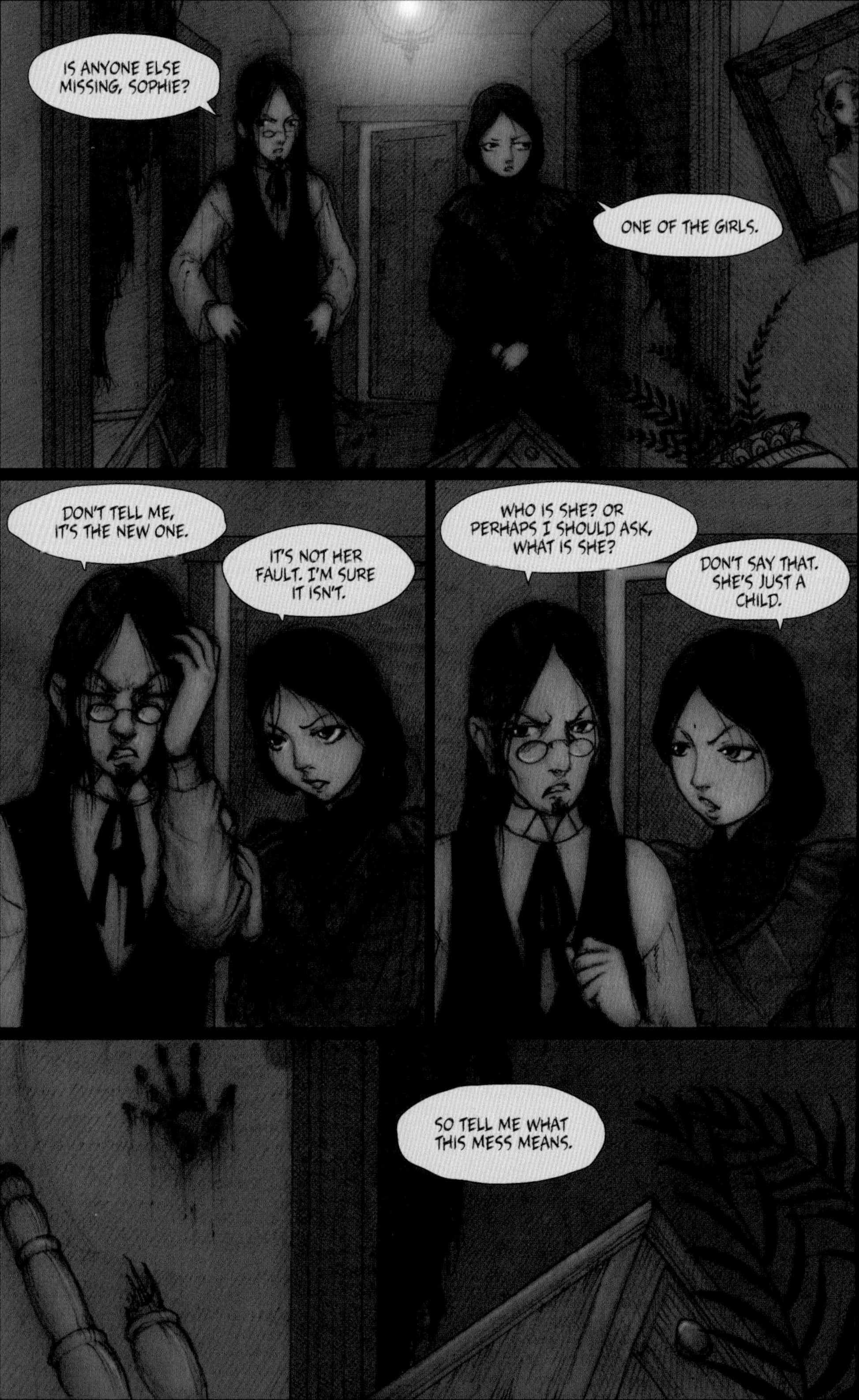
IS ANYONE ELSE MISSING, SOPHIE?
ONE OF THE GIRLS.
DON'T TELL ME, IT'S THE NEW ONE.
IT'S NOT HER FAULT. I'M SURE IT ISN'T.
WHO IS SHE? OR PERHAPS I SHOULD ASK, WHAT IS SHE?
DON'T SAY THAT. SHE'S JUST A CHILD.
SO TELL ME WHAT THIS MESS MEANS.

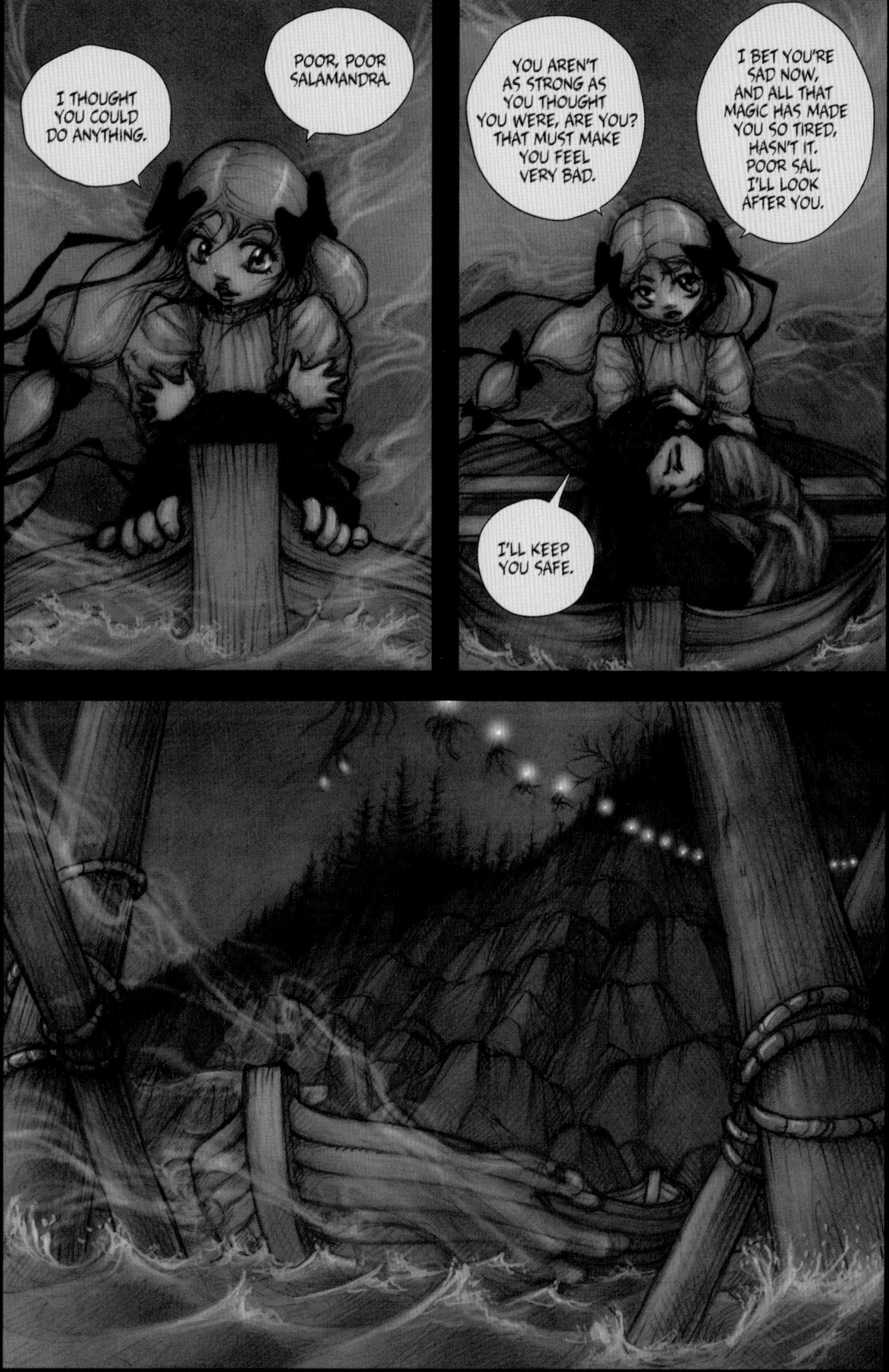
I THOUGHT YOU COULD DO ANYTHING.
POOR, POOR SALAMANDRA.
YOU AREN'T AS STRONG AS YOU THOUGHT YOU WERE, ARE YOU? THAT MUST MAKE YOU FEEL VERY BAD.
I BET YOU'RE SAD NOW, AND ALL THAT MAGIC HAS MADE YOU SO TIRED, HASN'T IT. POOR SAL. I'LL LOOK AFTER YOU.
I'LL KEEP YOU SAFE.

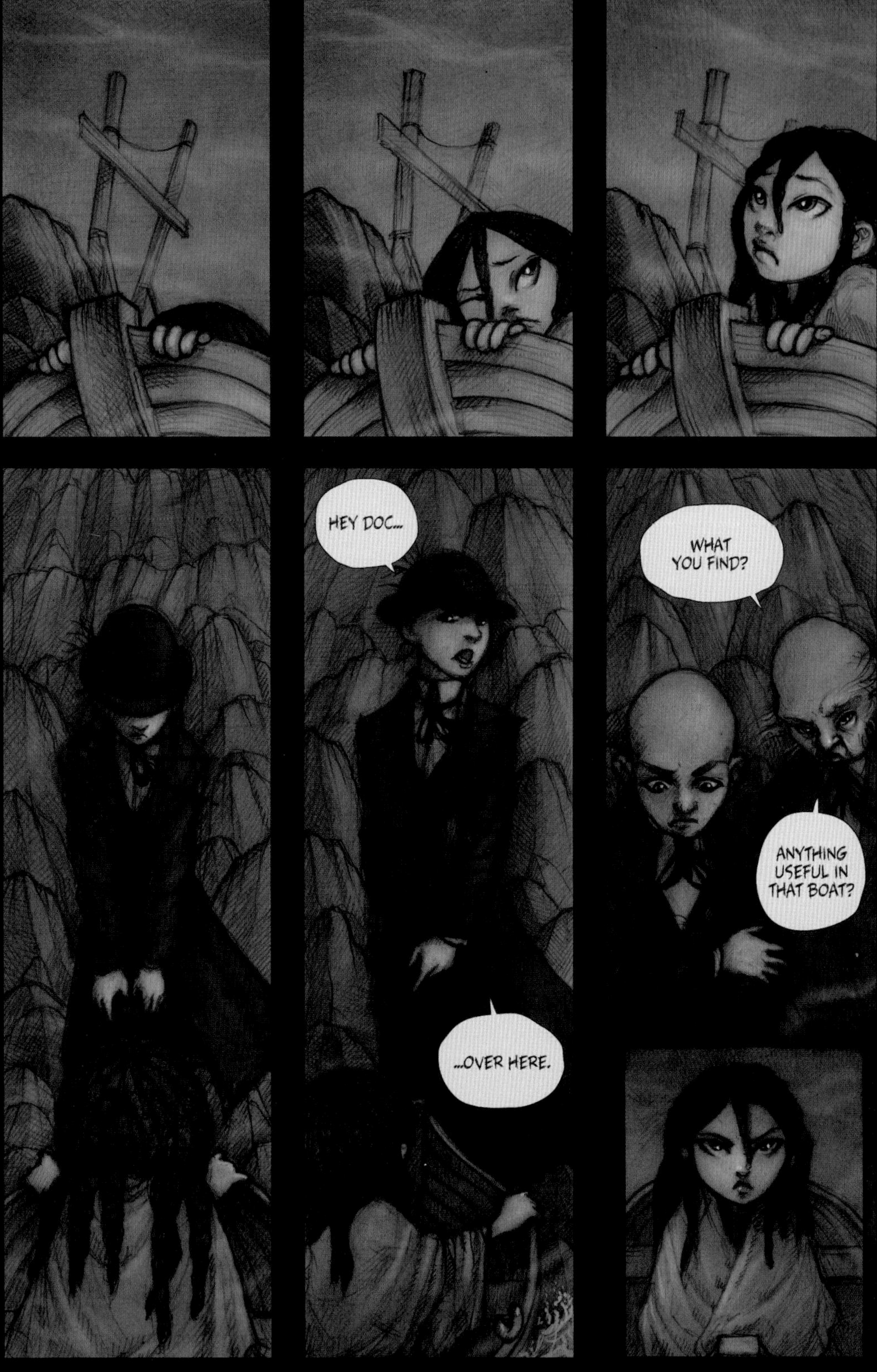
HEY DOC...
...OVER HERE.
WHAT YOU FIND?
ANYTHING USEFUL IN THAT BOAT?

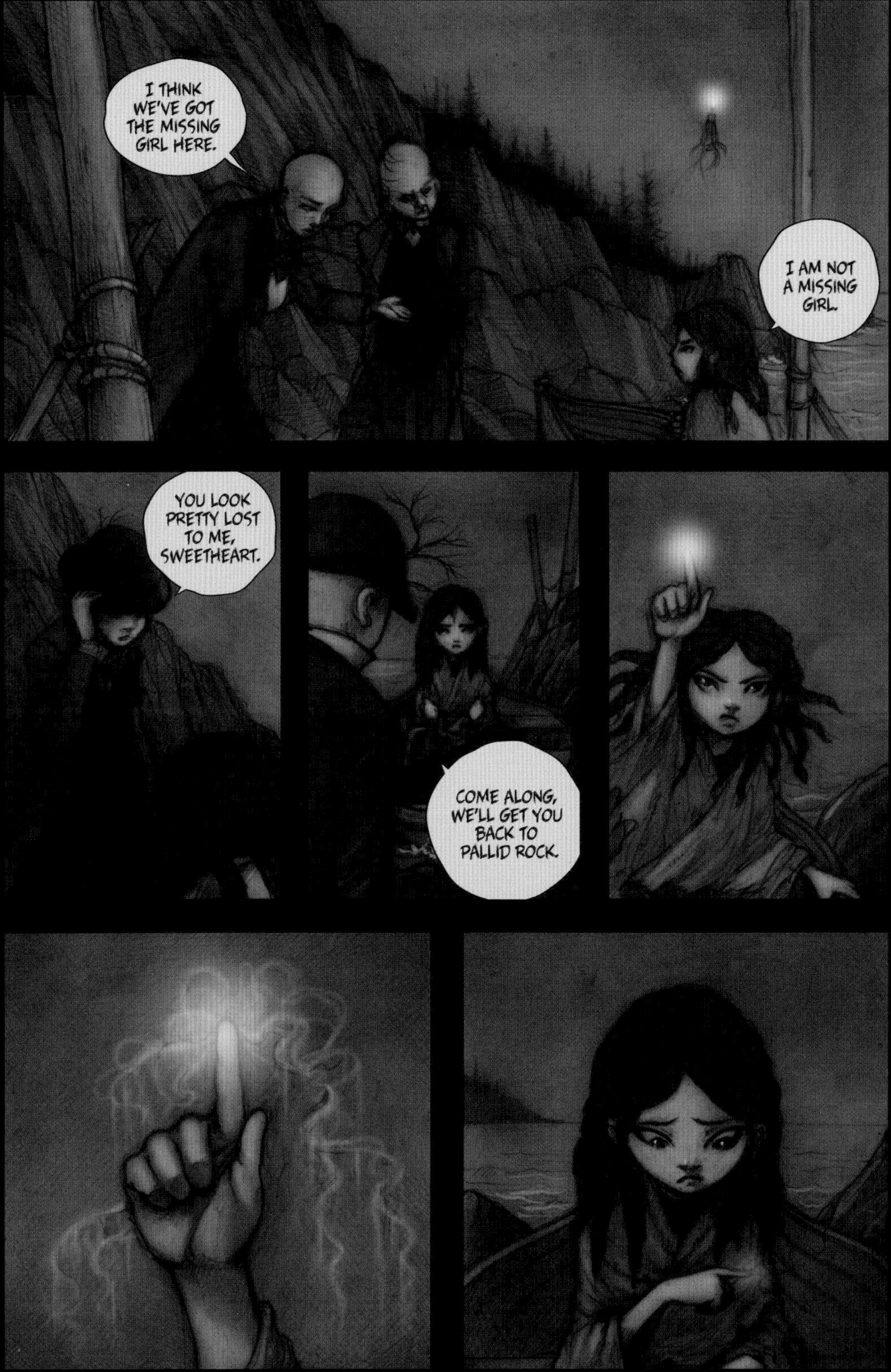
I THINK WE'VE GOT THE MISSING GIRL HERE.
I AM NOT A MISSING GIRL.
YOU LOOK PRETTY LOST TO ME, SWEETHEART.
COME ALONG, WE'LL GET YOU BACK TO PALLID ROCK.

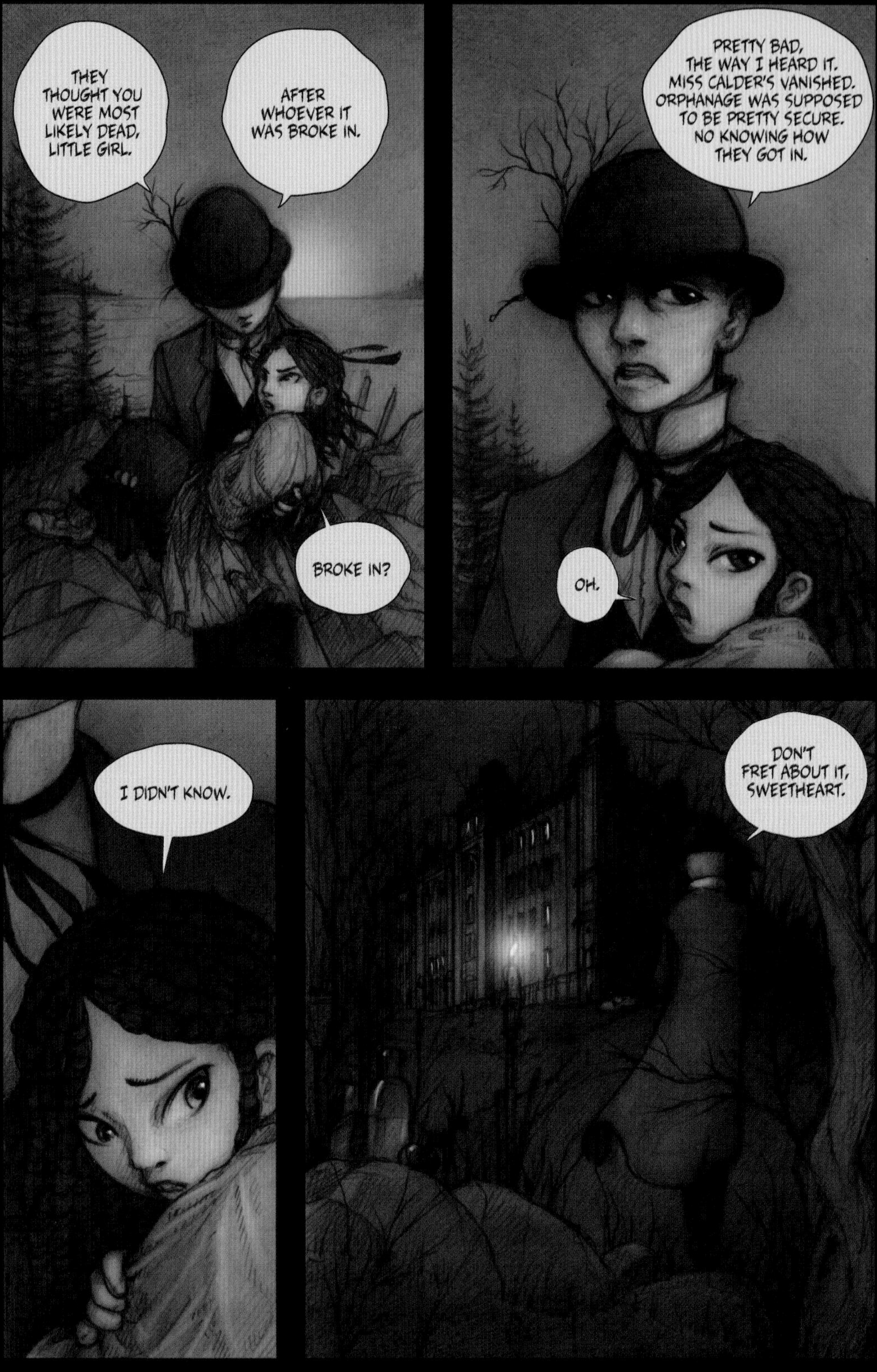
THEY THOUGHT YOU WERE MOST LIKELY DEAD, LITTLE GIRL.
AFTER WHOEVER IT WAS BROKE IN.
BROKE IN?
PRETTY BAD, THE WAY I HEARD IT. MISS CALDER'S VANISHED. ORPHANAGE WAS SUPPOSED TO BE PRETTY SECURE. NO KNOWING HOW THEY GOT IN.
OH.
I DIDN'T KNOW.
DON'T FRET ABOUT IT, SWEETHEART.

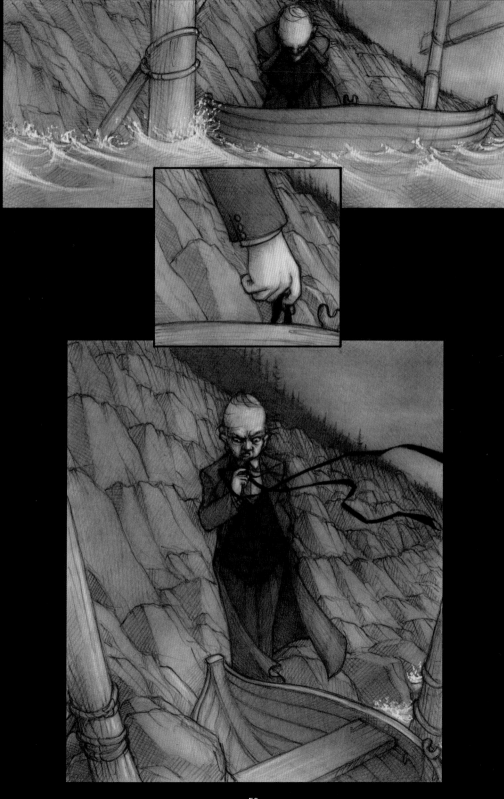

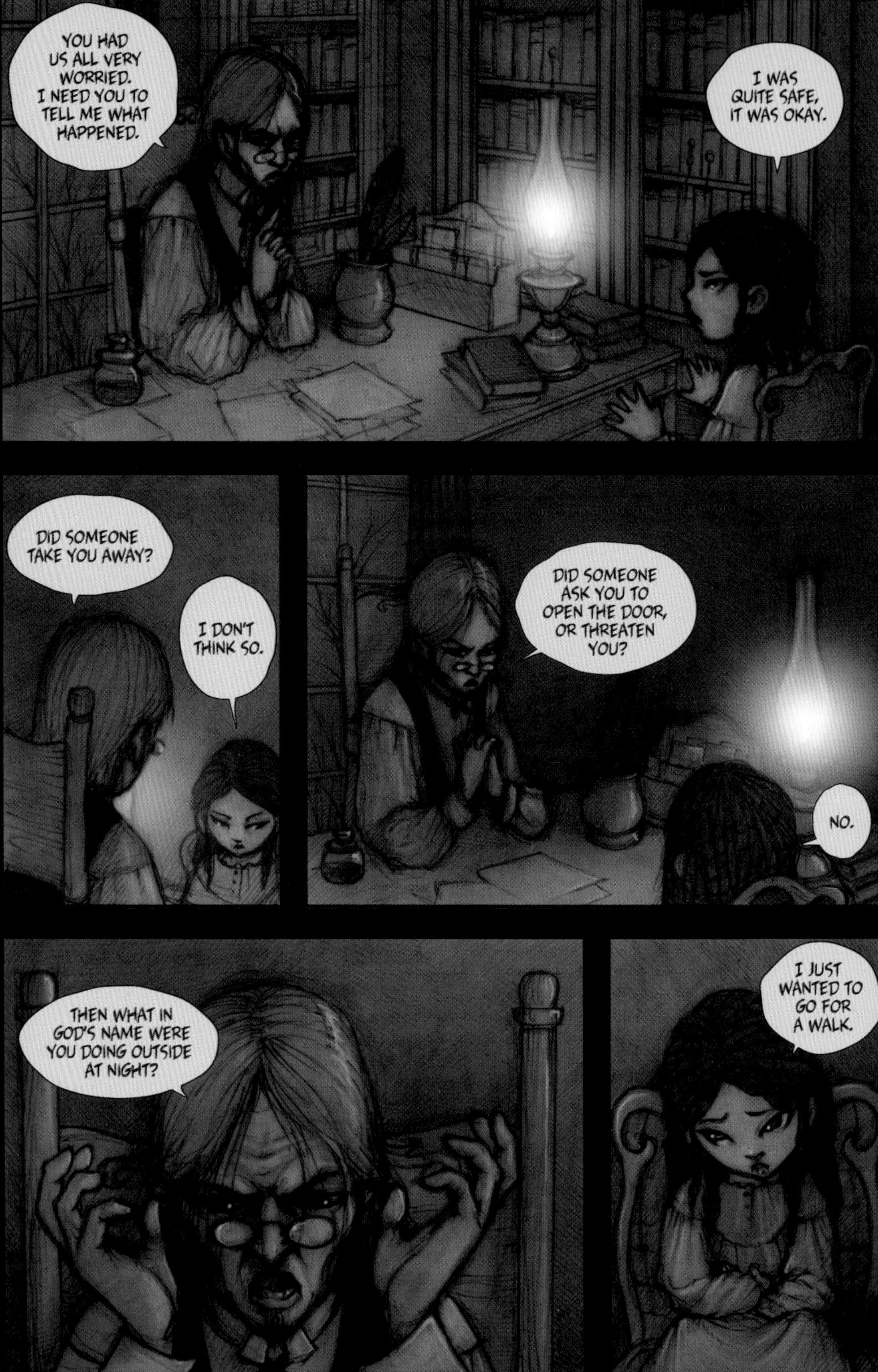
YOU HAD US ALL VERY WORRIED. I NEED YOU TO TELL ME WHAT HAPPENED.
I WAS QUITE SAFE, IT WAS OKAY.
DID SOMEONE TAKE YOU AWAY?
I DON'T THINK SO.
DID SOMEONE ASK YOU TO OPEN THE DOOR, OR THREATEN YOU?
NO.
THEN WHAT IN GOD'S NAME WERE YOU DOING OUTSIDE AT NIGHT?
I JUST WANTED TO GO FOR A WALK.

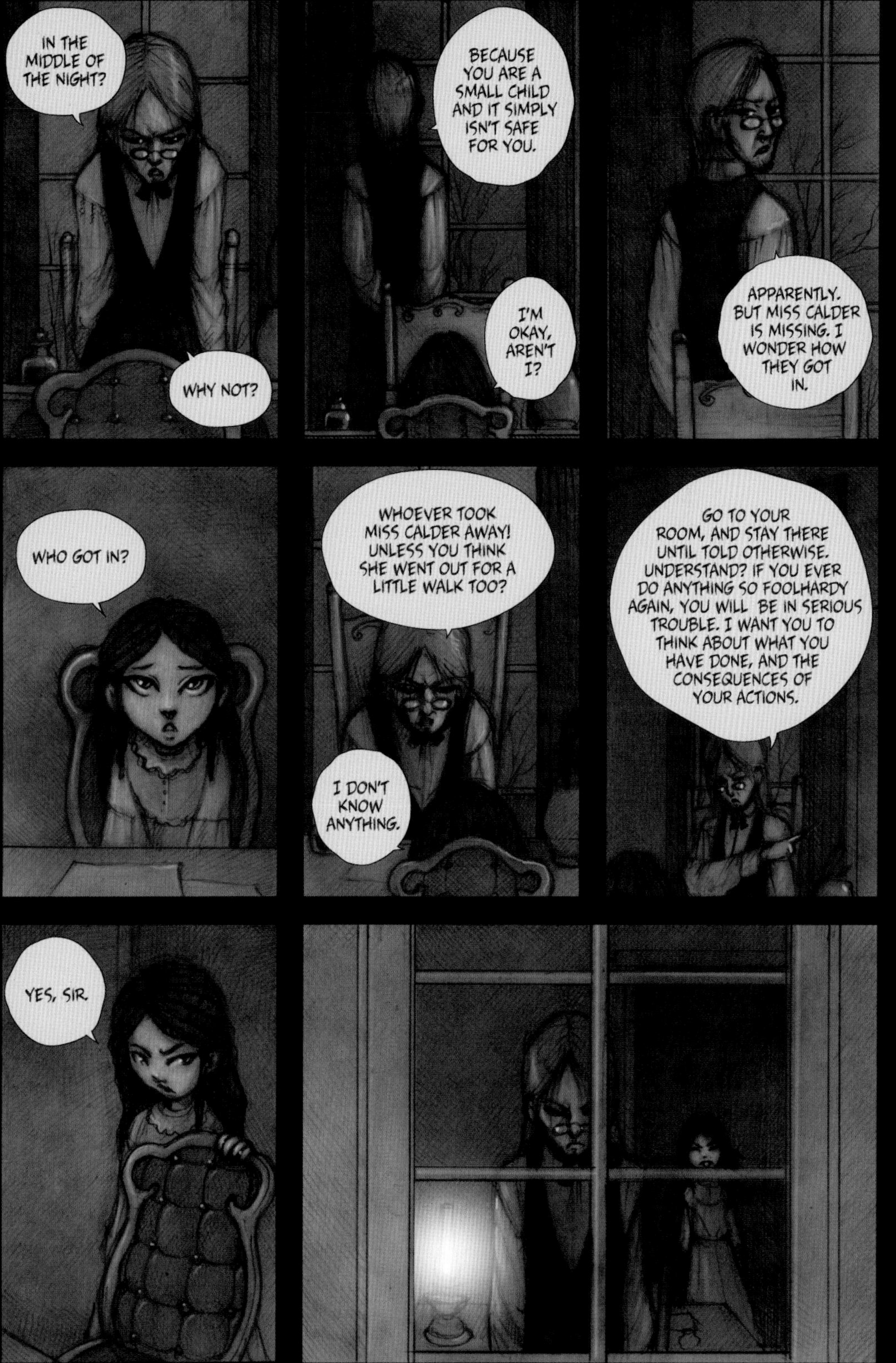
IN THE MIDDLE OF THE NIGHT?
WHY NOT?
BECAUSE YOU ARE A SMALL CHILD AND IT SIMPLY ISN'T SAFE FOR YOU.
I'M OKAY, AREN'T I?
APPARENTLY. BUT MISS CALDER IS MISSING. I WONDER HOW THEY GOT IN.
WHO GOT IN?
WHOEVER TOOK MISS CALDER AWAY! UNLESS YOU THINK SHE WENT OUT FOR A LITTLE WALK TOO?
I DON'T KNOW ANYTHING.
GO TO YOUR ROOM, AND STAY THERE UNTIL TOLD OTHERWISE. UNDERSTAND? IF YOU EVER DO ANYTHING SO FOOLHARDY AGAIN, YOU WILL BE IN SERIOUS TROUBLE. I WANT YOU TO THINK ABOUT WHAT YOU HAVE DONE, AND THE CONSEQUENCES OF YOUR ACTIONS.
YES, SIR.

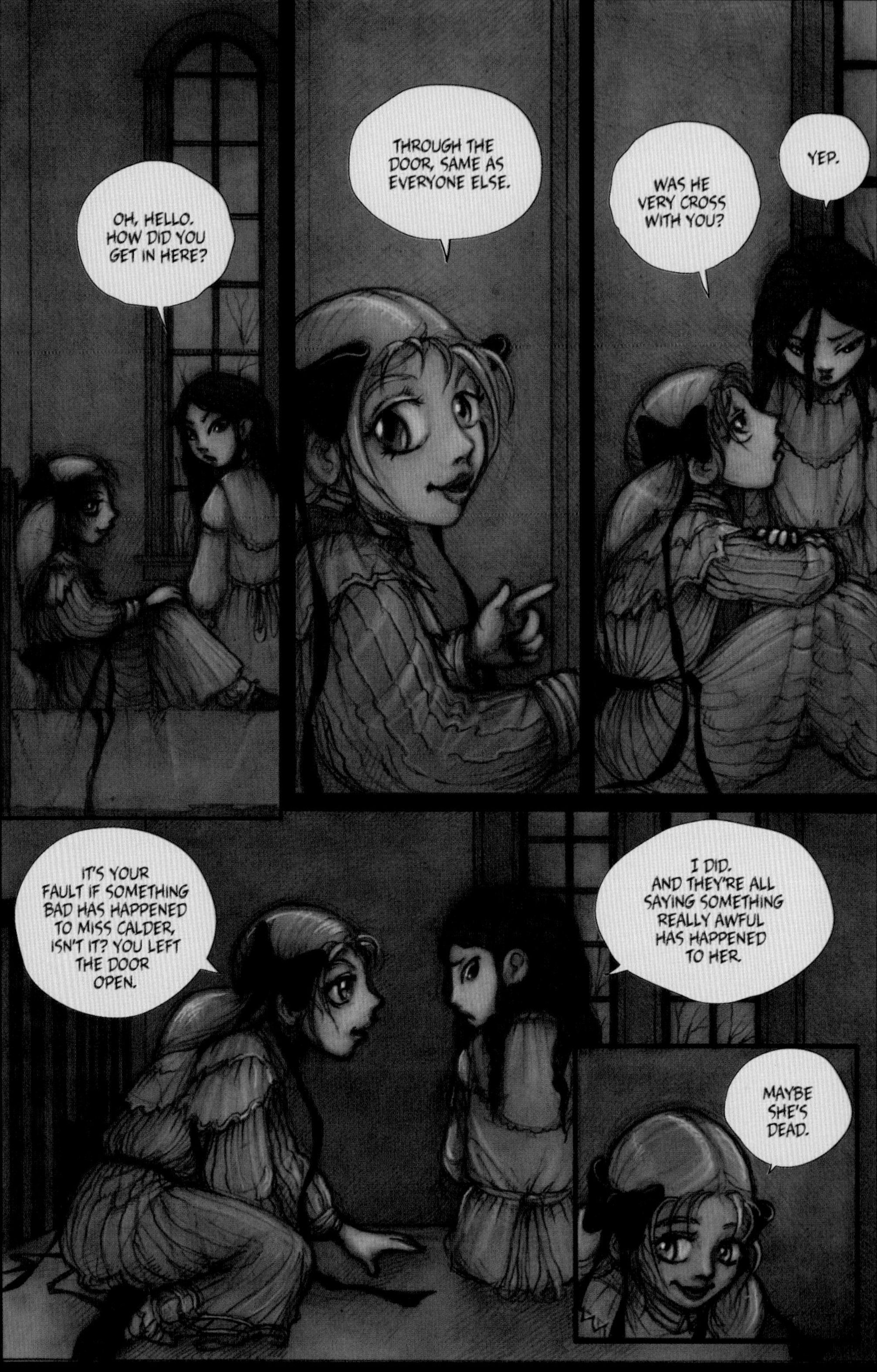
OH, HELLO. HOW DID YOU GET IN HERE?
THROUGH THE DOOR, SAME AS EVERYONE ELSE.
WAS HE VERY CROSS WITH YOU?
YEP.
IT'S YOUR FAULT IF SOMETHING BAD HAS HAPPENED TO MISS CALDER, ISN'T IT? YOU LEFT THE DOOR OPEN.
I DID. AND THEY'RE ALL SAYING SOMETHING REALLY AWFUL HAS HAPPENED TO HER.
MAYBE SHE'S DEAD.

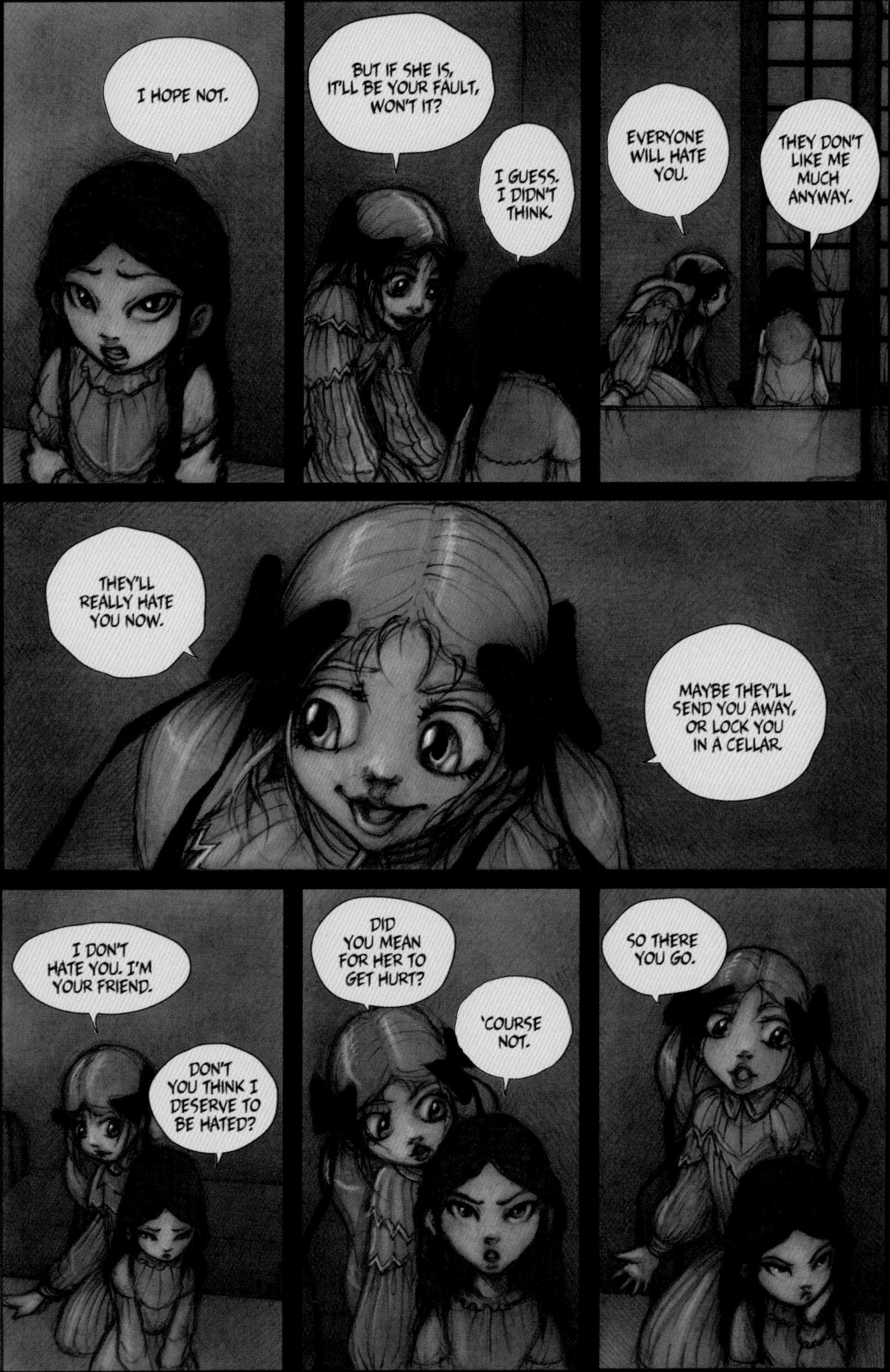
I HOPE NOT.
BUT IF SHE IS, IT'LL BE YOUR FAULT, WON'T IT?
I GUESS. I DIDN'T THINK.
EVERYONE WILL HATE YOU.
THEY DON'T LIKE ME MUCH ANYWAY.
THEY'LL REALLY HATE YOU NOW.
MAYBE THEY'LL SEND YOU AWAY, OR LOCK YOU IN A CELLAR.
I DON'T HATE YOU. I'M YOUR FRIEND.
DON'T YOU THINK I DESERVE TO BE HATED?
DID YOU MEAN FOR HER TO GET HURT?
'COURSE NOT.
SO THERE YOU GO.

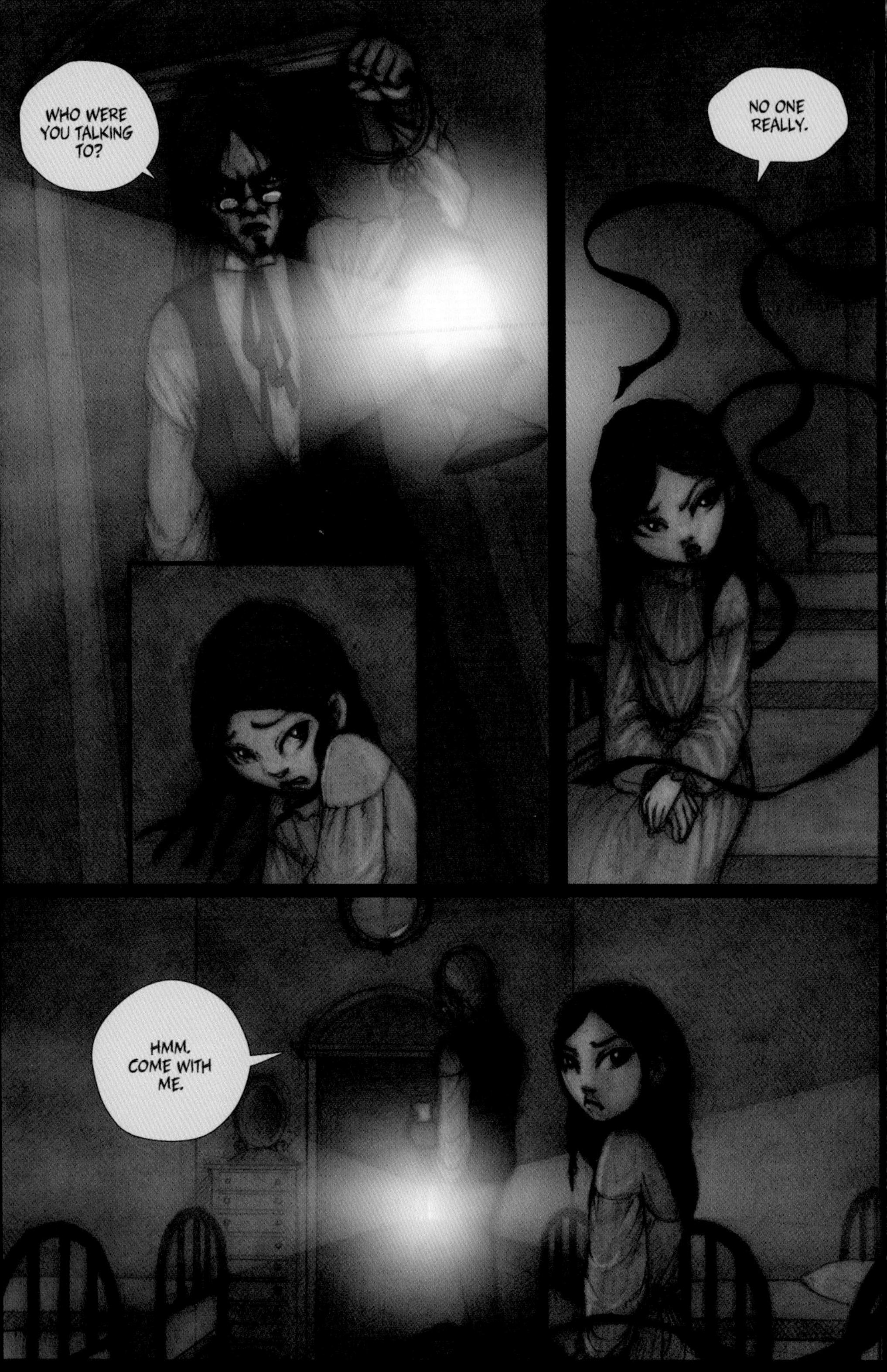
WHO WERE YOU TALKING TO?
NO ONE REALLY.
HMM. COME WITH ME.

CHAPTER FOUR

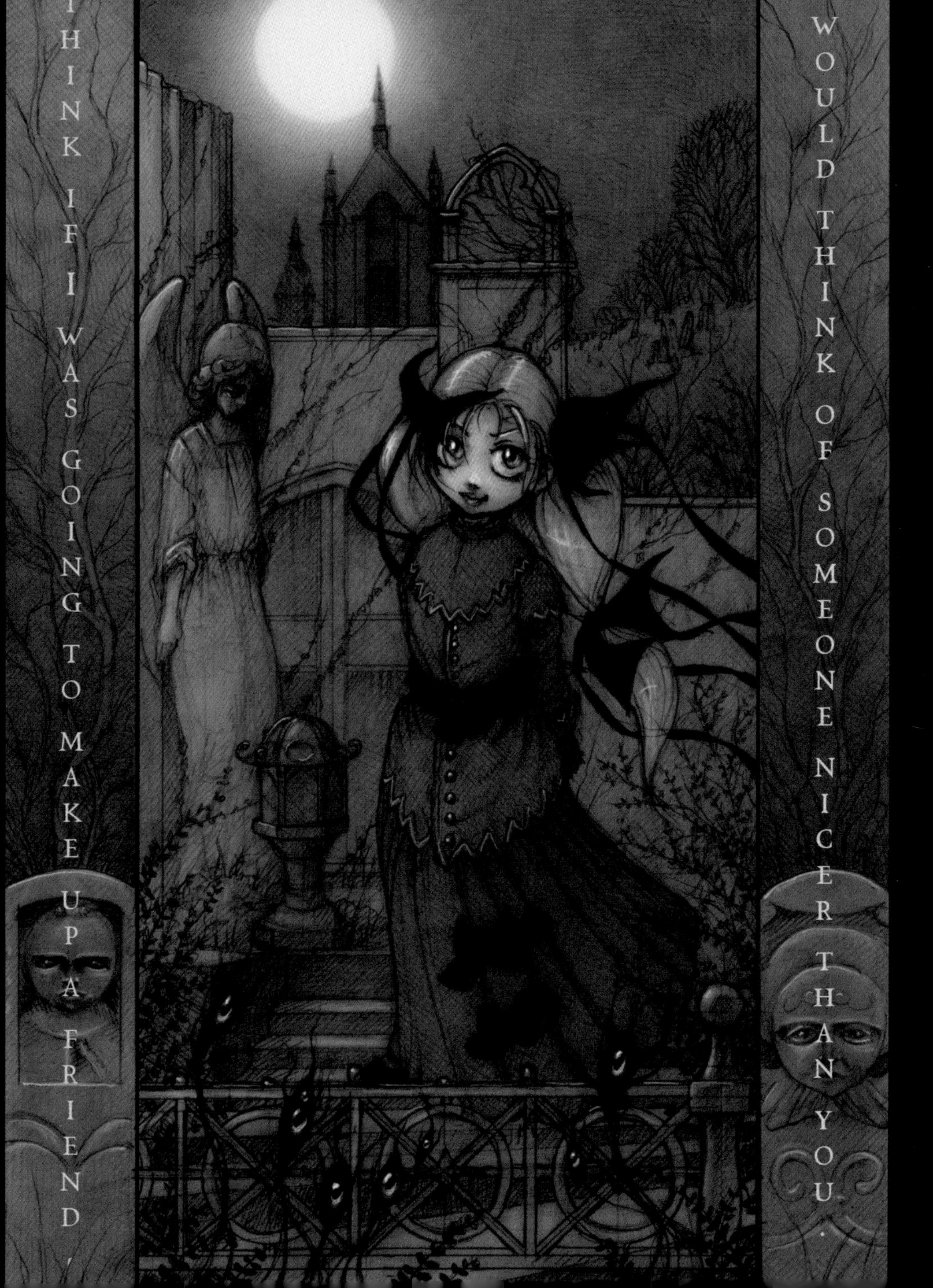
I THINK IF I WAS GOING TO MAKE UP A FRIEND,
I WOULD THINK OF SOMEONE NICER THAN YOU.

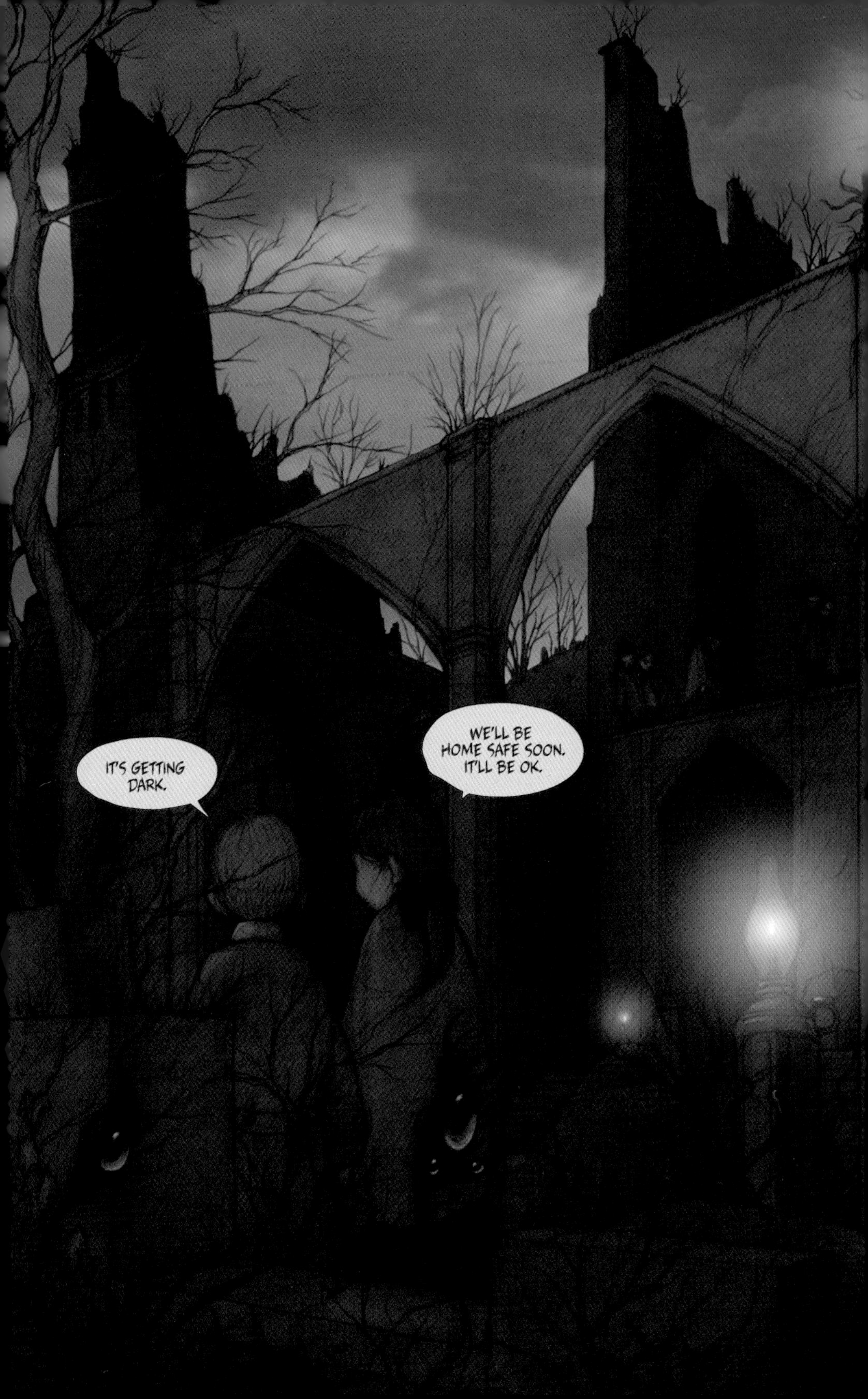
IT'S GETTING DARK.
WE'LL BE HOME SAFE SOON. IT'LL BE OK.

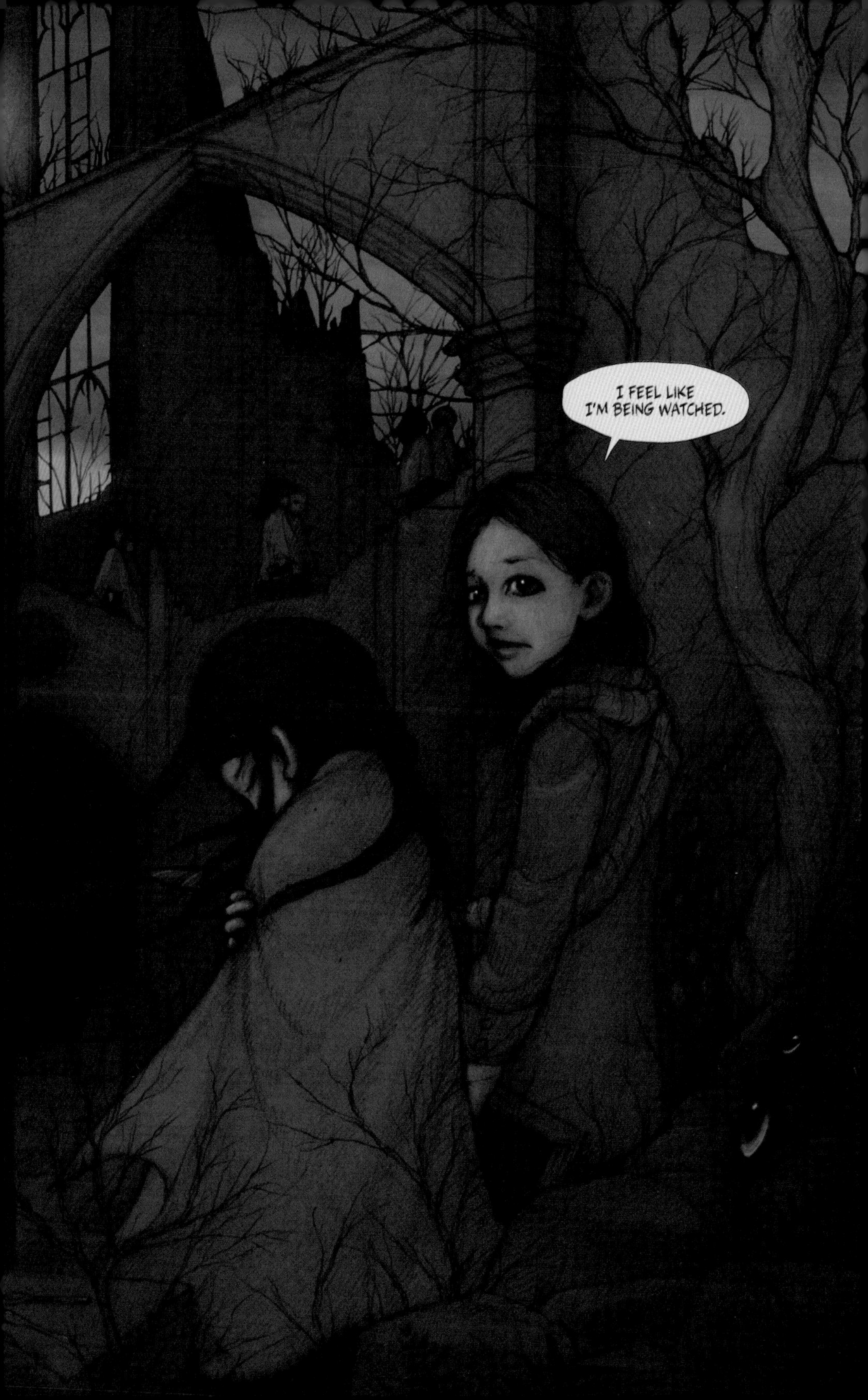
I FEEL LIKE I'M BEING WATCHED.

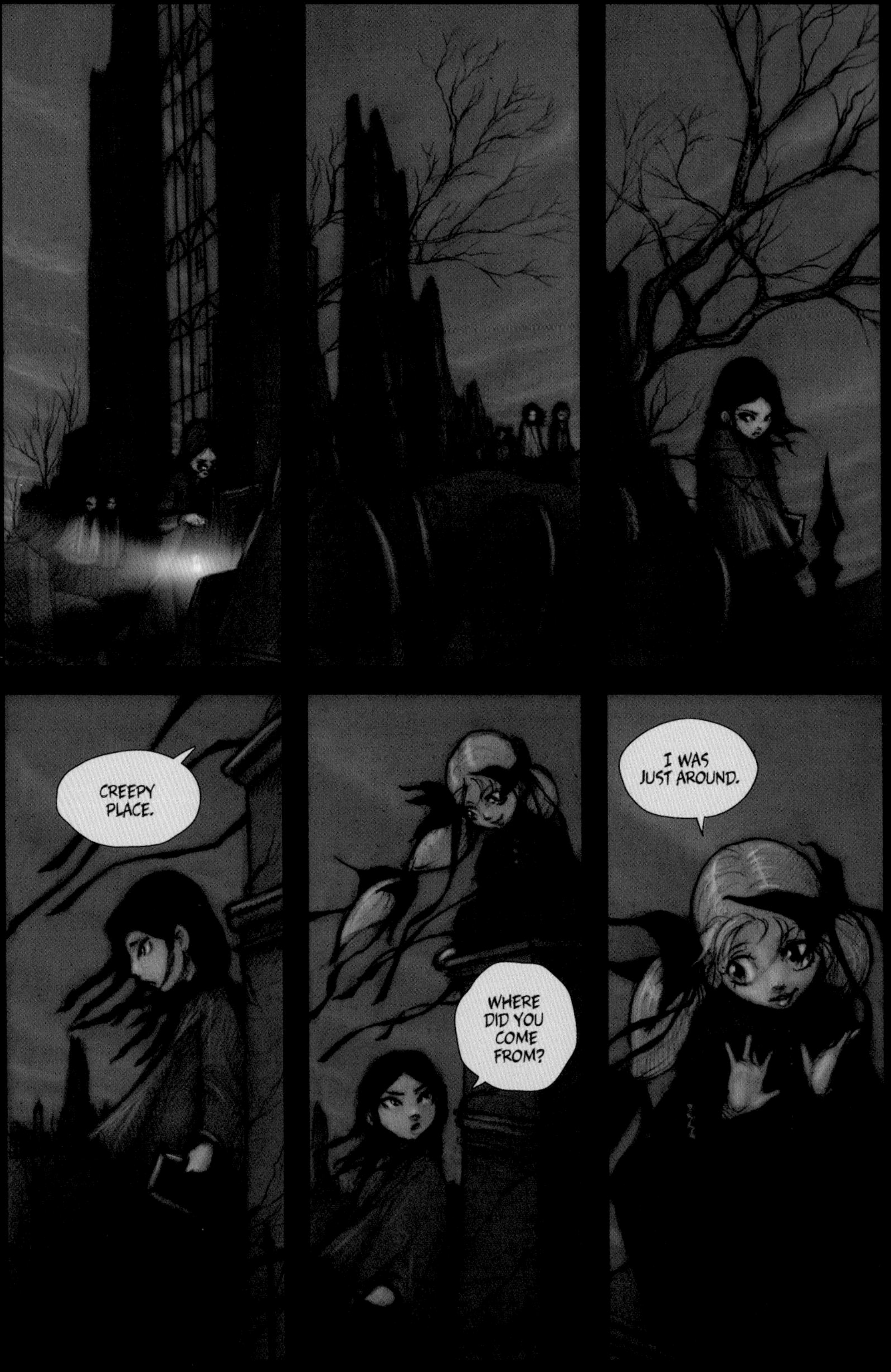
CREEPY PLACE.
WHERE DID YOU COME FROM?
I WAS JUST AROUND.

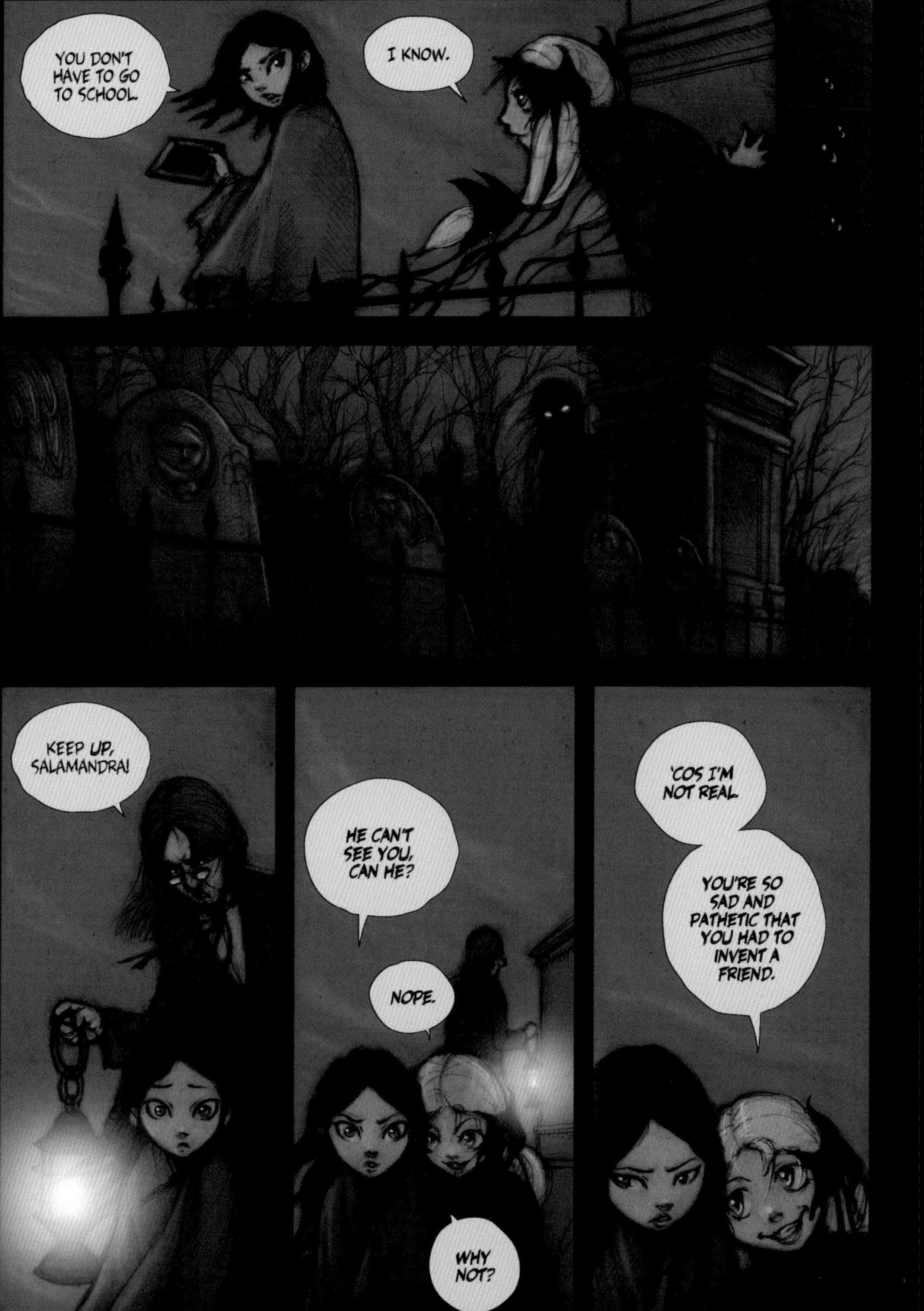
YOU DON'T HAVE TO GO TO SCHOOL.
I KNOW.
KEEP UP, SALAMANDRA!
HE CAN'T SEE YOU, CAN HE?
NOPE.
WHY NOT?
'COS I'M NOT REAL.
YOU'RE SO SAD AND PATHETIC THAT YOU HAD TO INVENT A FRIEND.

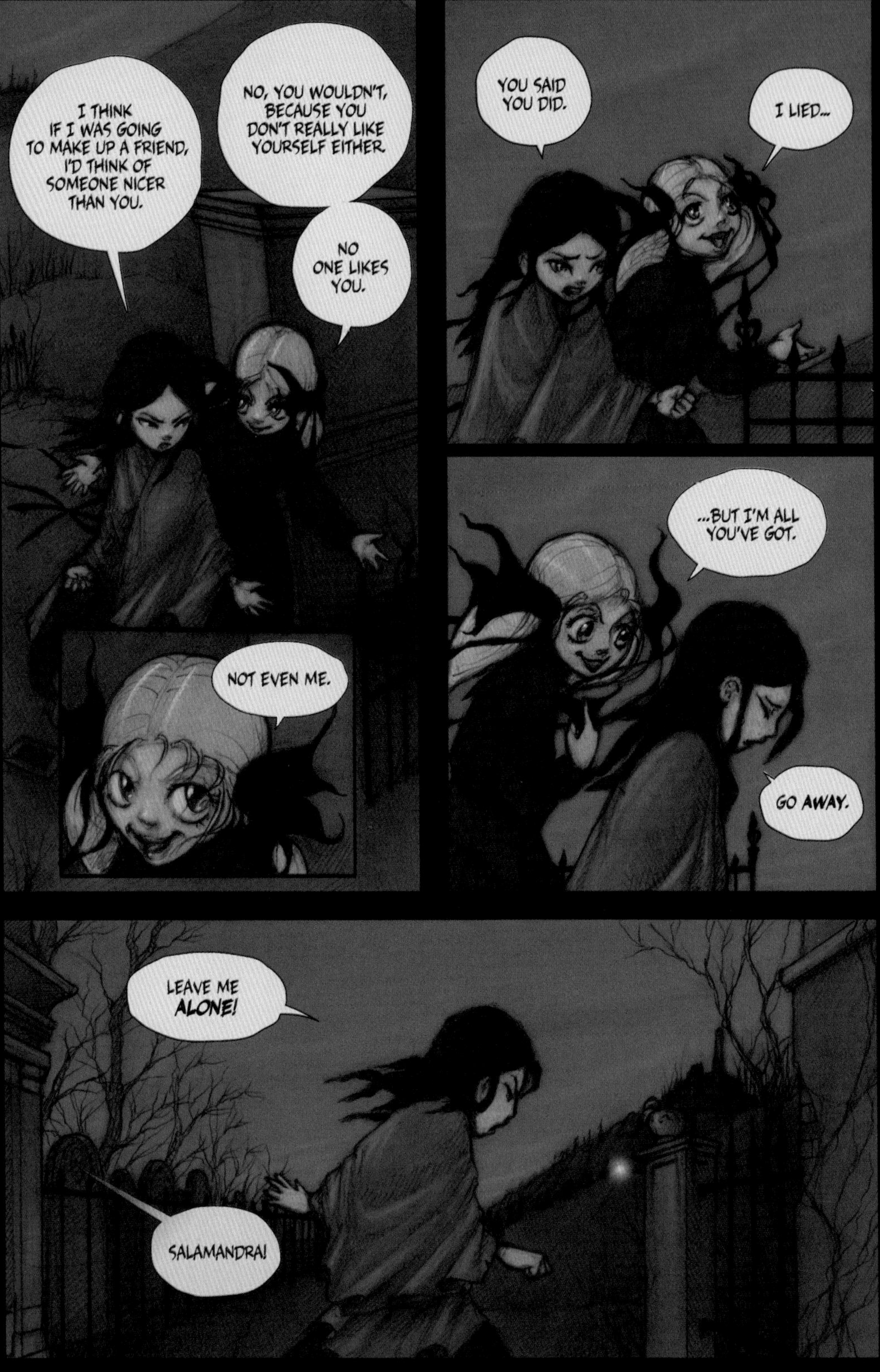
I THINK IF I WAS GOING TO MAKE UP A FRIEND, I'D THINK OF SOMEONE NICER THAN YOU.
NO, YOU WOULDN'T, BECAUSE YOU DON'T REALLY LIKE YOURSELF EITHER.
NO ONE LIKES YOU.
NOT EVEN ME.
YOU SAID YOU DID.
I LIED...
...BUT I'M ALL YOU'VE GOT.
GO AWAY.
LEAVE ME ALONE!
SALAMANDRA!

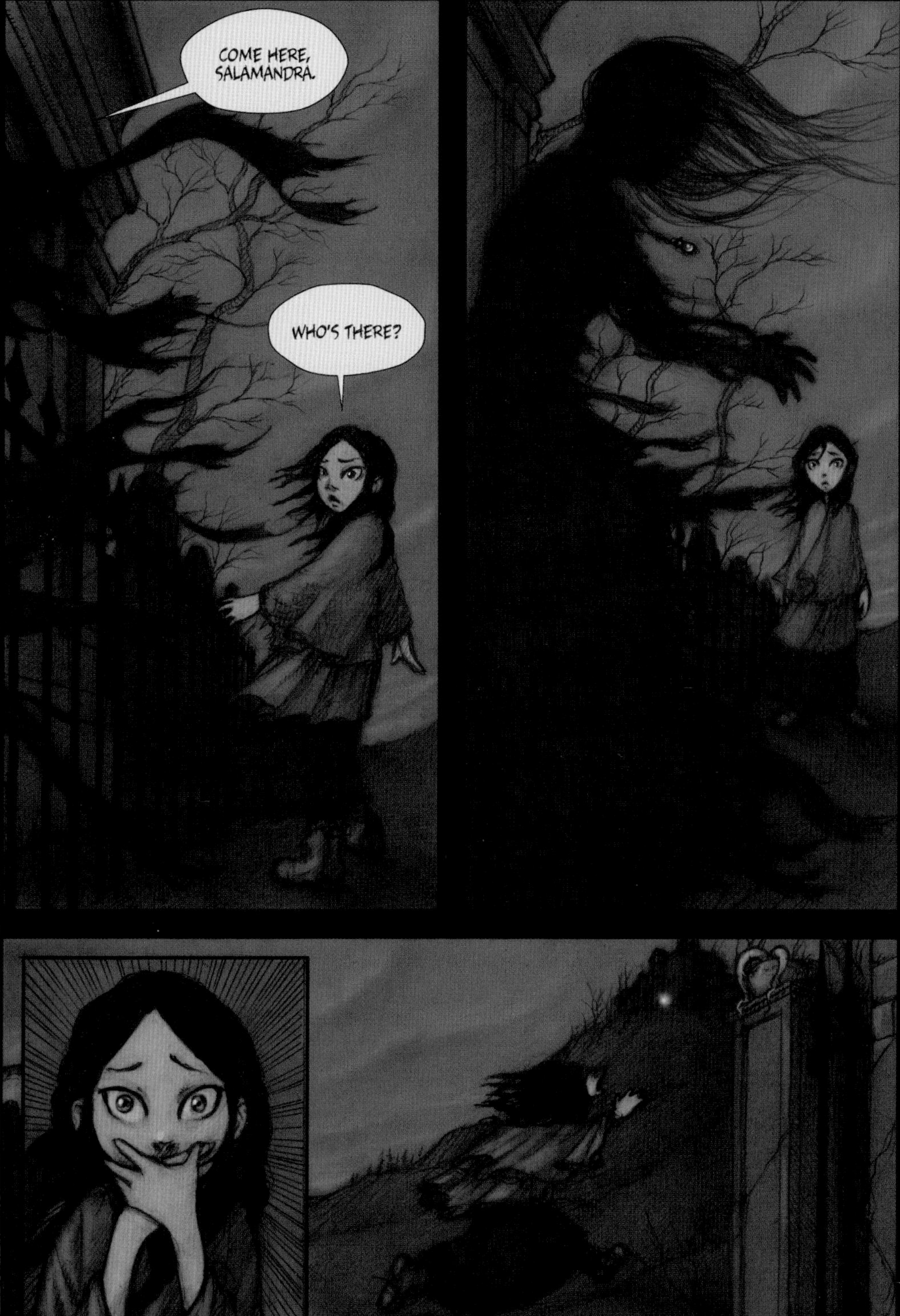
COME HERE, SALAMANDRA.
WHO'S THERE?

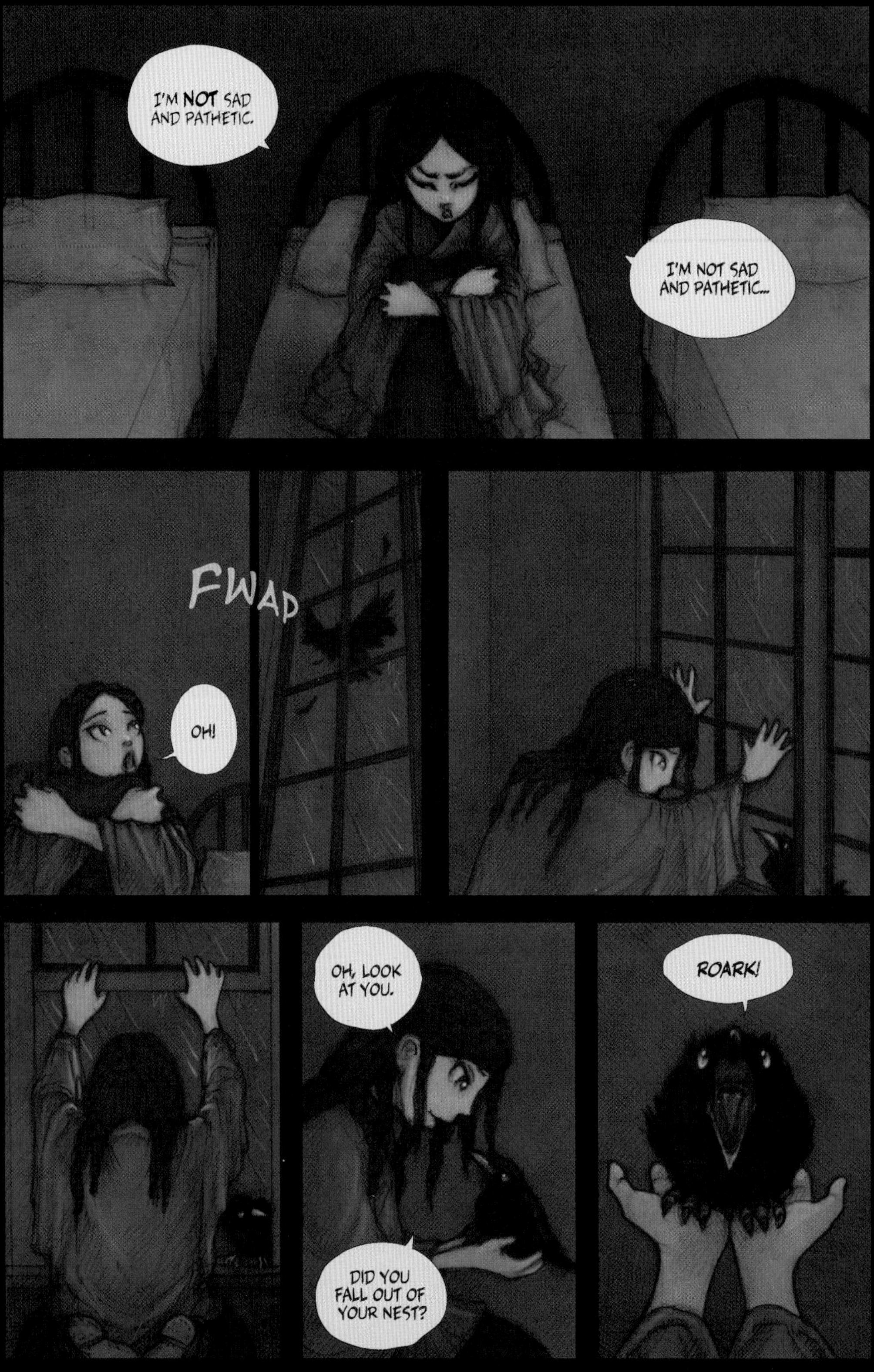
I'M NOT SAD AND PATHETIC.
I'M NOT SAD AND PATHETIC...
FWAP
OH!
OH, LOOK AT YOU.
DID YOU FALL OUT OF YOUR NEST?
ROARK!

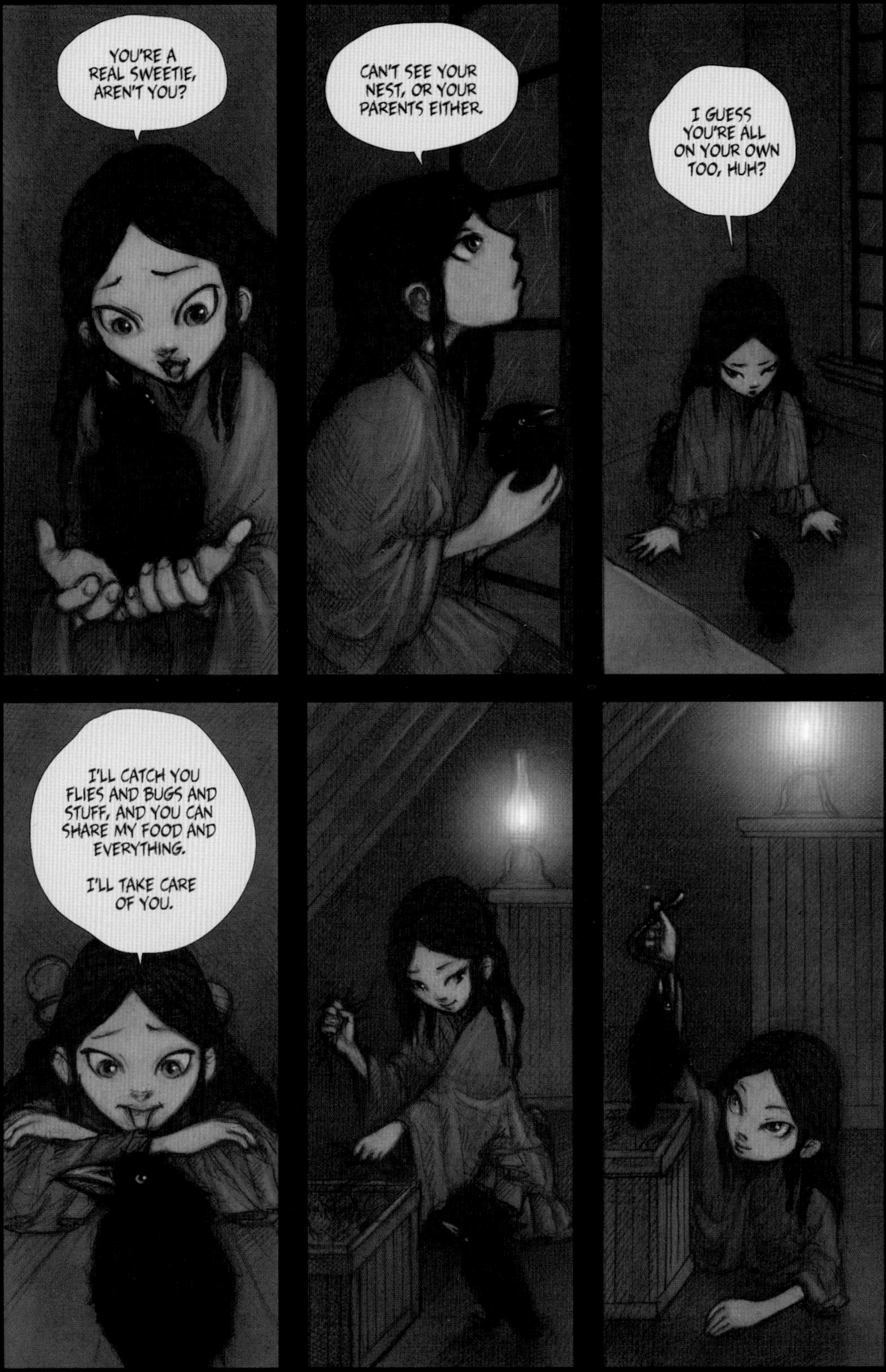
YOU'RE A REAL SWEETIE, AREN'T YOU?
CAN'T SEE YOUR NEST, OR YOUR PARENTS EITHER.
I GUESS YOU'RE ALL ON YOUR OWN TOO, HUH?
I'LL CATCH YOU FLIES AND BUGS AND STUFF, AND YOU CAN SHARE MY FOOD AND EVERYTHING.
I'LL TAKE CARE OF YOU.

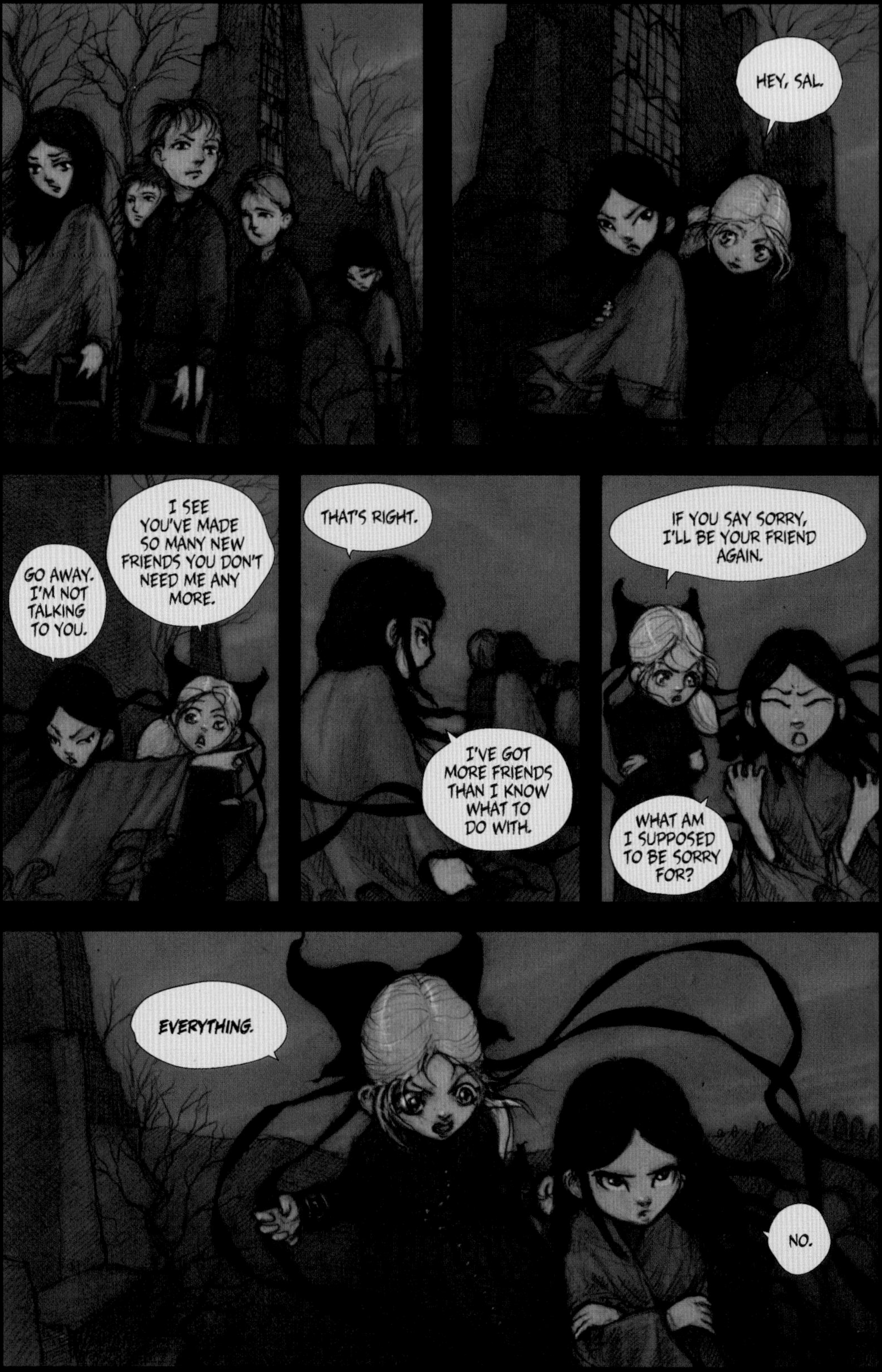
HEY, SAL.
GO AWAY. I'M NOT TALKING TO YOU.
I SEE YOU'VE MADE SO MANY NEW FRIENDS YOU DON'T NEED ME ANY MORE.
THAT'S RIGHT.
I'VE GOT MORE FRIENDS THAN I KNOW WHAT TO DO WITH.
IF YOU SAY SORRY, I'LL BE YOUR FRIEND AGAIN.
WHAT AM I SUPPOSED TO BE SORRY FOR?
EVERYTHING.
NO.

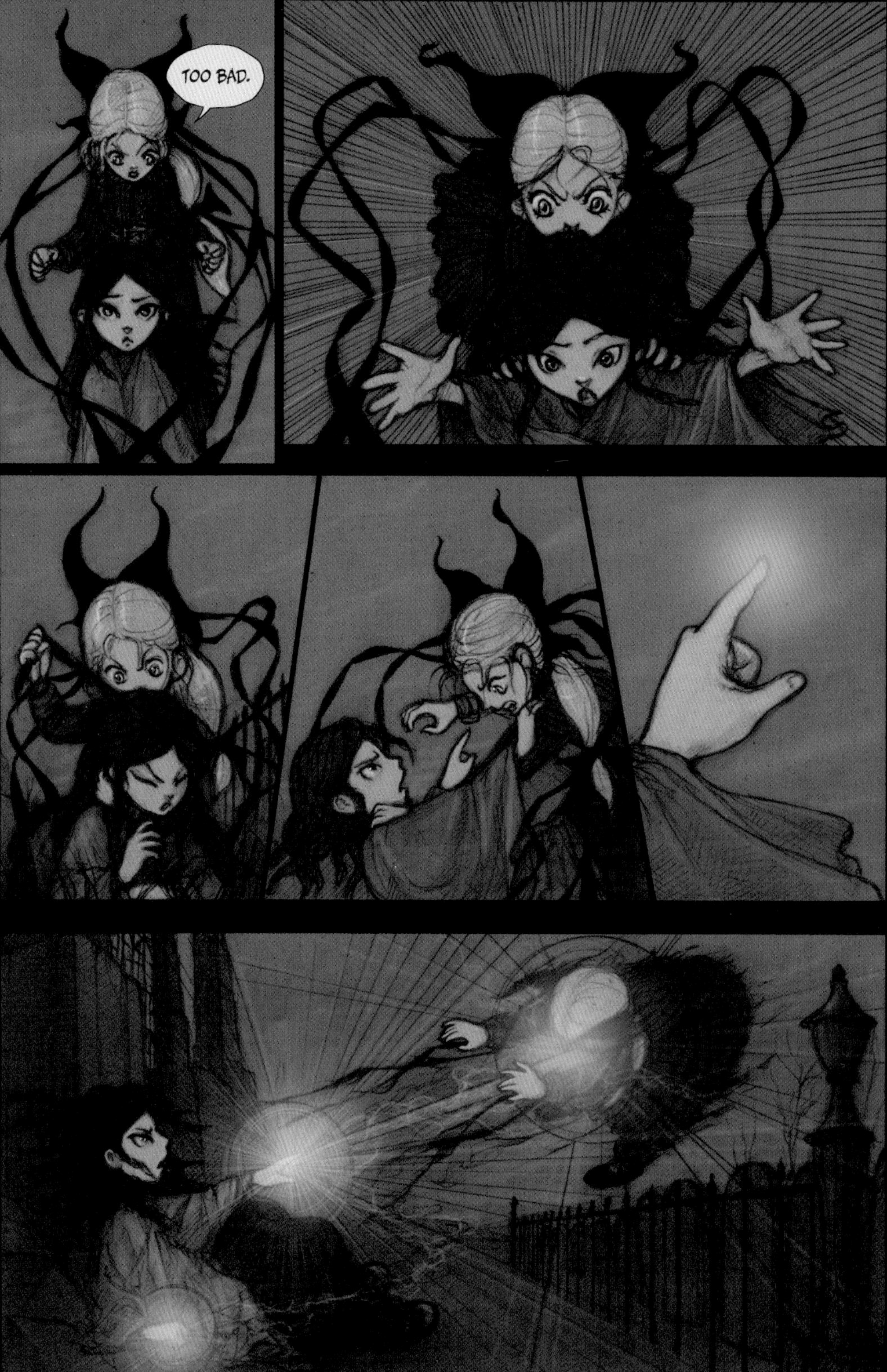
TOO BAD.

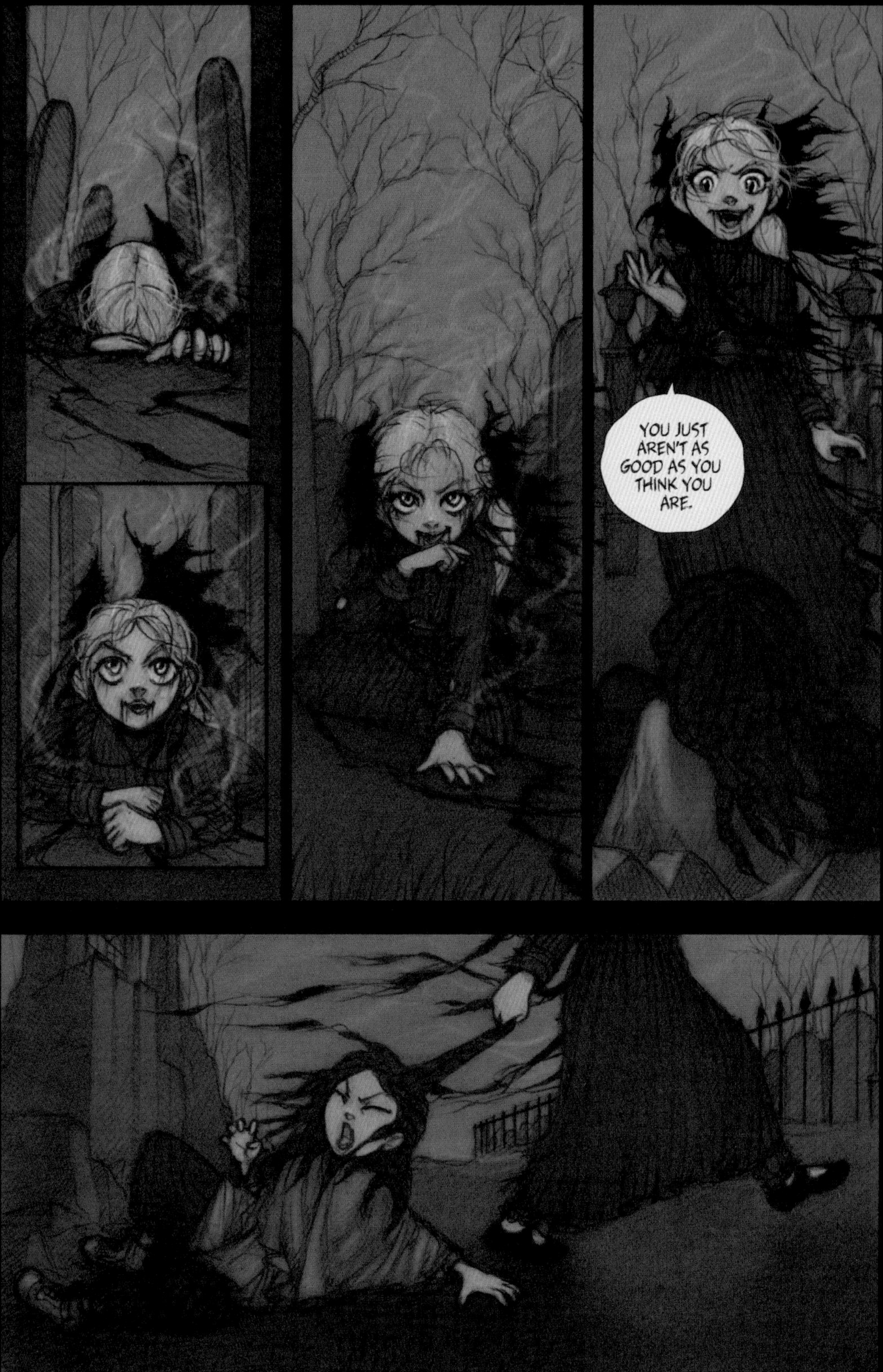
YOU JUST AREN'T AS GOOD AS YOU THINK YOU ARE.

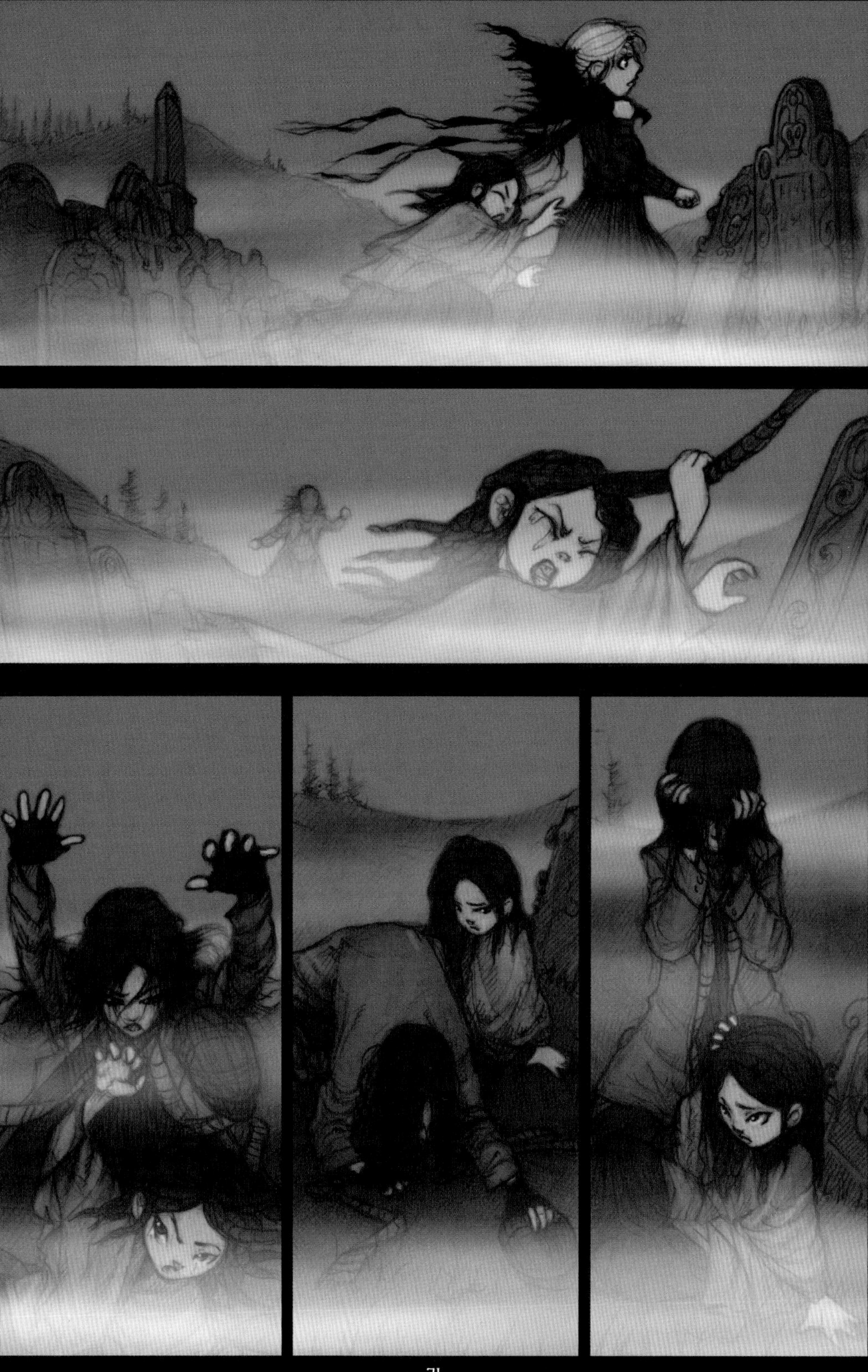

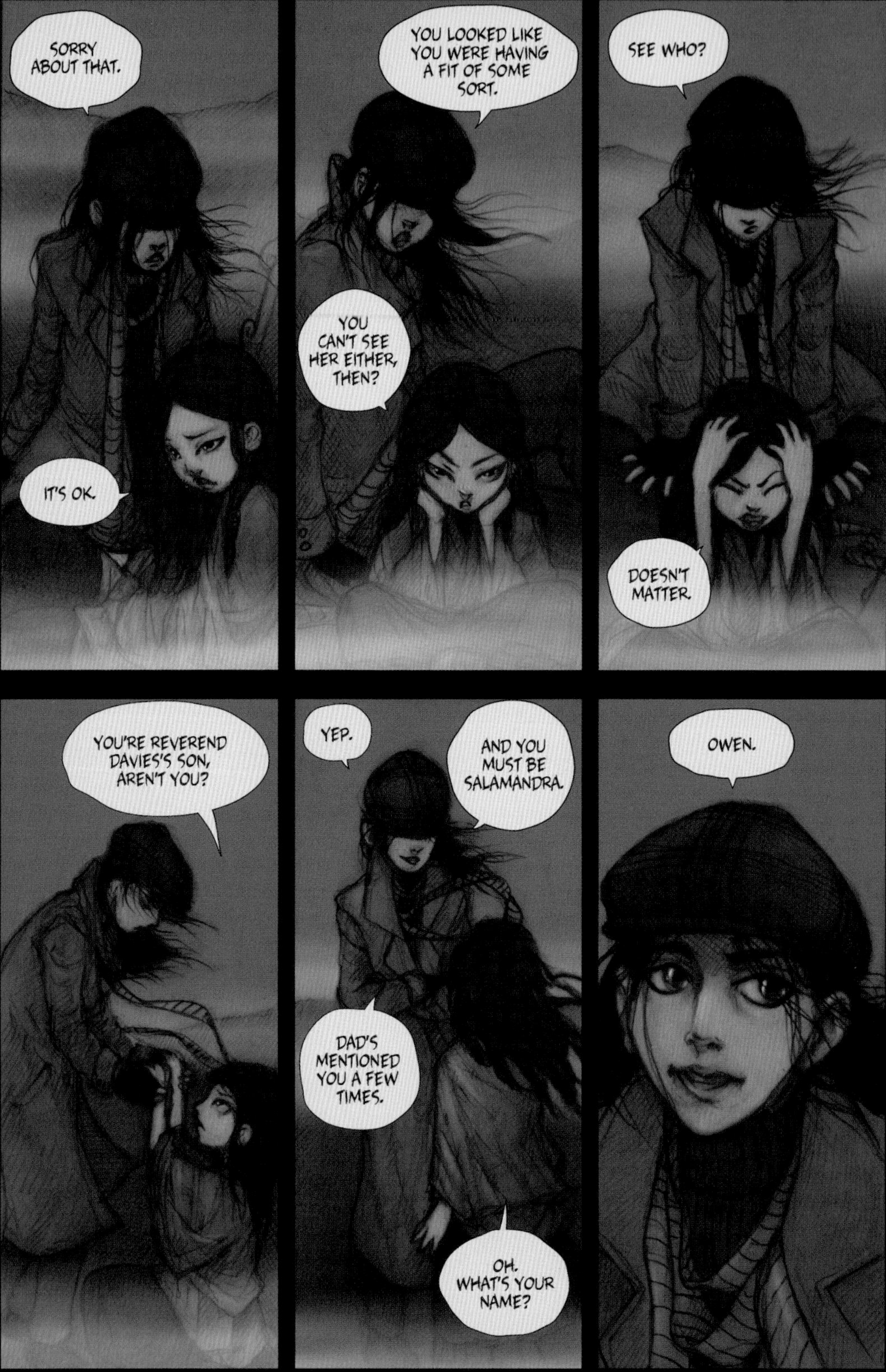
SORRY ABOUT THAT.
IT'S OK.
YOU LOOKED LIKE YOU WERE HAVING A FIT OF SOME SORT.
YOU CAN'T SEE HER EITHER, THEN?
SEE WHO?
DOESN'T MATTER.
YOU'RE REVEREND DAVIES'S SON, AREN'T YOU?
YEP.
AND YOU MUST BE SALAMANDRA.
DAD'S MENTIONED YOU A FEW TIMES.
OH. WHAT'S YOUR NAME?
OWEN.

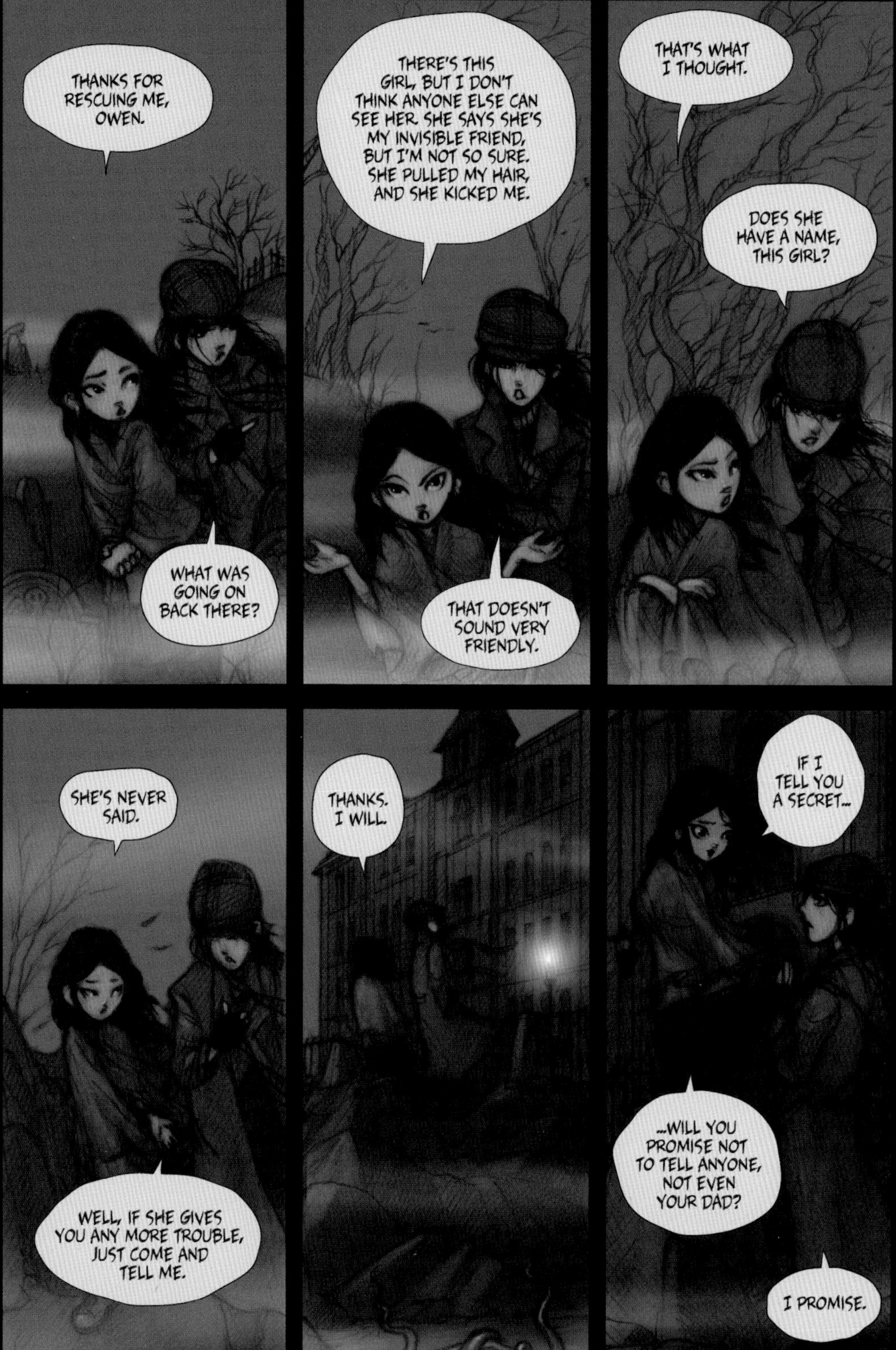
THANKS FOR RESCUING ME, OWEN.
WHAT WAS GOING ON BACK THERE?
THERE'S THIS GIRL, BUT I DON'T THINK ANYONE ELSE CAN SEE HER. SHE SAYS SHE'S MY INVISIBLE FRIEND, BUT I'M NOT SO SURE. SHE PULLED MY HAIR, AND SHE KICKED ME.
THAT DOESN'T SOUND VERY FRIENDLY.
THAT'S WHAT I THOUGHT.
DOES SHE HAVE A NAME, THIS GIRL?
SHE'S NEVER SAID.
WELL, IF SHE GIVES YOU ANY MORE TROUBLE, JUST COME AND TELL ME.
THANKS. I WILL.
IF I TELL YOU A SECRET...
...WILL YOU PROMISE NOT TO TELL ANYONE, NOT EVEN YOUR DAD?
I PROMISE.

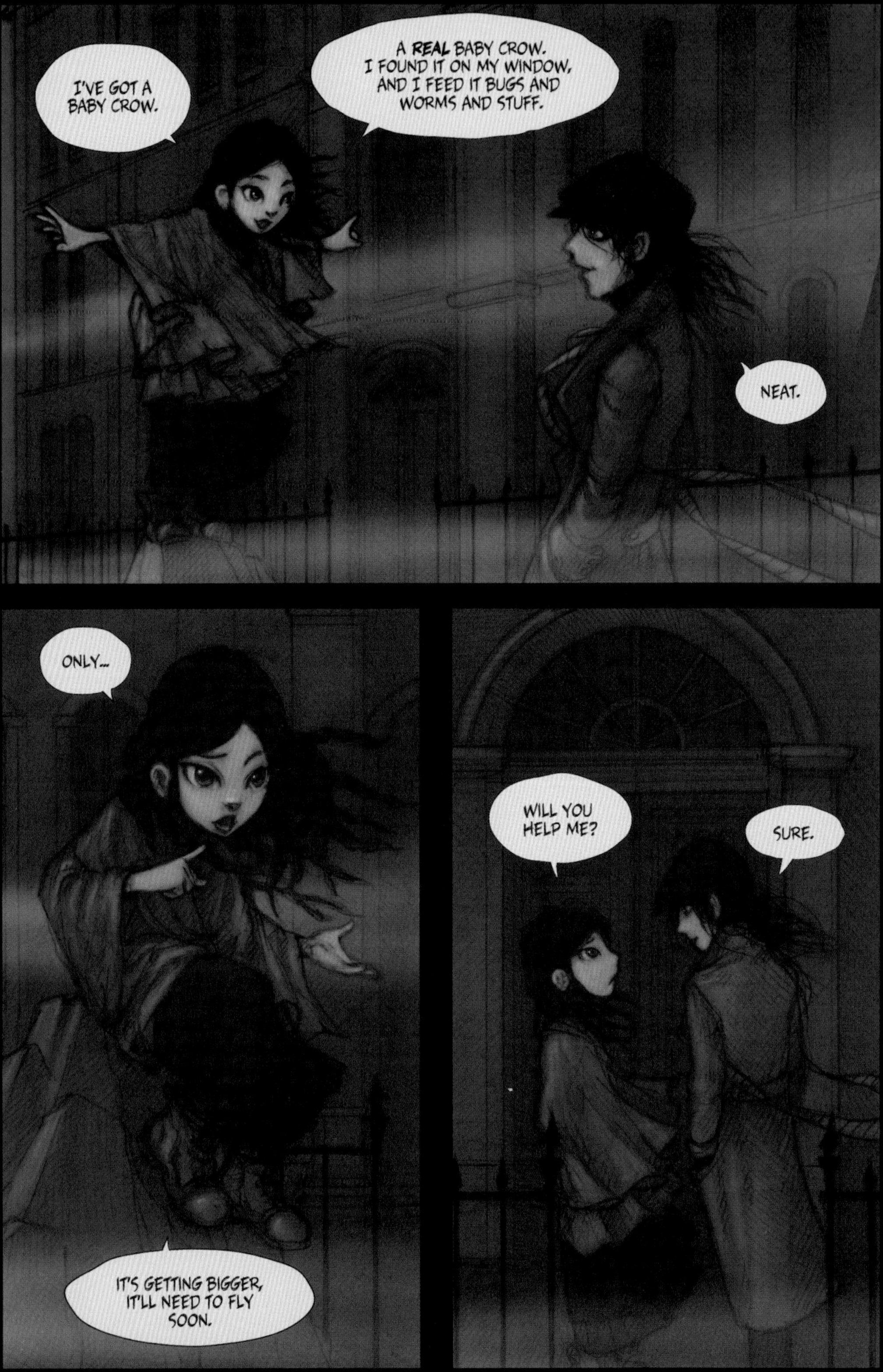
I'VE GOT A BABY CROW.
A REAL BABY CROW. I FOUND IT ON MY WINDOW, AND I FEED IT BUGS AND WORMS AND STUFF.
NEAT.
ONLY...
IT'S GETTING BIGGER, IT'LL NEED TO FLY SOON.
WILL YOU HELP ME?
SURE.

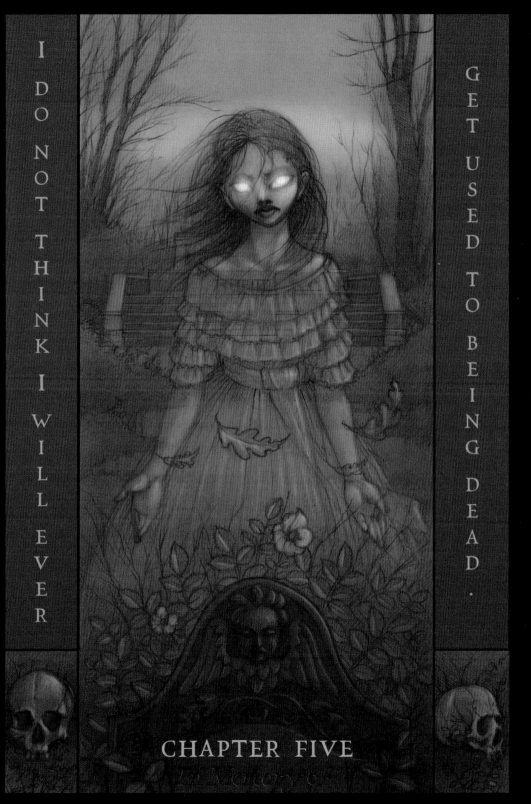

I DO NOT THINK I WILL EVER GET USED TO BEING DEAD.

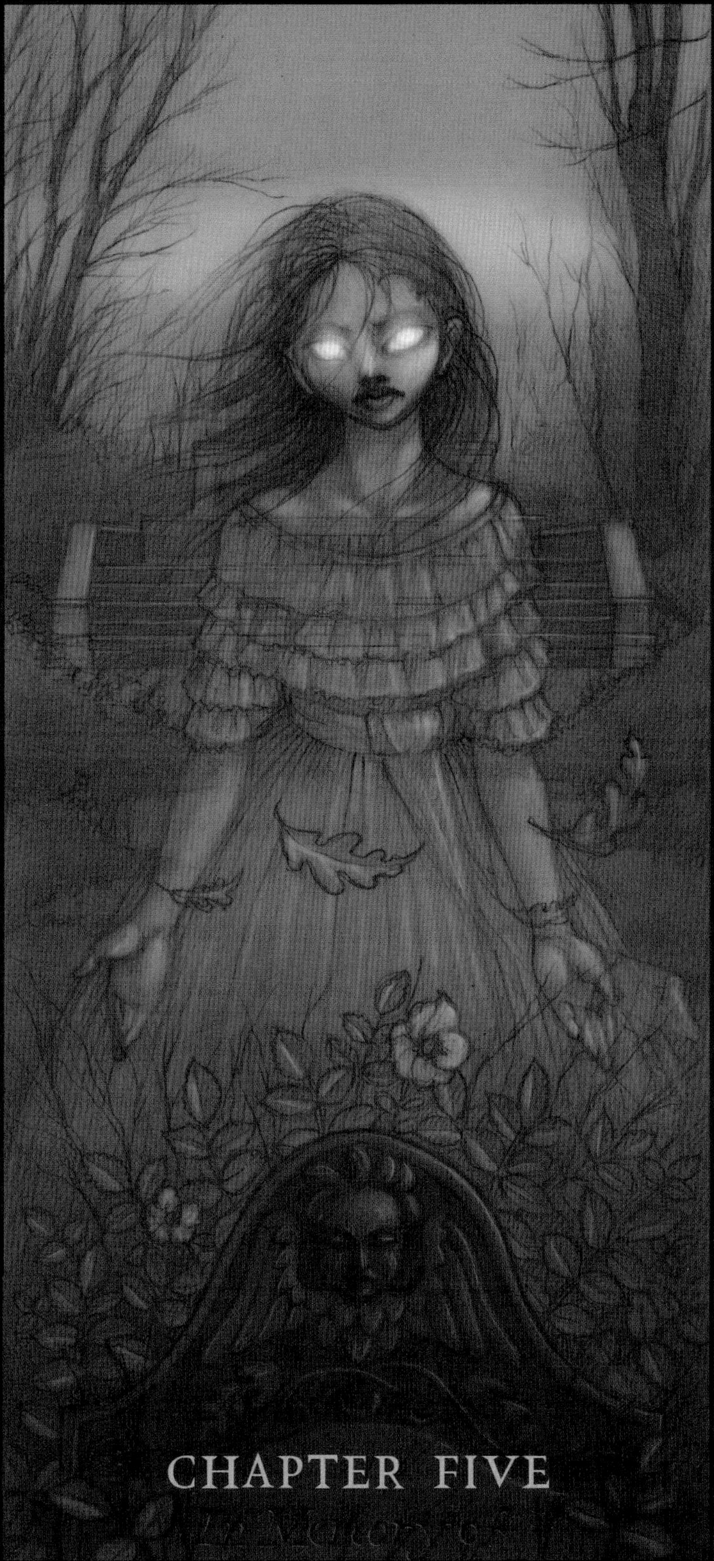

CHAPTER FIVE

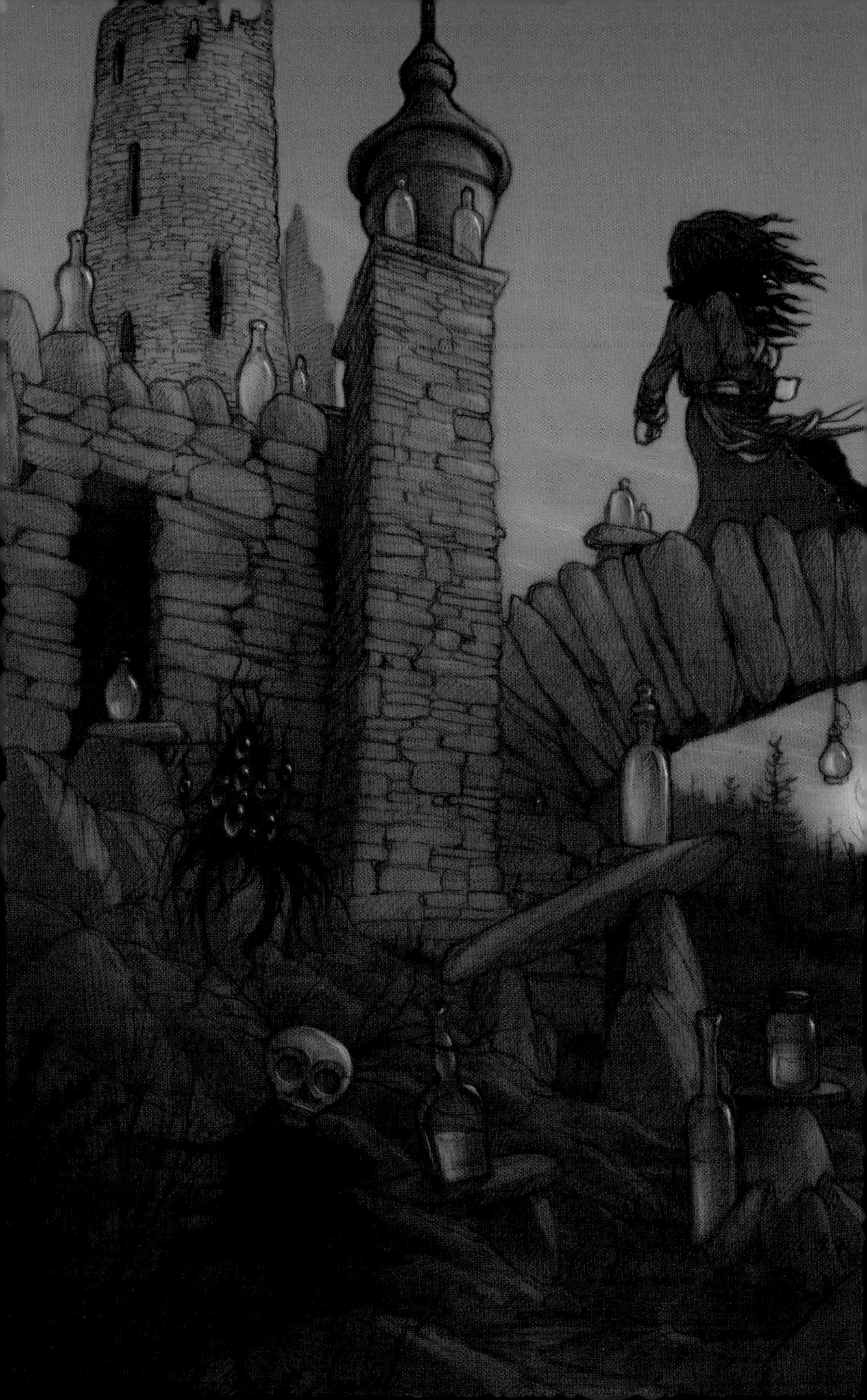

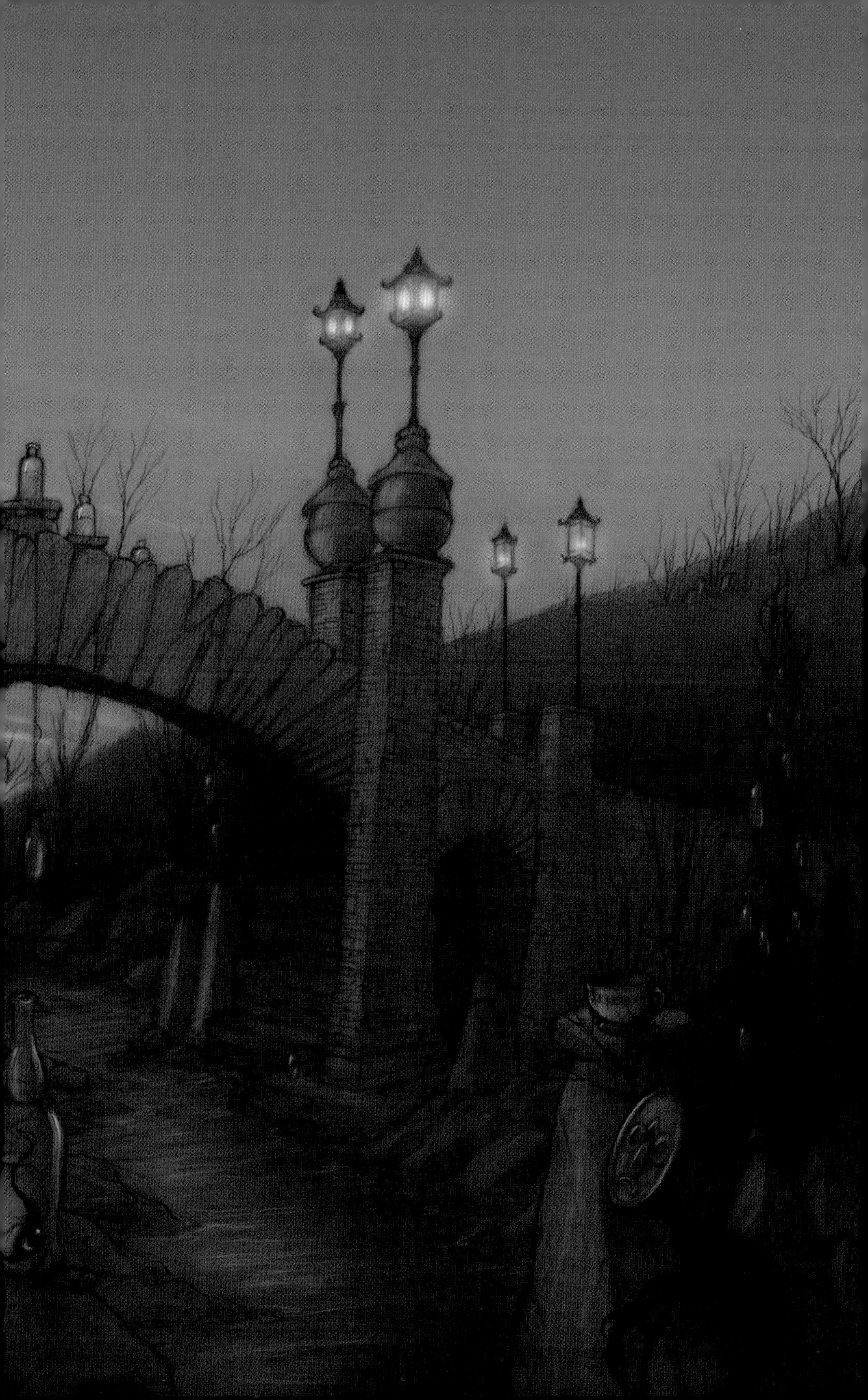

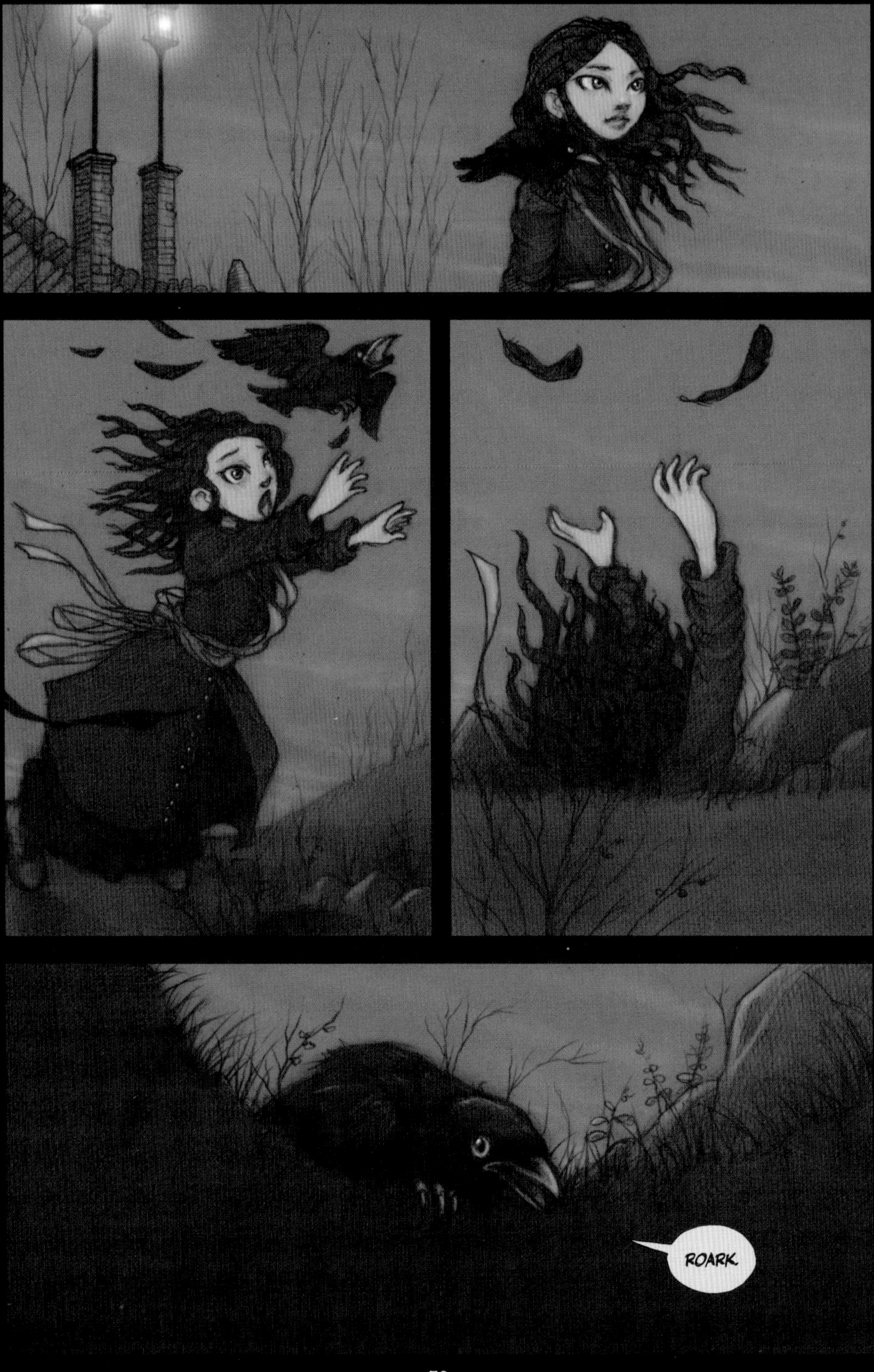
ROARK

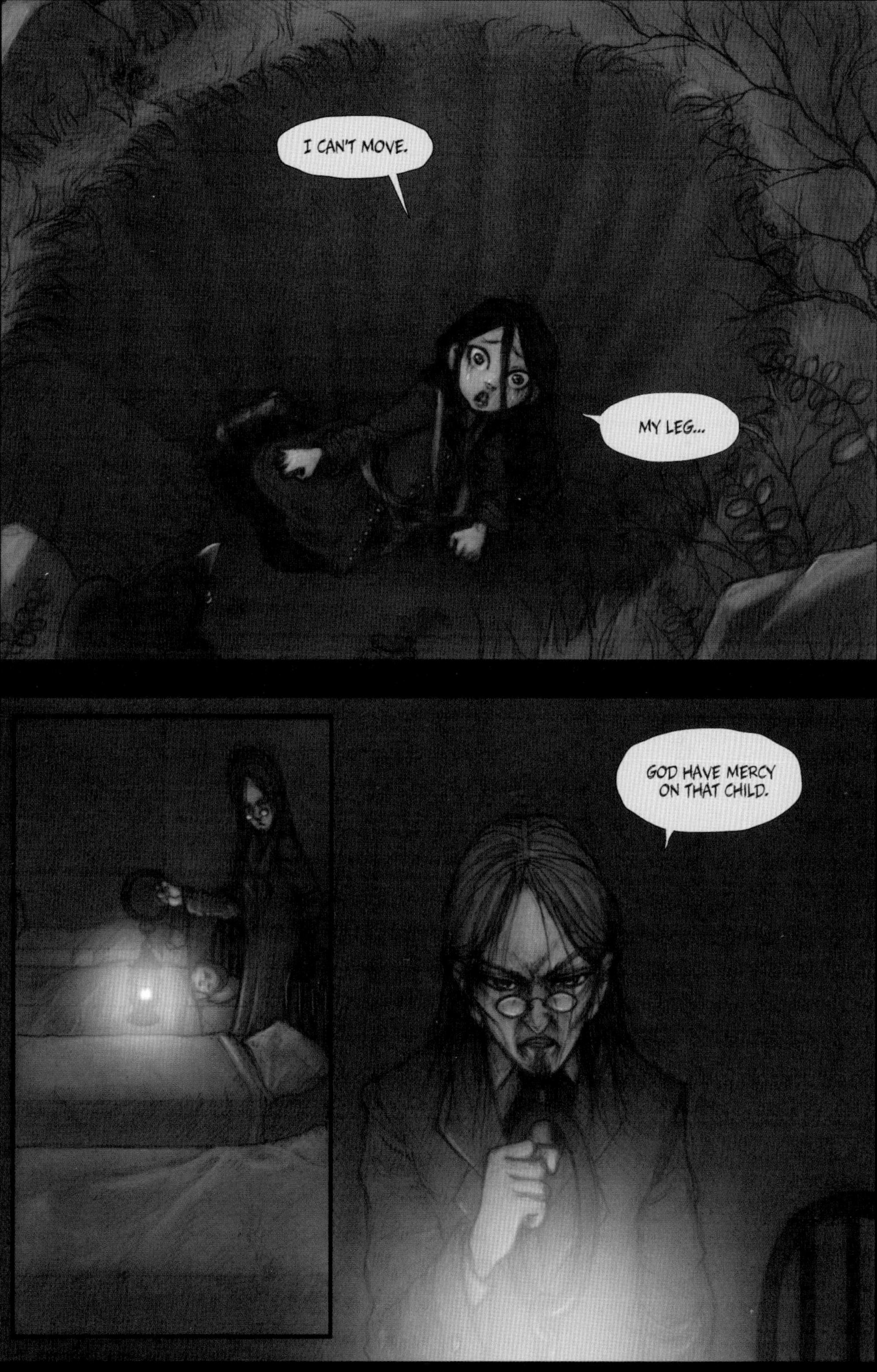
I CAN'T MOVE.
MY LEG...
GOD HAVE MERCY ON THAT CHILD.

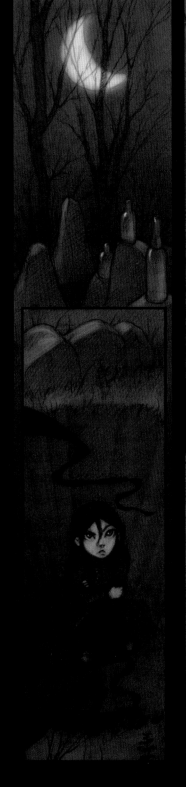

READY TO SAY SORRY YET?

NO.

I COULD HELP YOU ESCAPE.

I DON'T BELIEVE YOU.

DO YOU HAVE ANY CHOICE?

YES.

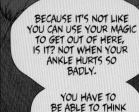

BECAUSE IT'S NOT LIKE YOU CAN USE YOUR MAGIC TO GET OUT OF HERE, IS IT? NOT WHEN YOUR ANKLE HURTS SO BADLY.

YOU HAVE TO BE ABLE TO THINK CLEARLY TO DO MAGIC, DON'T YOU?

WE'LL SEE.

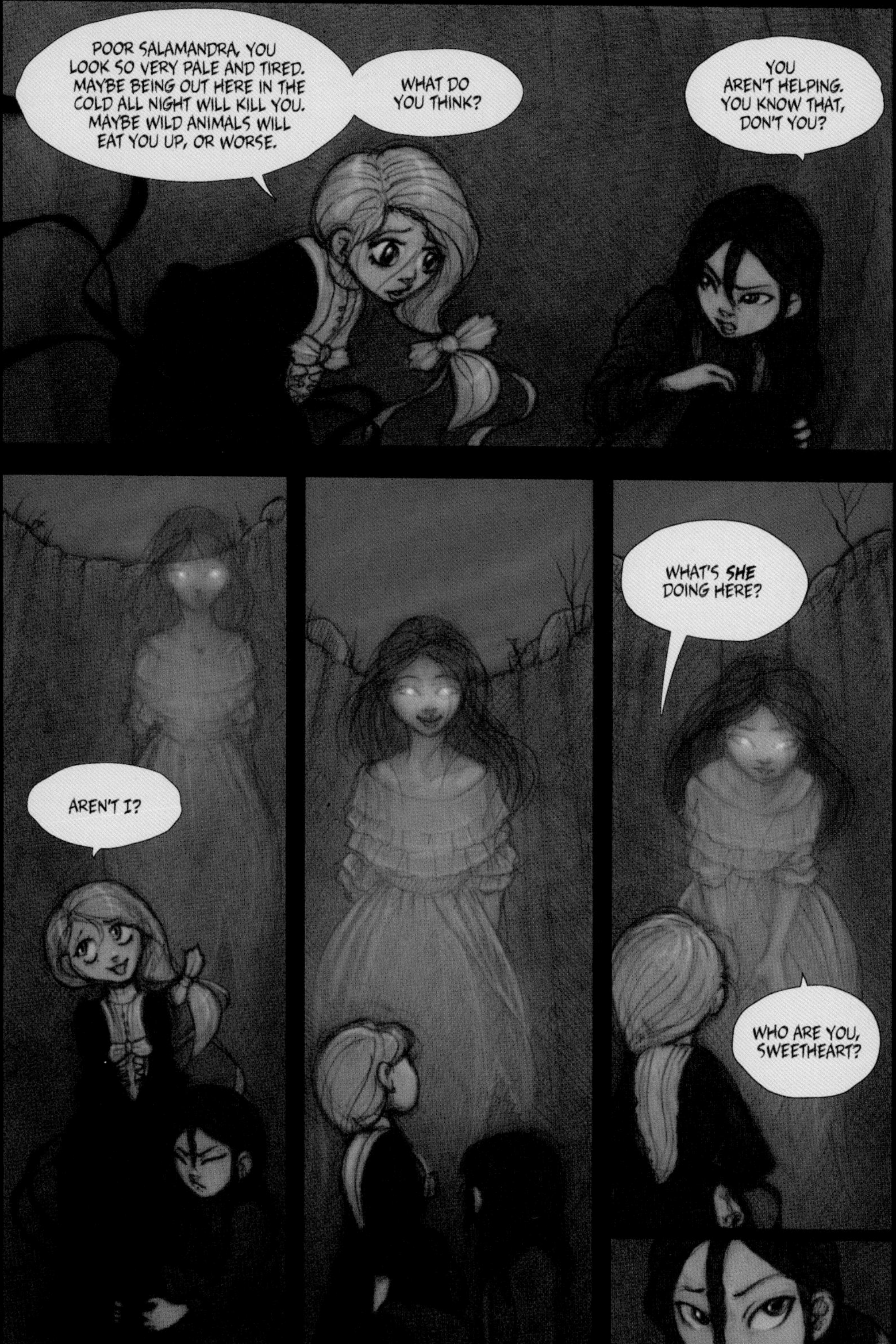
POOR SALAMANDRA, YOU LOOK SO VERY PALE AND TIRED. MAYBE BEING OUT HERE IN THE COLD ALL NIGHT WILL KILL YOU. MAYBE WILD ANIMALS WILL EAT YOU UP, OR WORSE.
WHAT DO YOU THINK?
YOU AREN'T HELPING. YOU KNOW THAT, DON'T YOU?
AREN'T I?
WHAT'S **SHE** DOING HERE?
WHO ARE YOU, SWEETHEART?

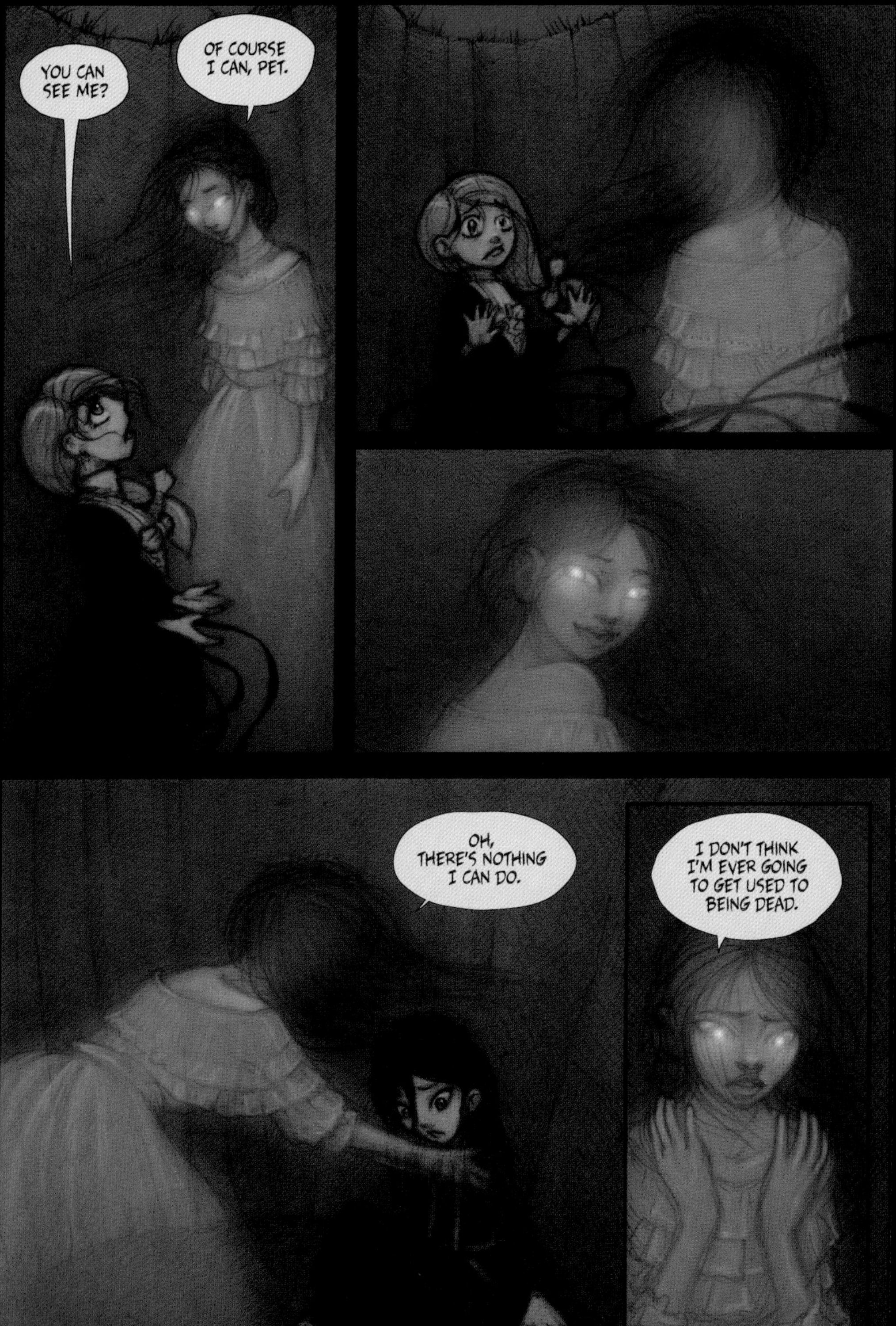
YOU CAN SEE ME?
OF COURSE I CAN, PET.
OH, THERE'S NOTHING I CAN DO.
I DON'T THINK I'M EVER GOING TO GET USED TO BEING DEAD.

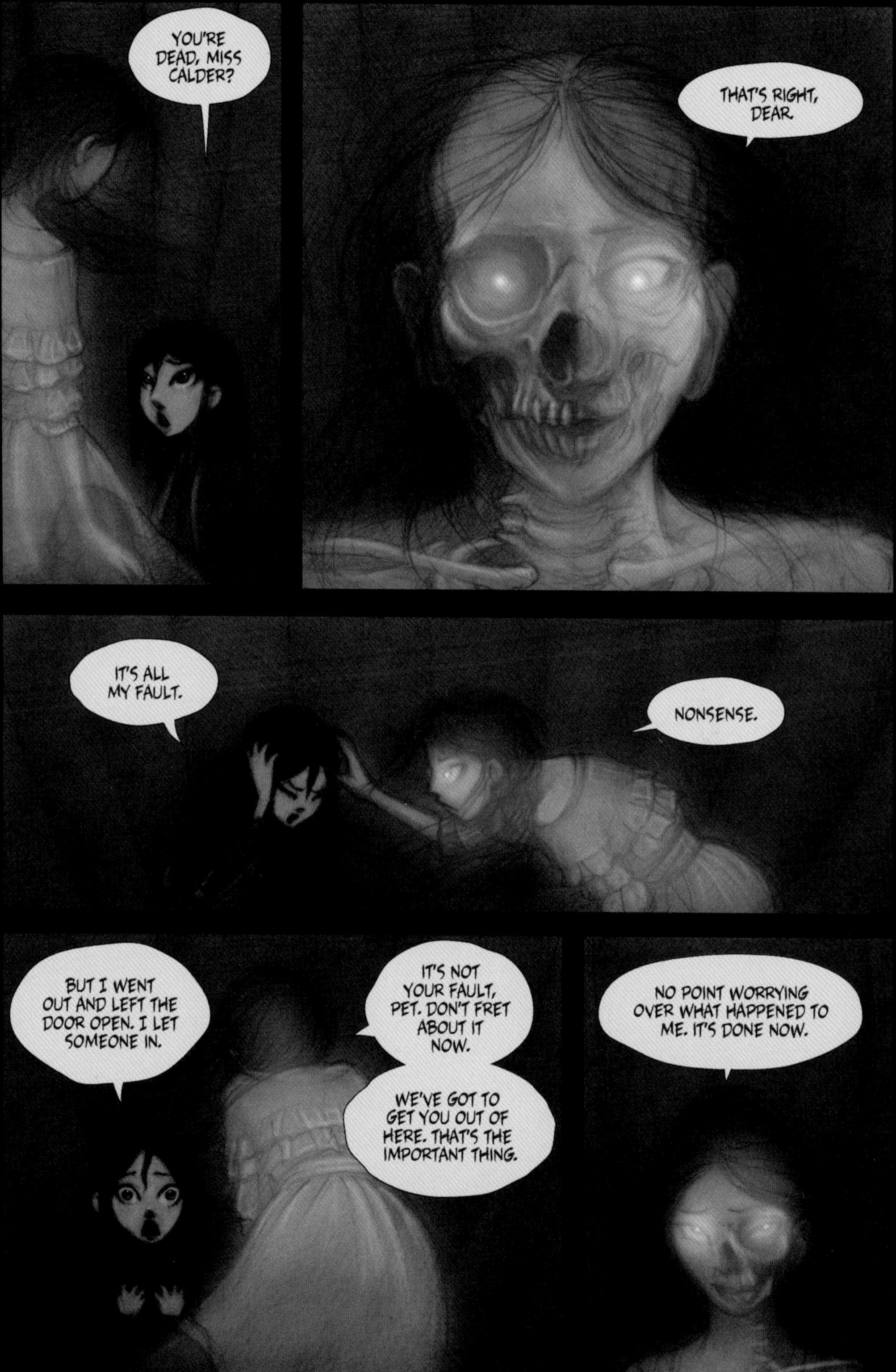
YOU'RE DEAD, MISS CALDER?
THAT'S RIGHT, DEAR.
IT'S ALL MY FAULT.
NONSENSE.
BUT I WENT OUT AND LEFT THE DOOR OPEN. I LET SOMEONE IN.
IT'S NOT YOUR FAULT, PET. DON'T FRET ABOUT IT NOW.
WE'VE GOT TO GET YOU OUT OF HERE. THAT'S THE IMPORTANT THING.
NO POINT WORRYING OVER WHAT HAPPENED TO ME. IT'S DONE NOW.

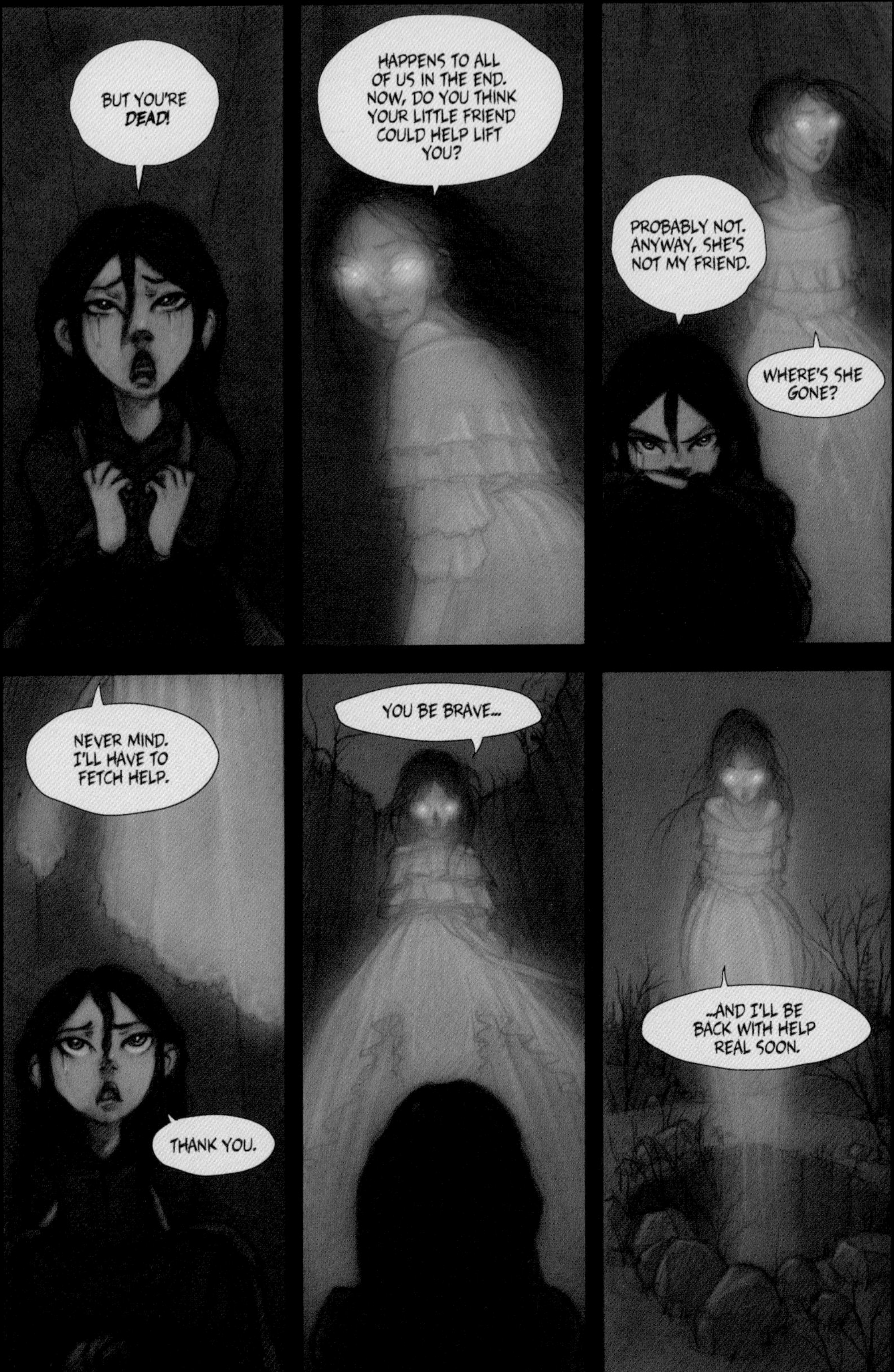
BUT YOU'RE DEAD!
HAPPENS TO ALL OF US IN THE END. NOW, DO YOU THINK YOUR LITTLE FRIEND COULD HELP LIFT YOU?
PROBABLY NOT. ANYWAY, SHE'S NOT MY FRIEND.
WHERE'S SHE GONE?
NEVER MIND. I'LL HAVE TO FETCH HELP.
THANK YOU.
YOU BE BRAVE...
...AND I'LL BE BACK WITH HELP REAL SOON.

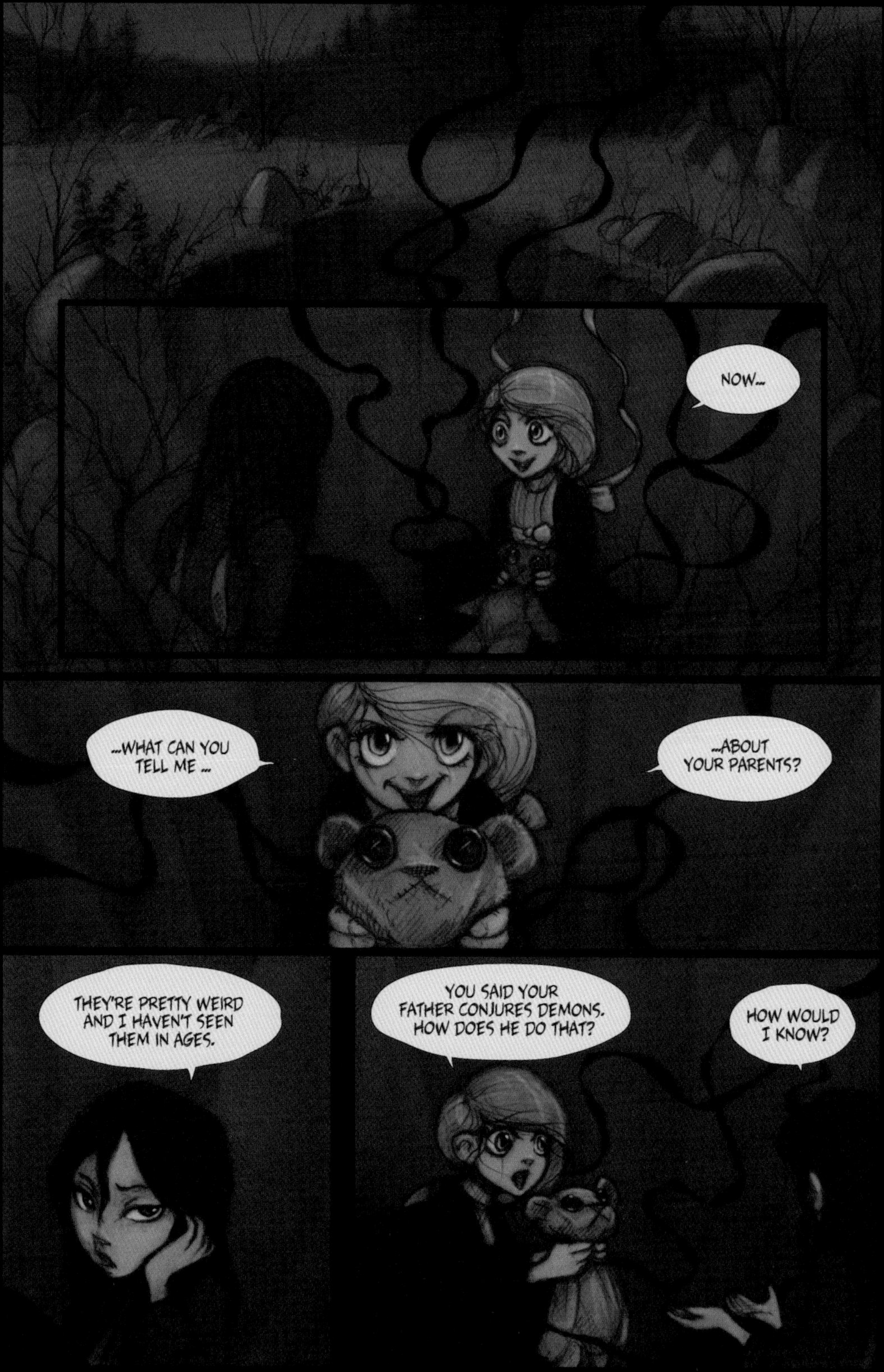
NOW...
...WHAT CAN YOU TELL ME ...
...ABOUT YOUR PARENTS?
THEY'RE PRETTY WEIRD AND I HAVEN'T SEEN THEM IN AGES.
YOU SAID YOUR FATHER CONJURES DEMONS. HOW DOES HE DO THAT?
HOW WOULD I KNOW?

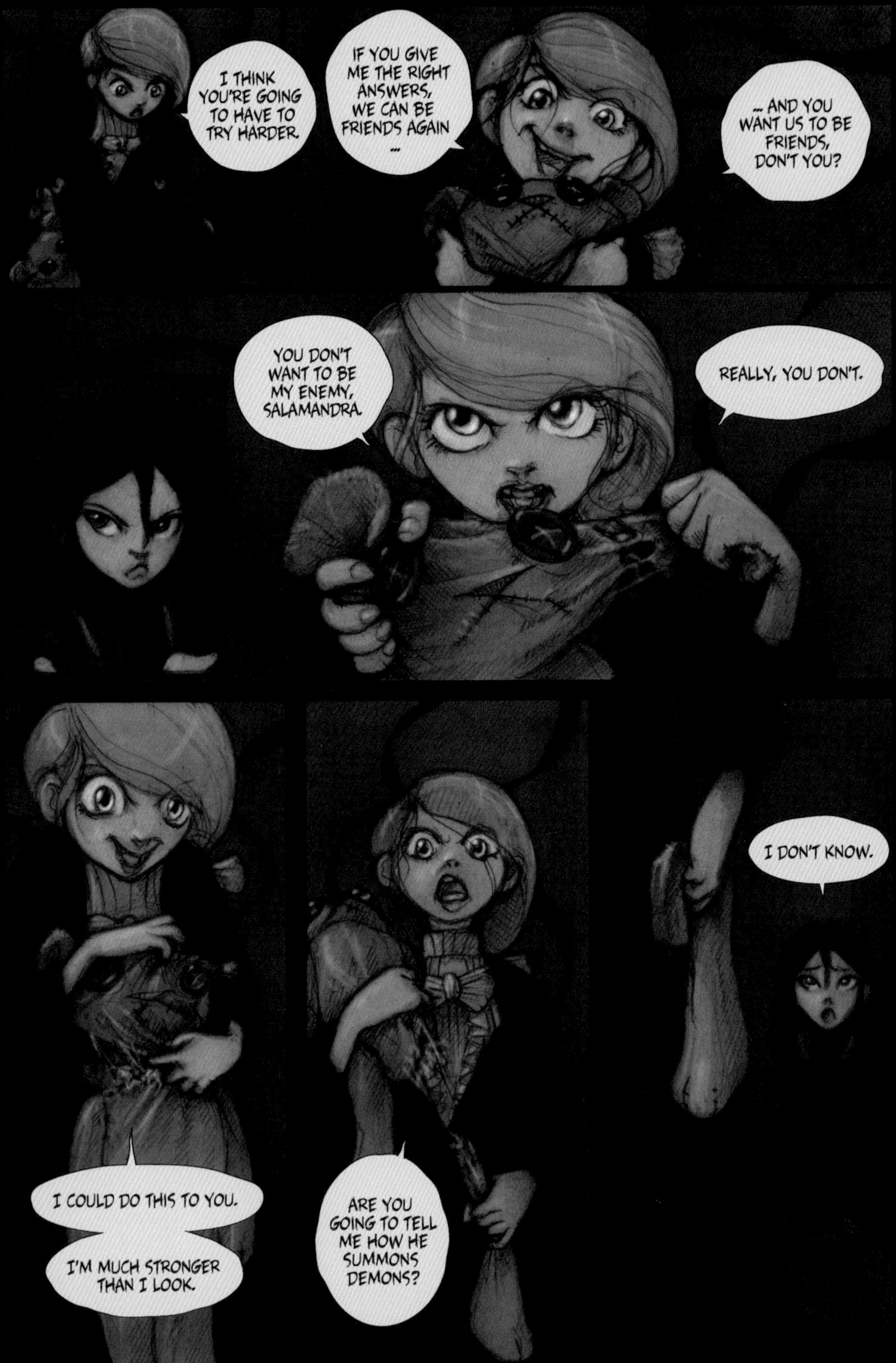
I THINK YOU'RE GOING TO HAVE TO TRY HARDER.
IF YOU GIVE ME THE RIGHT ANSWERS, WE CAN BE FRIENDS AGAIN ...
... AND YOU WANT US TO BE FRIENDS, DON'T YOU?
YOU DON'T WANT TO BE MY ENEMY, SALAMANDRA.
REALLY, YOU DON'T.
I COULD DO THIS TO YOU.
I'M MUCH STRONGER THAN I LOOK.
ARE YOU GOING TO TELL ME HOW HE SUMMONS DEMONS?
I DON'T KNOW.

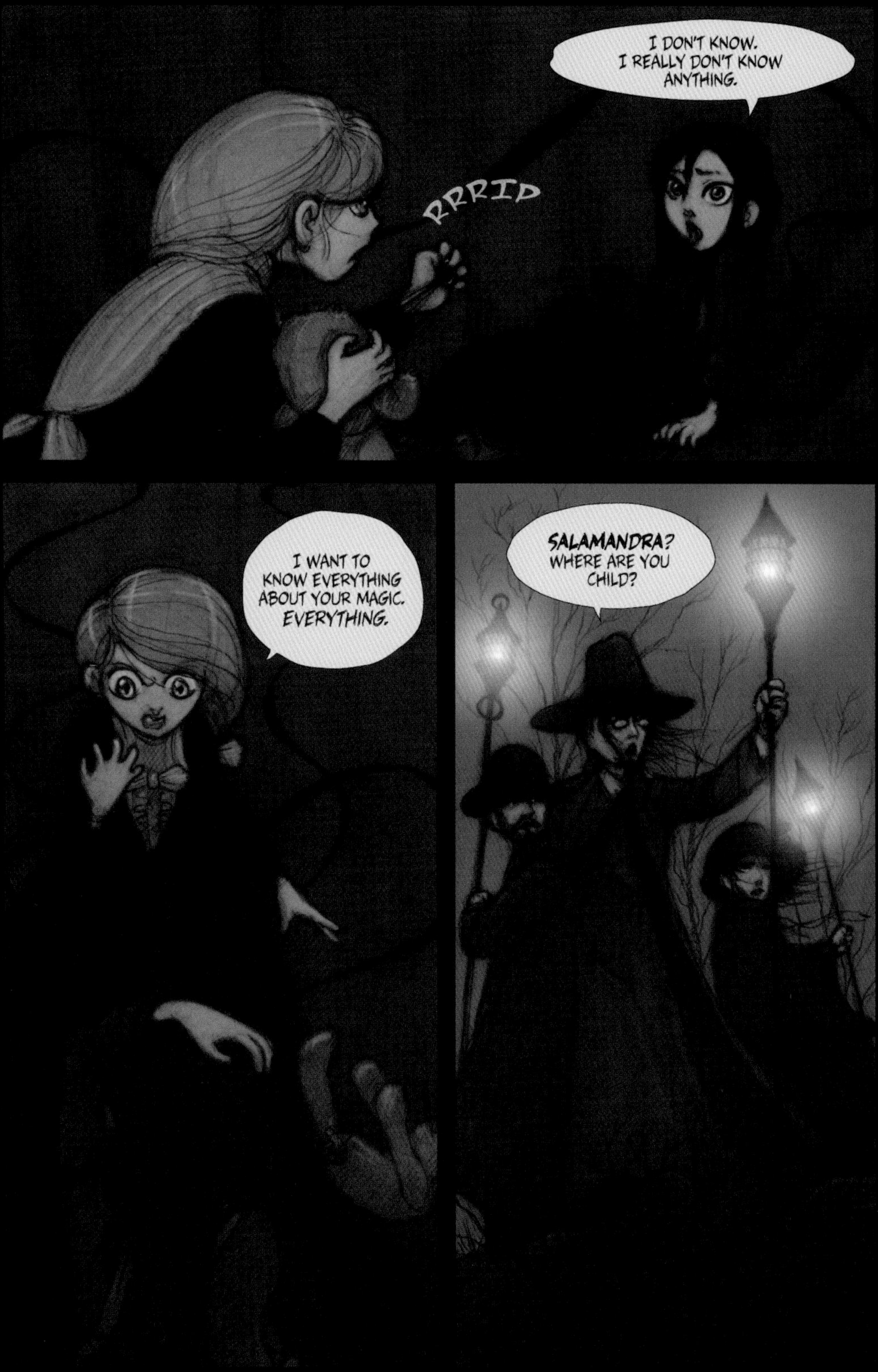
I DON'T KNOW. I REALLY DON'T KNOW ANYTHING.
RRRIP
I WANT TO KNOW EVERYTHING ABOUT YOUR MAGIC. EVERYTHING.
SALAMANDRA? WHERE ARE YOU CHILD?

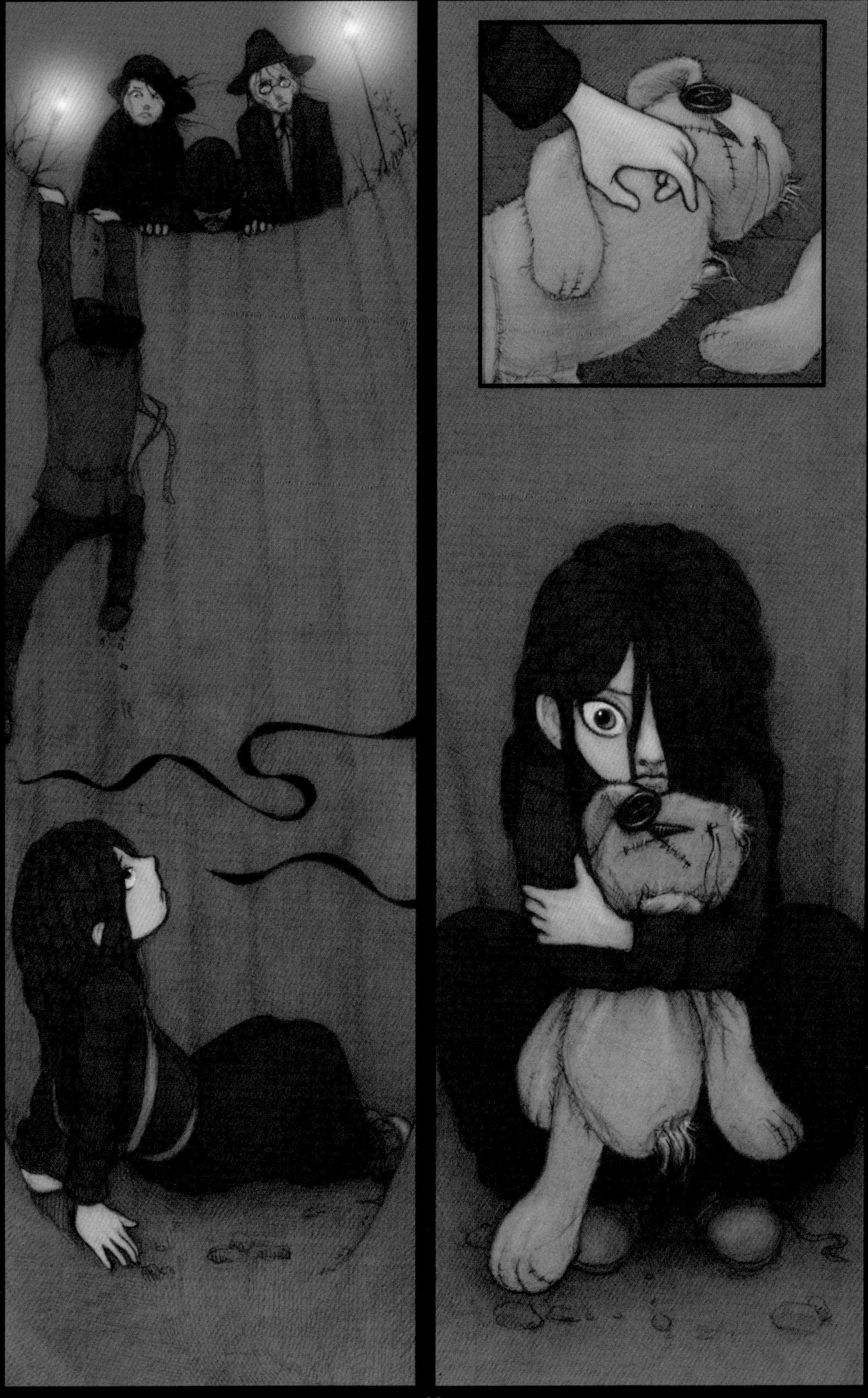

CHAPTER SIX

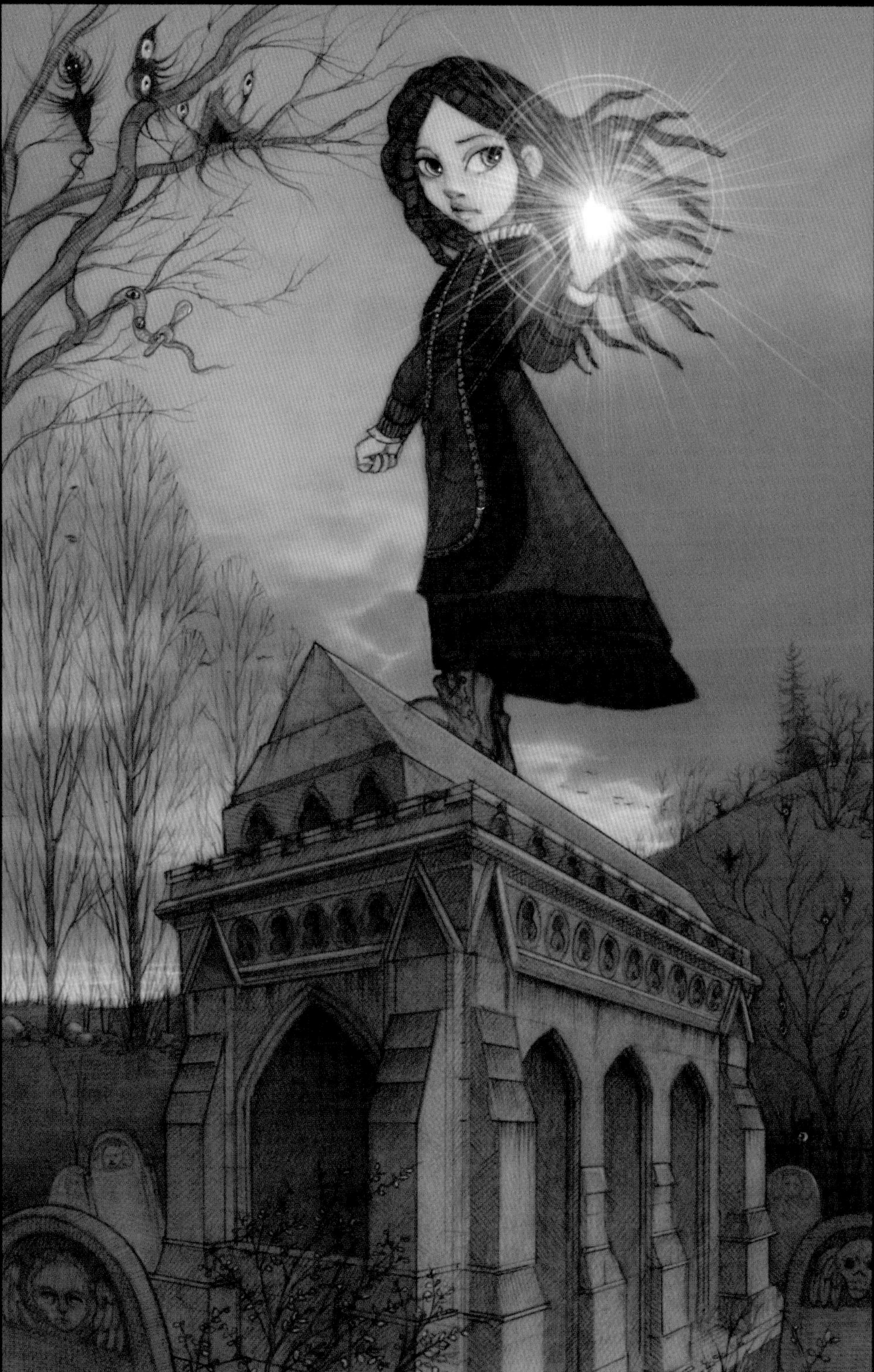

DO YOU THINK PEOPLE WHO DO MAGIC ARE BAD

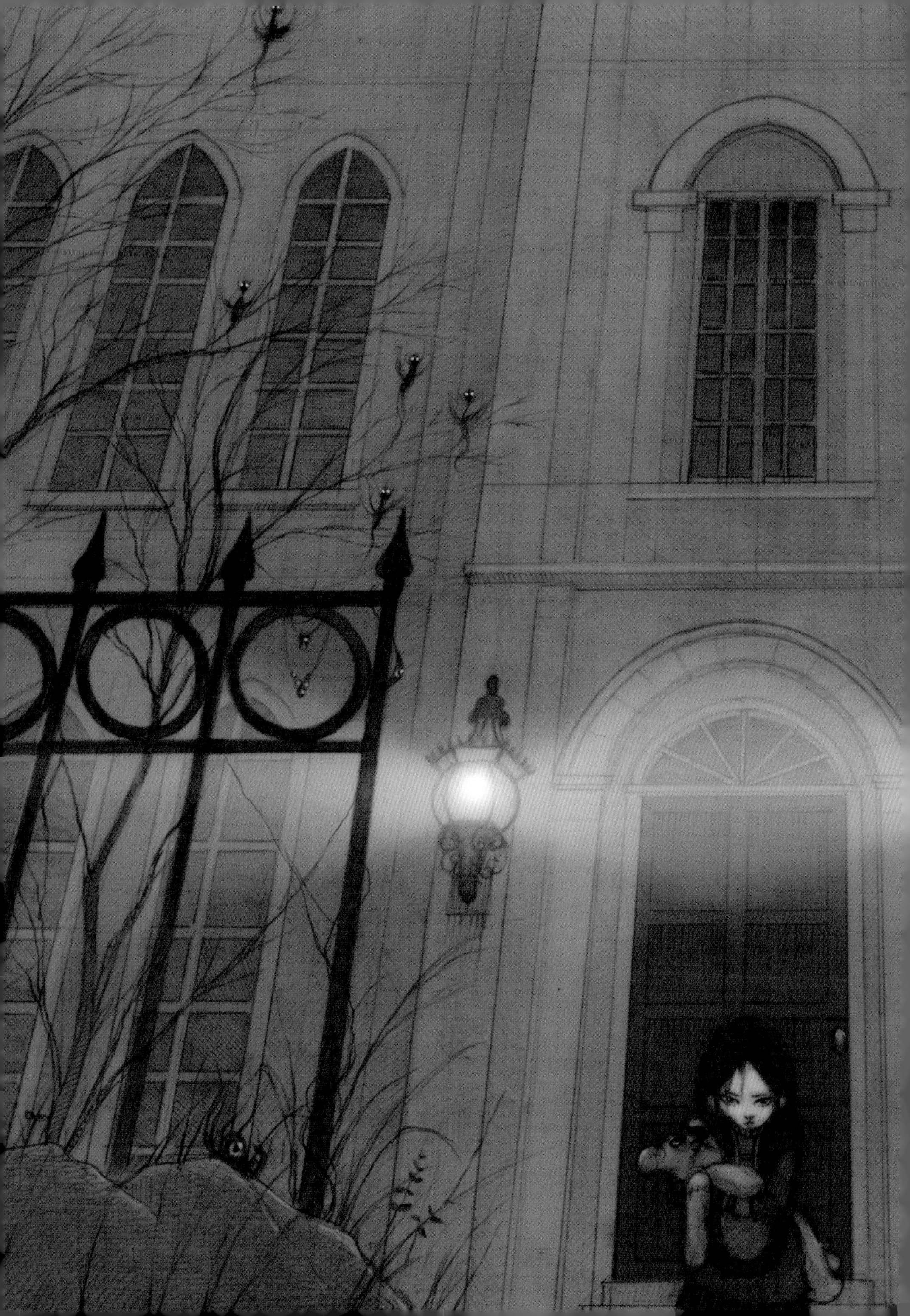

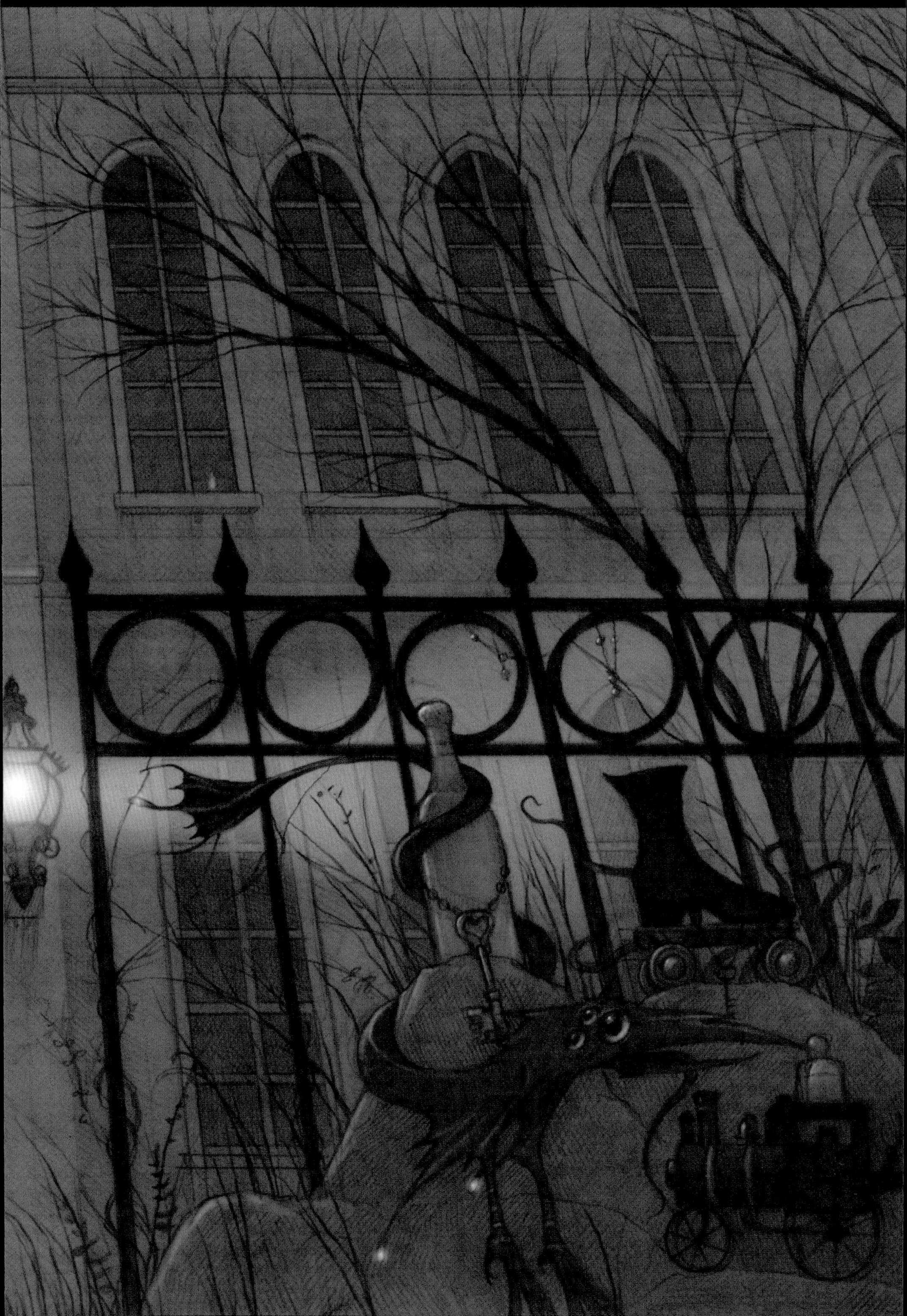

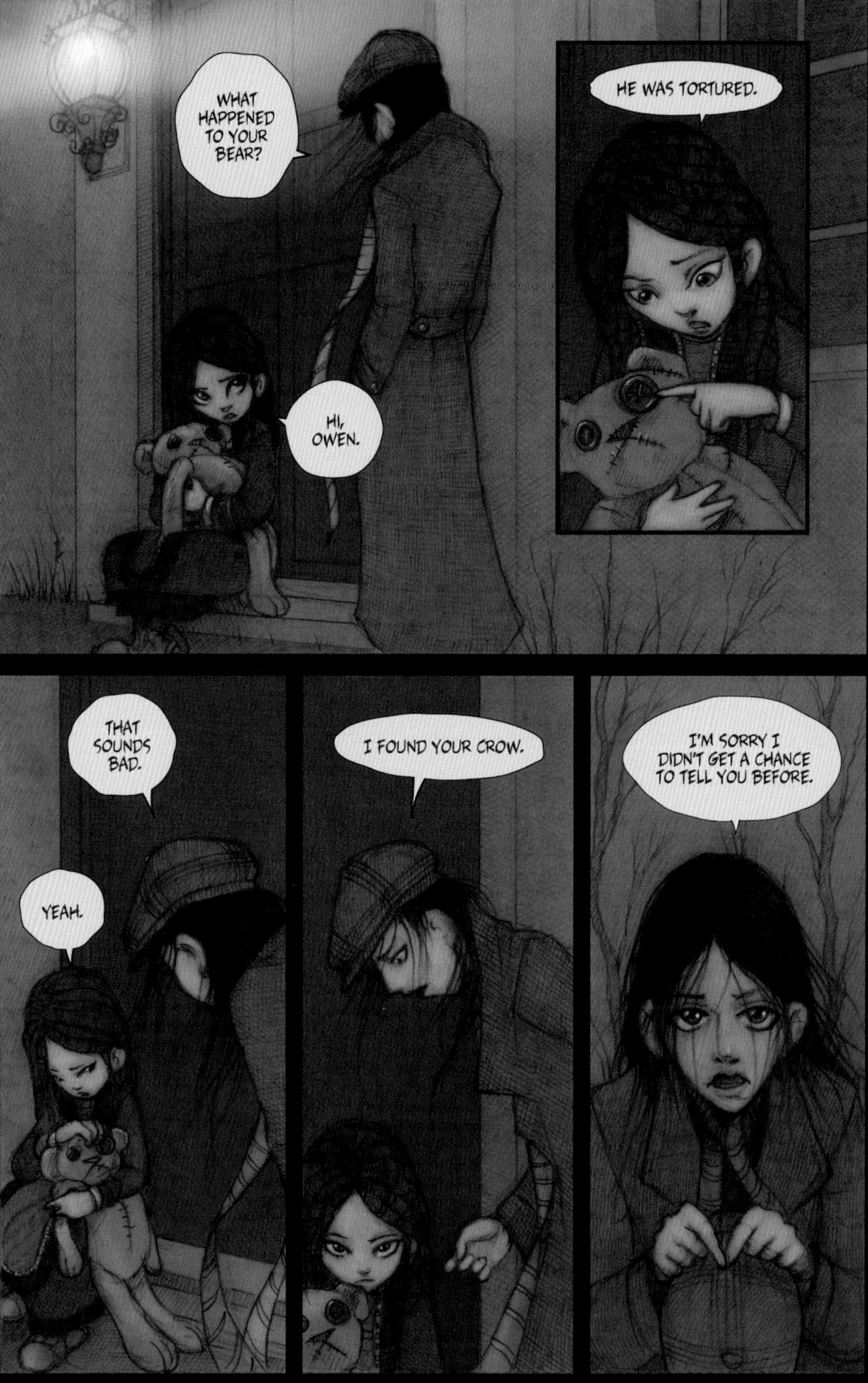

WHAT HAPPENED TO YOUR BEAR?
HI, OWEN.
HE WAS TORTURED.
THAT SOUNDS BAD.
YEAH.
I FOUND YOUR CROW.
I'M SORRY I DIDN'T GET A CHANCE TO TELL YOU BEFORE.

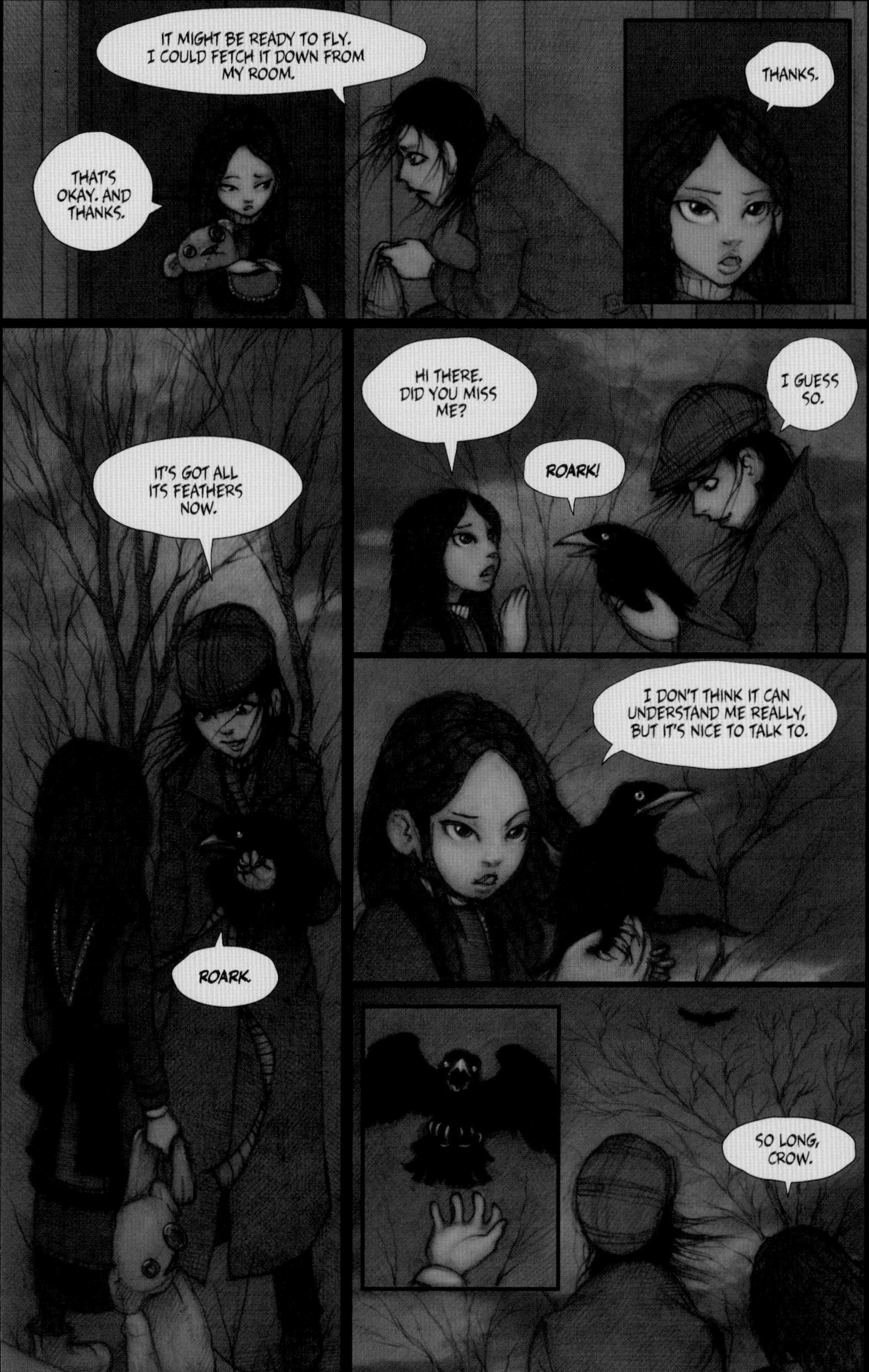
IT MIGHT BE READY TO FLY. I COULD FETCH IT DOWN FROM MY ROOM.
THAT'S OKAY. AND THANKS.
THANKS.
IT'S GOT ALL ITS FEATHERS NOW.
ROARK.
HI THERE. DID YOU MISS ME?
ROARK!
I GUESS SO.
I DON'T THINK IT CAN UNDERSTAND ME REALLY, BUT IT'S NICE TO TALK TO.
SO LONG, CROW.

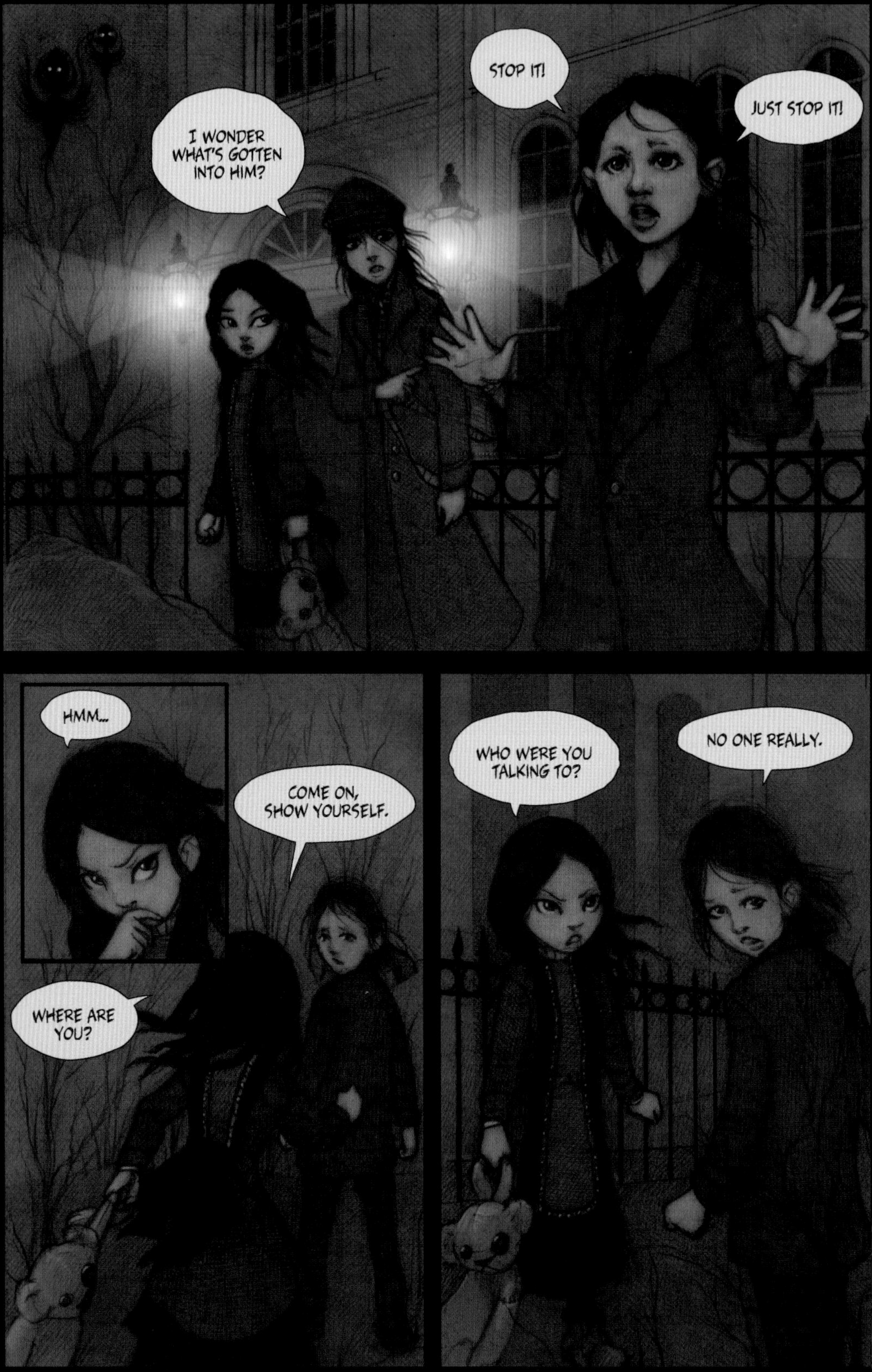
I WONDER WHAT'S GOTTEN INTO HIM?
STOP IT!
JUST STOP IT!
HMM...
COME ON, SHOW YOURSELF.
WHERE ARE YOU?
WHO WERE YOU TALKING TO?
NO ONE REALLY.

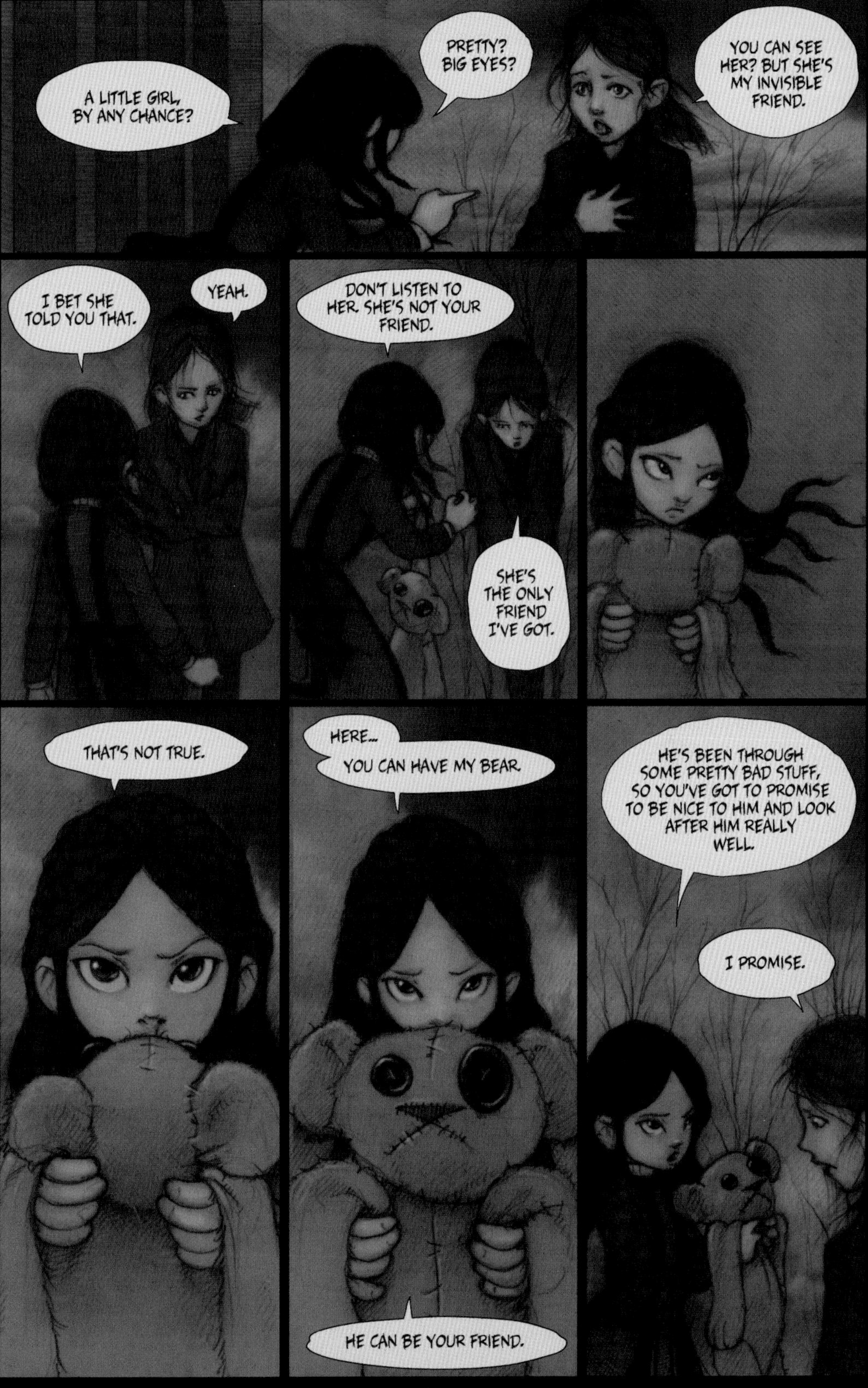
A LITTLE GIRL, BY ANY CHANCE?
PRETTY? BIG EYES?
YOU CAN SEE HER? BUT SHE'S MY INVISIBLE FRIEND.
I BET SHE TOLD YOU THAT.
YEAH.
DON'T LISTEN TO HER. SHE'S NOT YOUR FRIEND.
SHE'S THE ONLY FRIEND I'VE GOT.
THAT'S NOT TRUE.
HERE...
YOU CAN HAVE MY BEAR.
HE CAN BE YOUR FRIEND.
HE'S BEEN THROUGH SOME PRETTY BAD STUFF, SO YOU'VE GOT TO PROMISE TO BE NICE TO HIM AND LOOK AFTER HIM REALLY WELL.
I PROMISE.

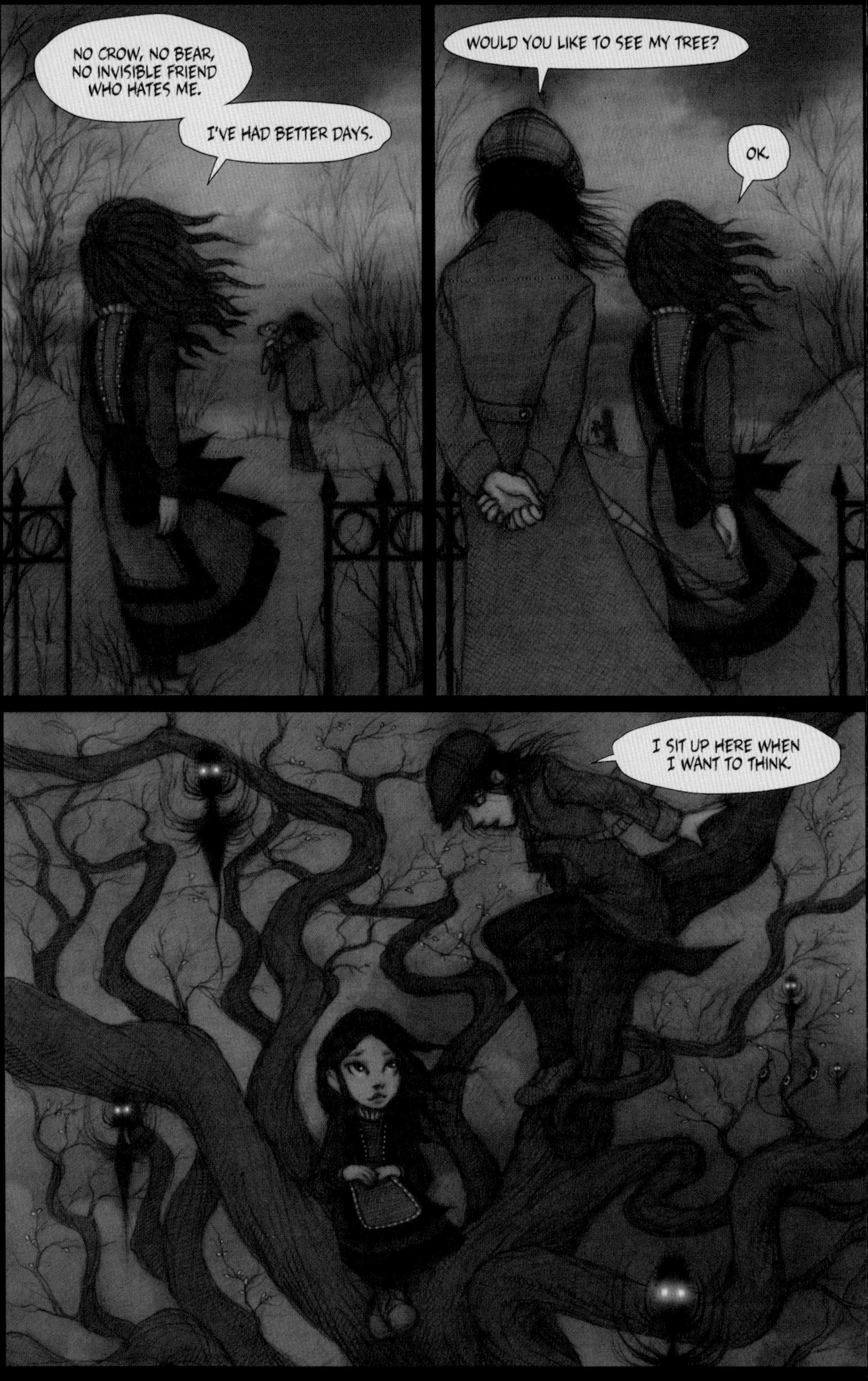
NO CROW, NO BEAR, NO INVISIBLE FRIEND WHO HATES ME.
I'VE HAD BETTER DAYS.
WOULD YOU LIKE TO SEE MY TREE?
OK.
I SIT UP HERE WHEN I WANT TO THINK.

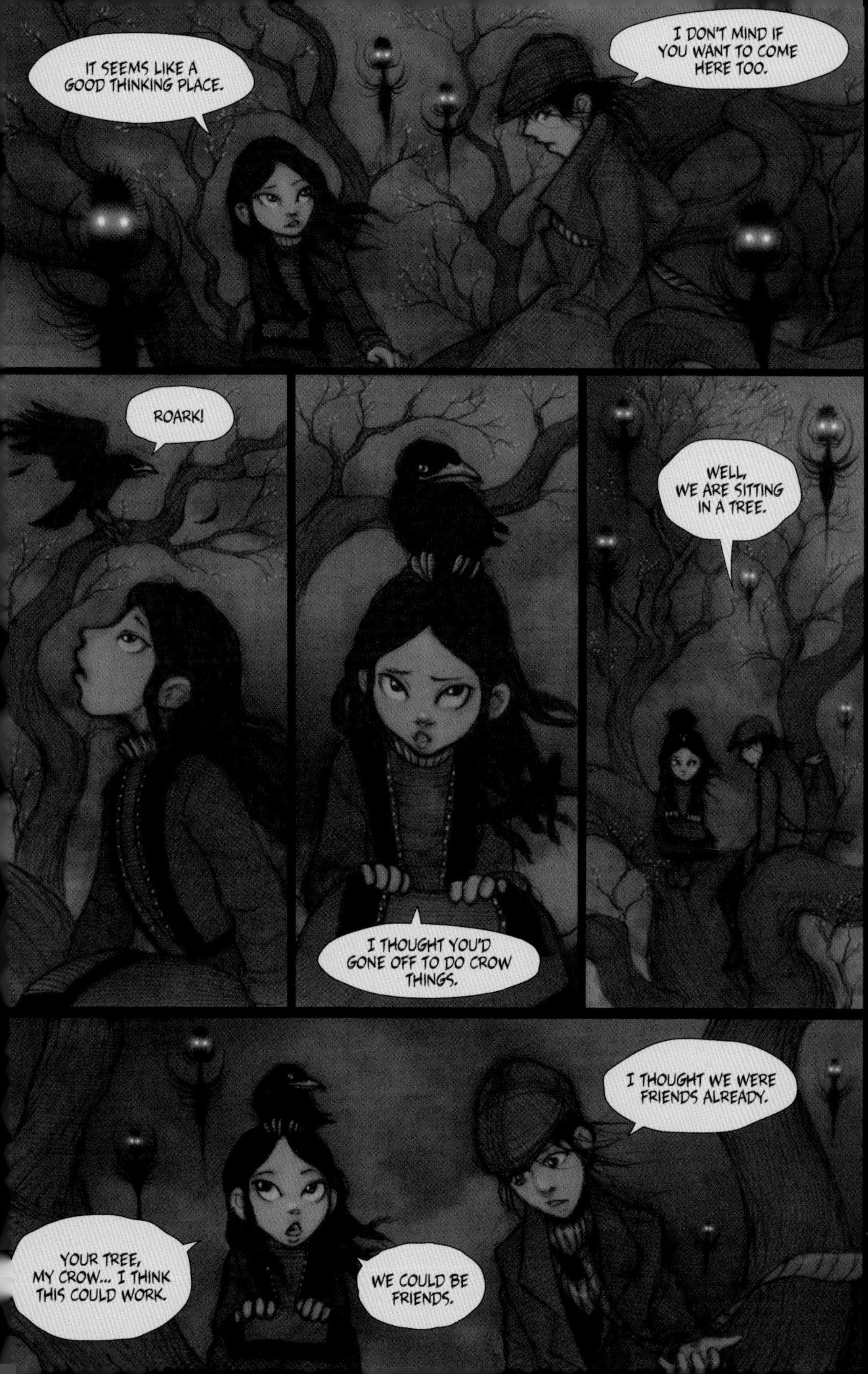
IT SEEMS LIKE A GOOD THINKING PLACE.
I DON'T MIND IF YOU WANT TO COME HERE TOO.
ROARK!
I THOUGHT YOU'D GONE OFF TO DO CROW THINGS.
WELL, WE ARE SITTING IN A TREE.
I THOUGHT WE WERE FRIENDS ALREADY.
YOUR TREE, MY CROW... I THINK THIS COULD WORK.
WE COULD BE FRIENDS.

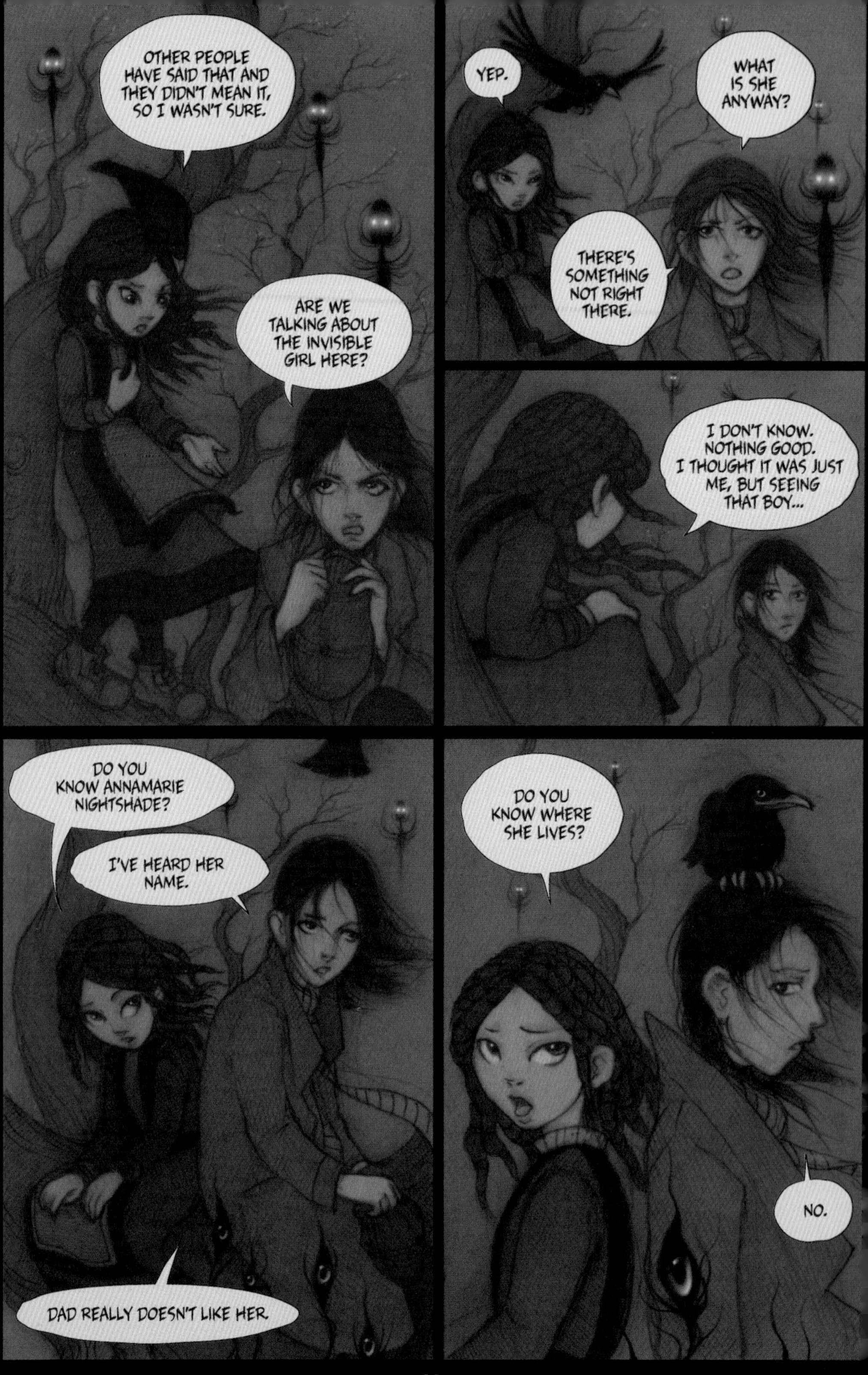
OTHER PEOPLE HAVE SAID THAT AND THEY DIDN'T MEAN IT, SO I WASN'T SURE.
ARE WE TALKING ABOUT THE INVISIBLE GIRL HERE?
YEP.
WHAT IS SHE ANYWAY?
THERE'S SOMETHING NOT RIGHT THERE.
I DON'T KNOW. NOTHING GOOD. I THOUGHT IT WAS JUST ME, BUT SEEING THAT BOY...
DO YOU KNOW ANNAMARIE NIGHTSHADE?
I'VE HEARD HER NAME.
DAD REALLY DOESN'T LIKE HER.
DO YOU KNOW WHERE SHE LIVES?
NO.

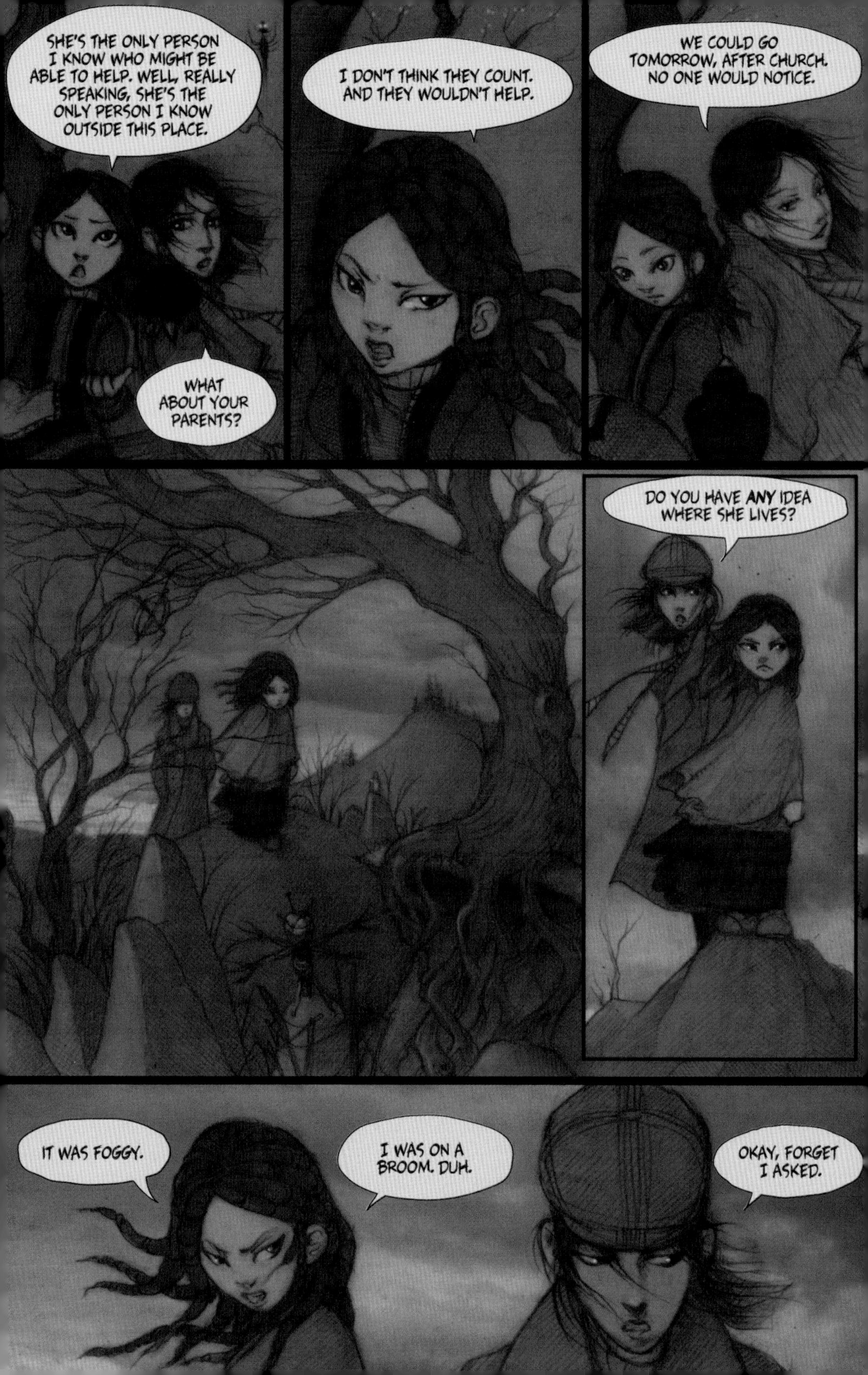
SHE'S THE ONLY PERSON I KNOW WHO MIGHT BE ABLE TO HELP. WELL, REALLY SPEAKING, SHE'S THE ONLY PERSON I KNOW OUTSIDE THIS PLACE.
WHAT ABOUT YOUR PARENTS?
I DON'T THINK THEY COUNT. AND THEY WOULDN'T HELP.
WE COULD GO TOMORROW, AFTER CHURCH. NO ONE WOULD NOTICE.
DO YOU HAVE ANY IDEA WHERE SHE LIVES?
IT WAS FOGGY.
I WAS ON A BROOM. DUH.
OKAY, FORGET I ASKED.

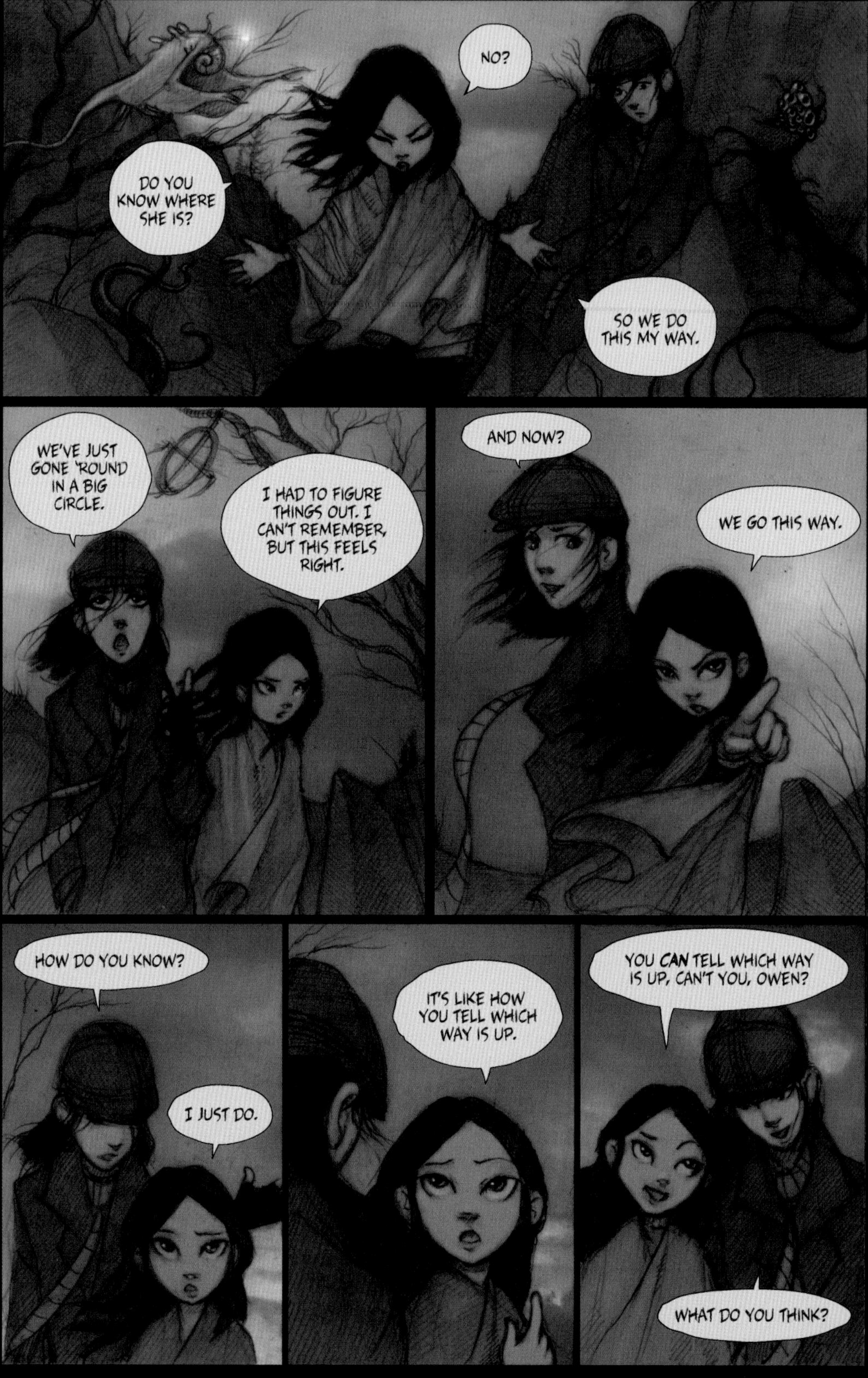
NO?
DO YOU KNOW WHERE SHE IS?
SO WE DO THIS MY WAY.
WE'VE JUST GONE 'ROUND IN A BIG CIRCLE.
I HAD TO FIGURE THINGS OUT. I CAN'T REMEMBER, BUT THIS FEELS RIGHT.
AND NOW?
WE GO THIS WAY.
HOW DO YOU KNOW?
I JUST DO.
IT'S LIKE HOW YOU TELL WHICH WAY IS UP.
YOU CAN TELL WHICH WAY IS UP, CAN'T YOU, OWEN?
WHAT DO YOU THINK?

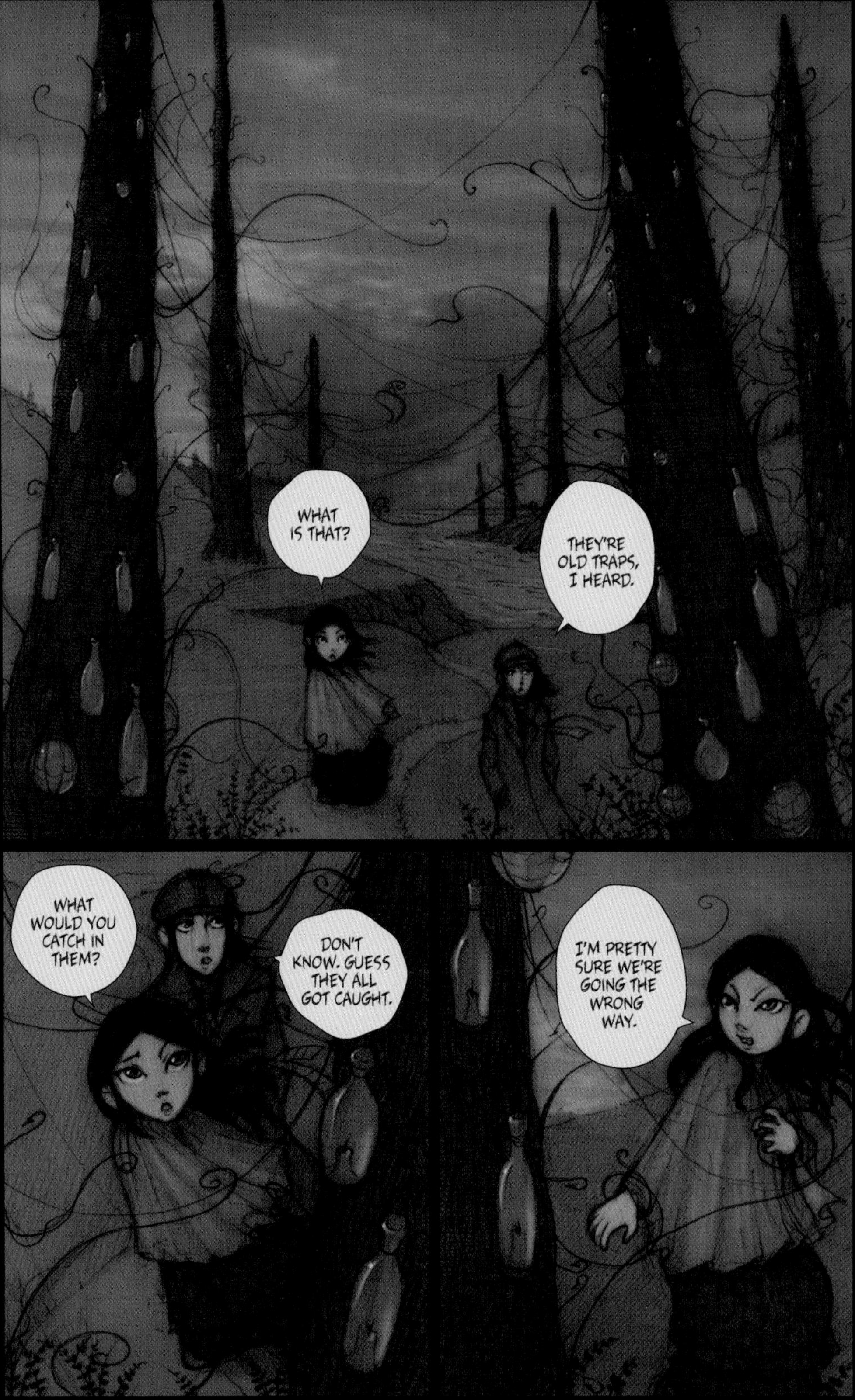
WHAT IS THAT?
THEY'RE OLD TRAPS, I HEARD.
WHAT WOULD YOU CATCH IN THEM?
DON'T KNOW. GUESS THEY ALL GOT CAUGHT.
I'M PRETTY SURE WE'RE GOING THE WRONG WAY.

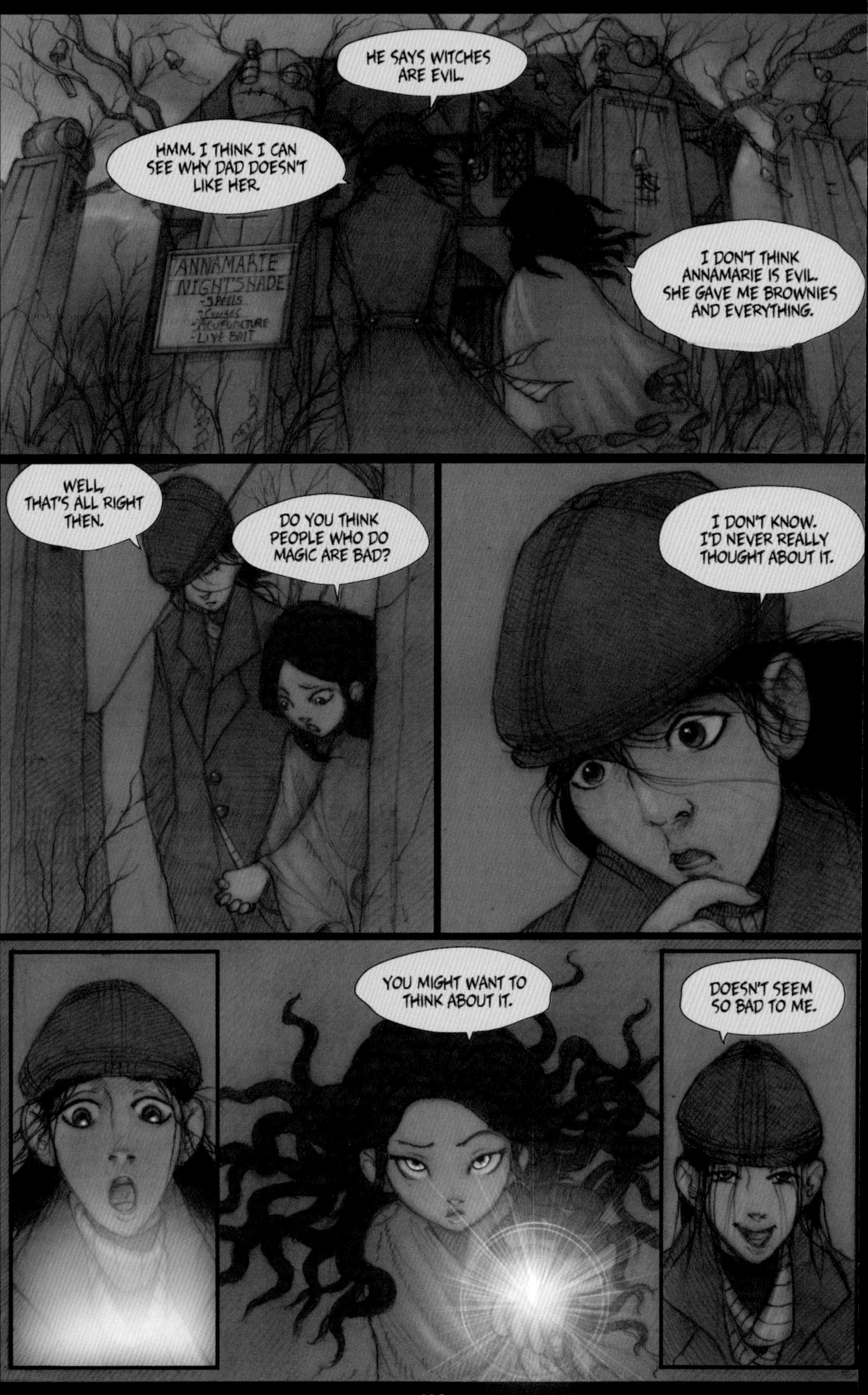
HE SAYS WITCHES ARE EVIL.
HMM. I THINK I CAN SEE WHY DAD DOESN'T LIKE HER.
ANNAMARIE NIGHTSHADE
-SPELLS
-CURSES
-LIVE BAIT
I DON'T THINK ANNAMARIE IS EVIL. SHE GAVE ME BROWNIES AND EVERYTHING.
WELL, THAT'S ALL RIGHT THEN.
DO YOU THINK PEOPLE WHO DO MAGIC ARE BAD?
I DON'T KNOW. I'D NEVER REALLY THOUGHT ABOUT IT.
YOU MIGHT WANT TO THINK ABOUT IT.
DOESN'T SEEM SO BAD TO ME.

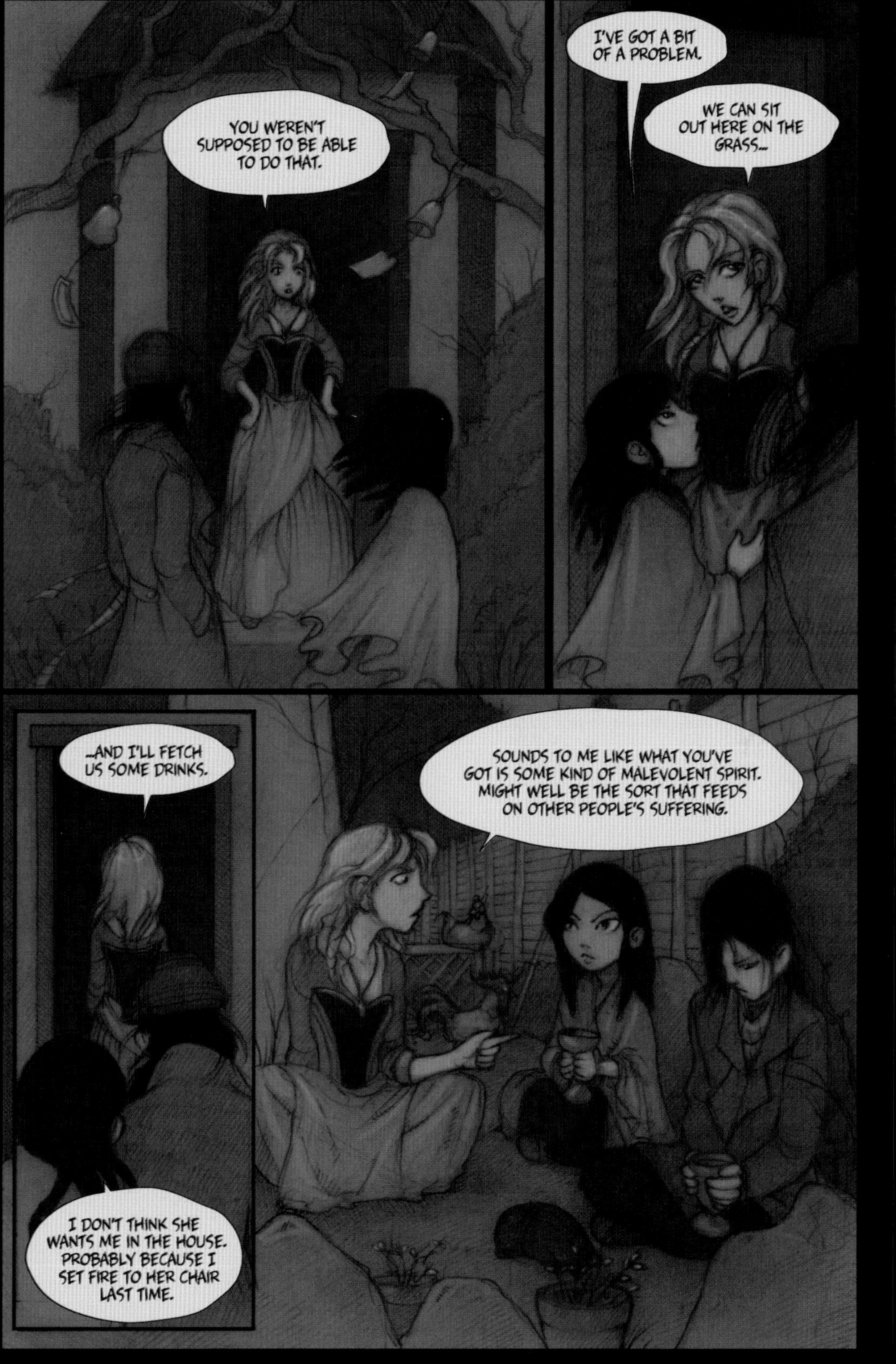
YOU WEREN'T SUPPOSED TO BE ABLE TO DO THAT.
I'VE GOT A BIT OF A PROBLEM.
WE CAN SIT OUT HERE ON THE GRASS...
...AND I'LL FETCH US SOME DRINKS.
I DON'T THINK SHE WANTS ME IN THE HOUSE. PROBABLY BECAUSE I SET FIRE TO HER CHAIR LAST TIME.
SOUNDS TO ME LIKE WHAT YOU'VE GOT IS SOME KIND OF MALEVOLENT SPIRIT. MIGHT WELL BE THE SORT THAT FEEDS ON OTHER PEOPLE'S SUFFERING.

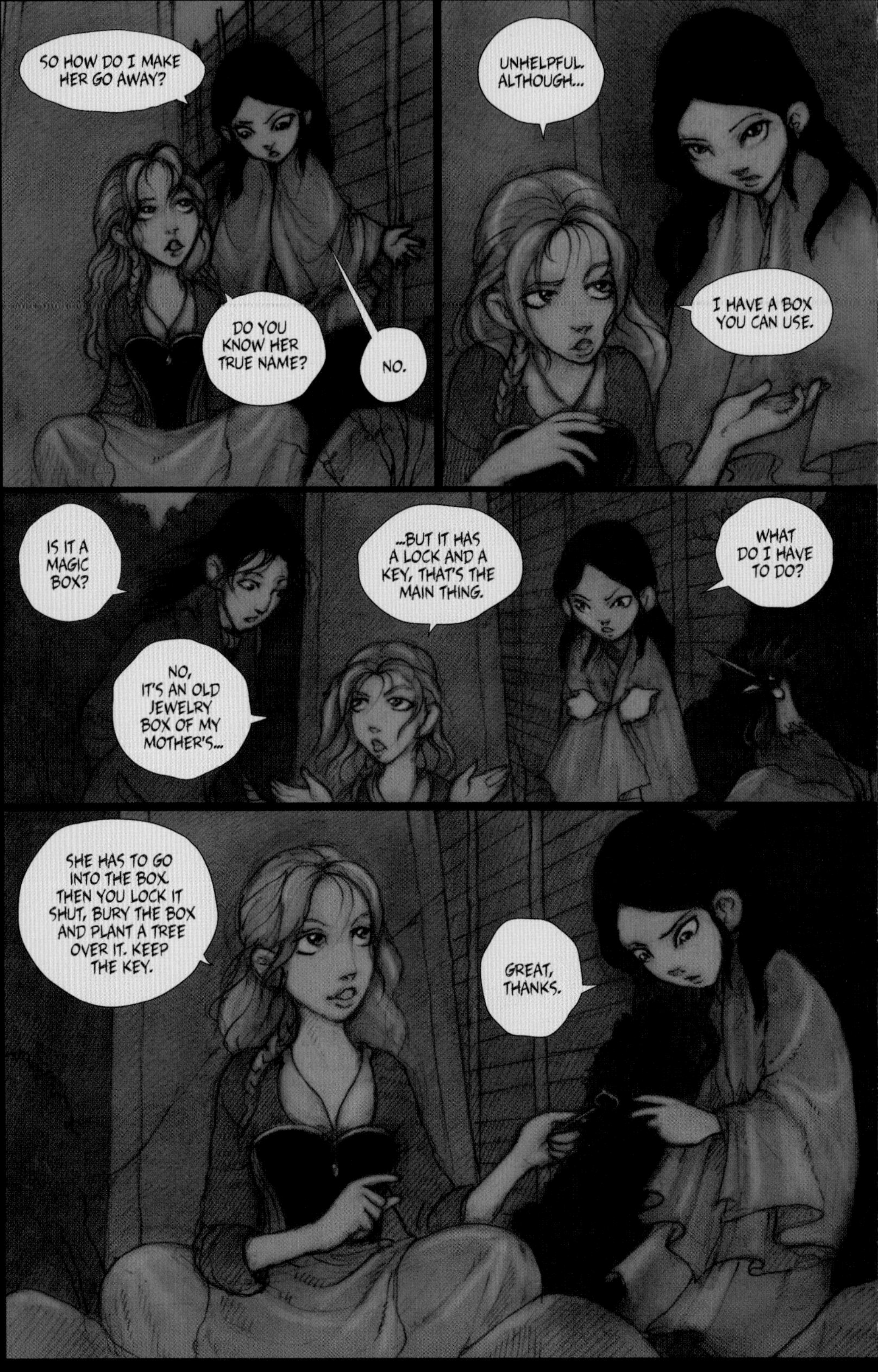
SO HOW DO I MAKE HER GO AWAY?
DO YOU KNOW HER TRUE NAME?
NO.
UNHELPFUL. ALTHOUGH...
I HAVE A BOX YOU CAN USE.
IS IT A MAGIC BOX?
NO, IT'S AN OLD JEWELRY BOX OF MY MOTHER'S...
...BUT IT HAS A LOCK AND A KEY, THAT'S THE MAIN THING.
WHAT DO I HAVE TO DO?
SHE HAS TO GO INTO THE BOX. THEN YOU LOCK IT SHUT, BURY THE BOX AND PLANT A TREE OVER IT. KEEP THE KEY.
GREAT, THANKS.

CHAPTER SEVEN

I AM NOT A WITCH · I AM A · · SOMETHING ELSE ·

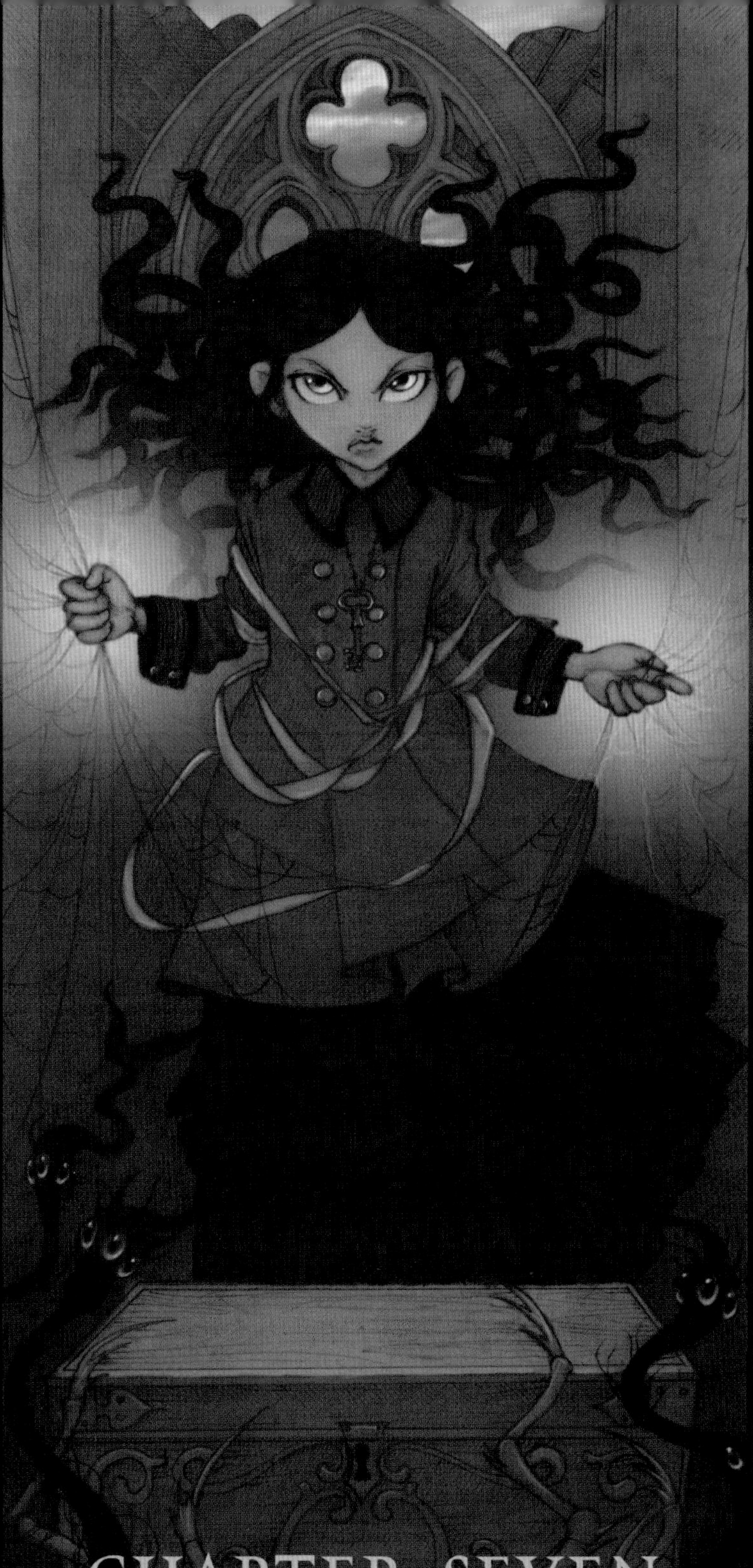

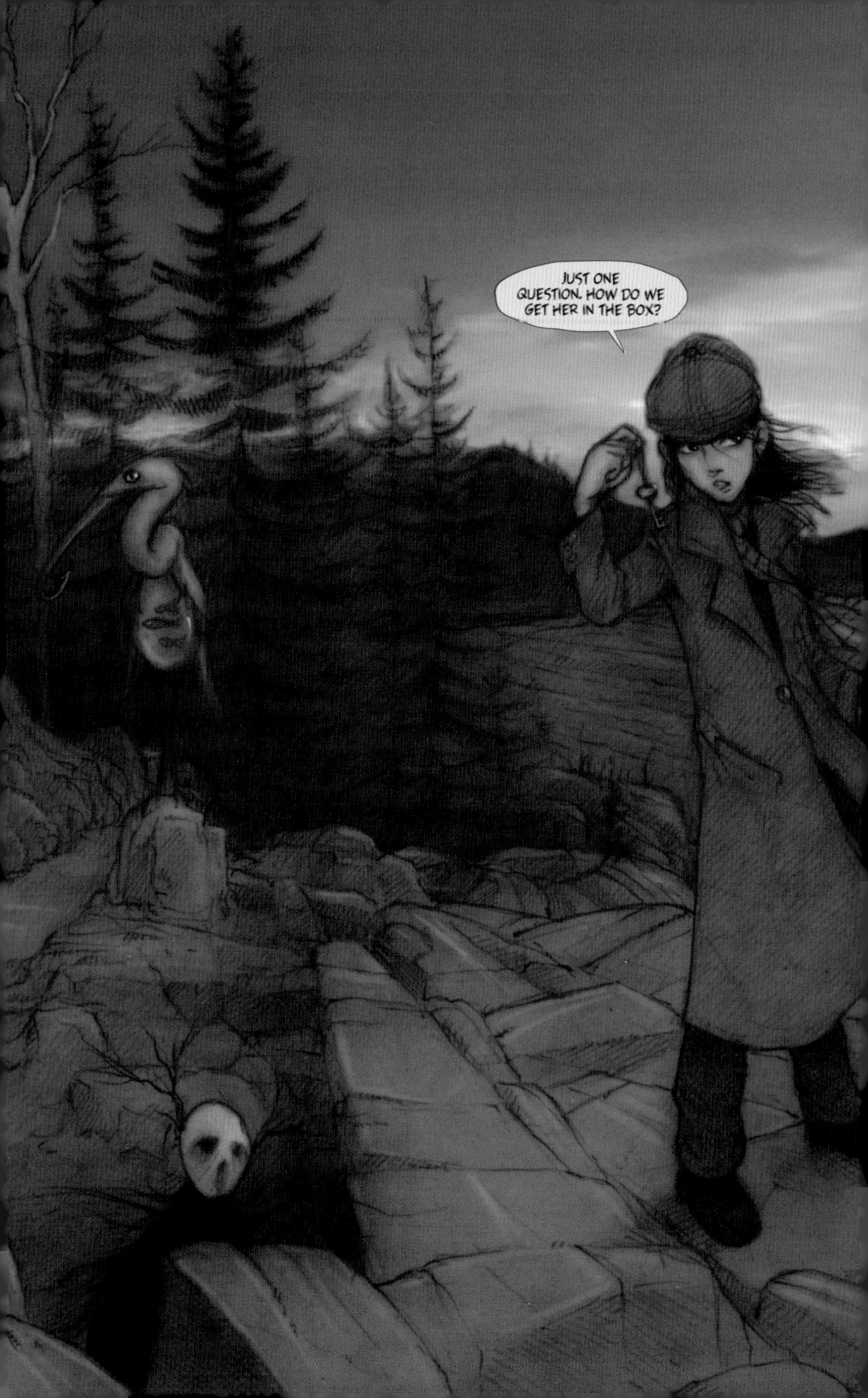
JUST ONE QUESTION. HOW DO WE GET HER IN THE BOX?

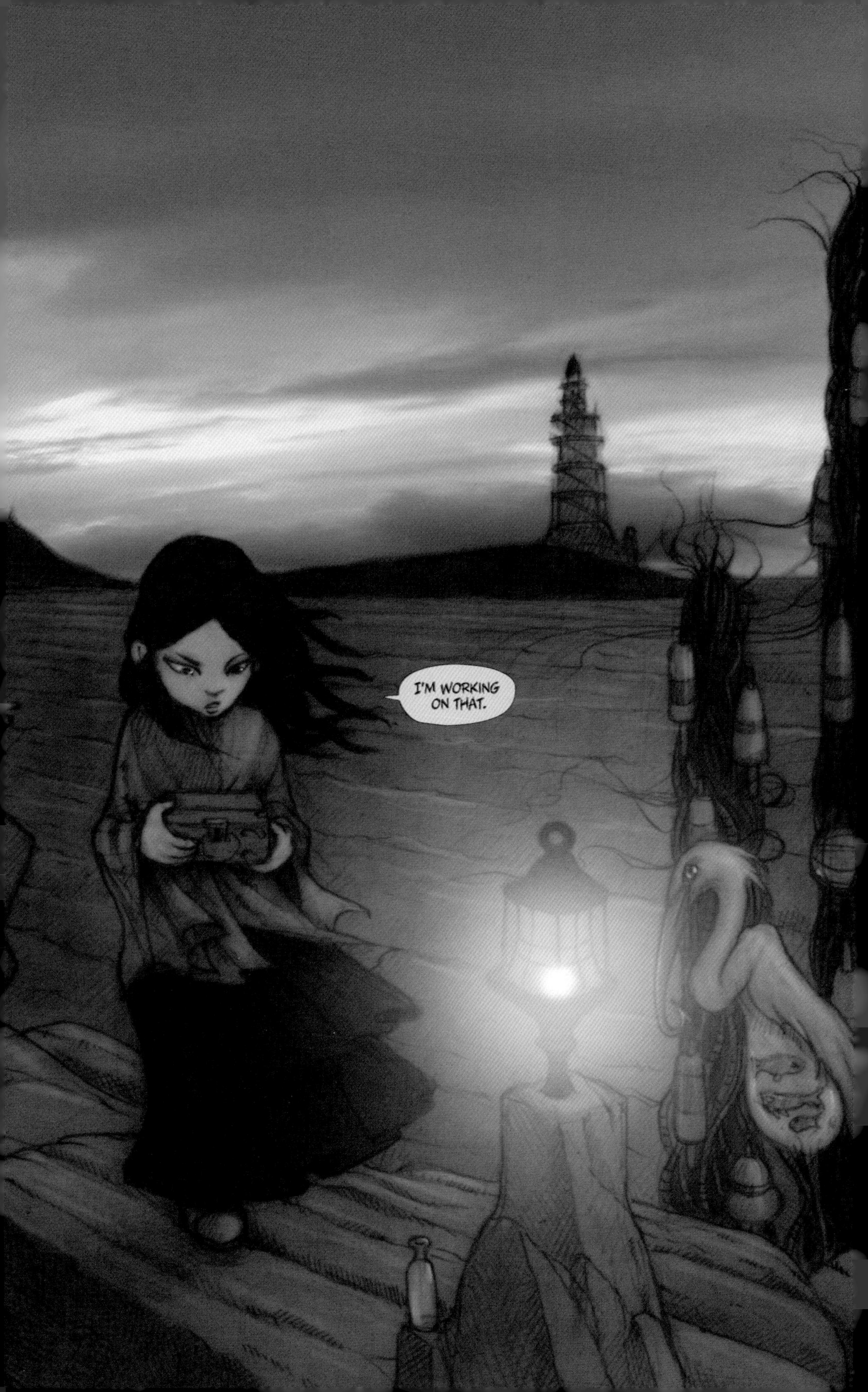
I'M WORKING ON THAT.

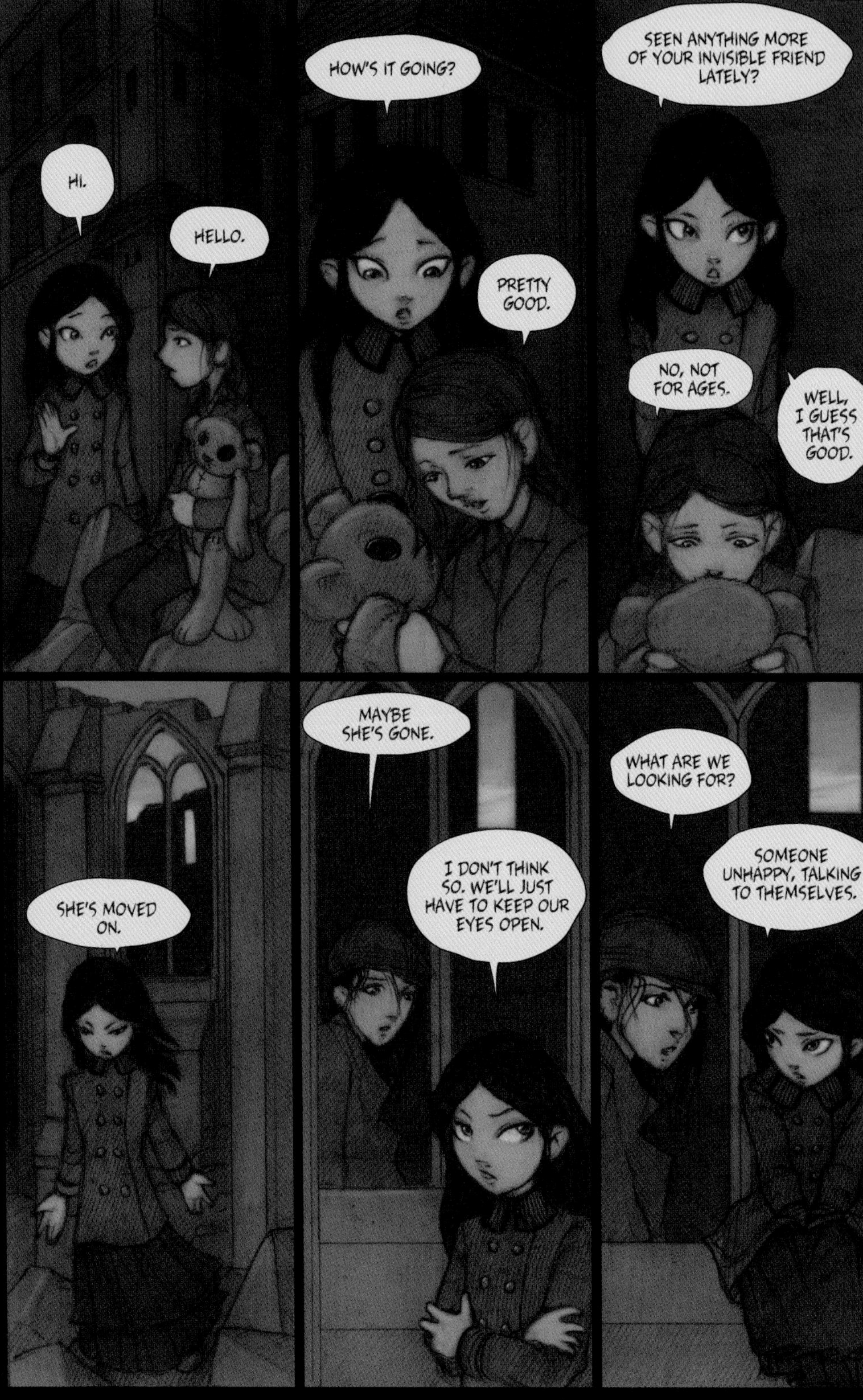
HI.
HELLO.
HOW'S IT GOING?
PRETTY GOOD.
SEEN ANYTHING MORE OF YOUR INVISIBLE FRIEND LATELY?
NO, NOT FOR AGES.
WELL, I GUESS THAT'S GOOD.
SHE'S MOVED ON.
MAYBE SHE'S GONE.
I DON'T THINK SO. WE'LL JUST HAVE TO KEEP OUR EYES OPEN.
WHAT ARE WE LOOKING FOR?
SOMEONE UNHAPPY, TALKING TO THEMSELVES.

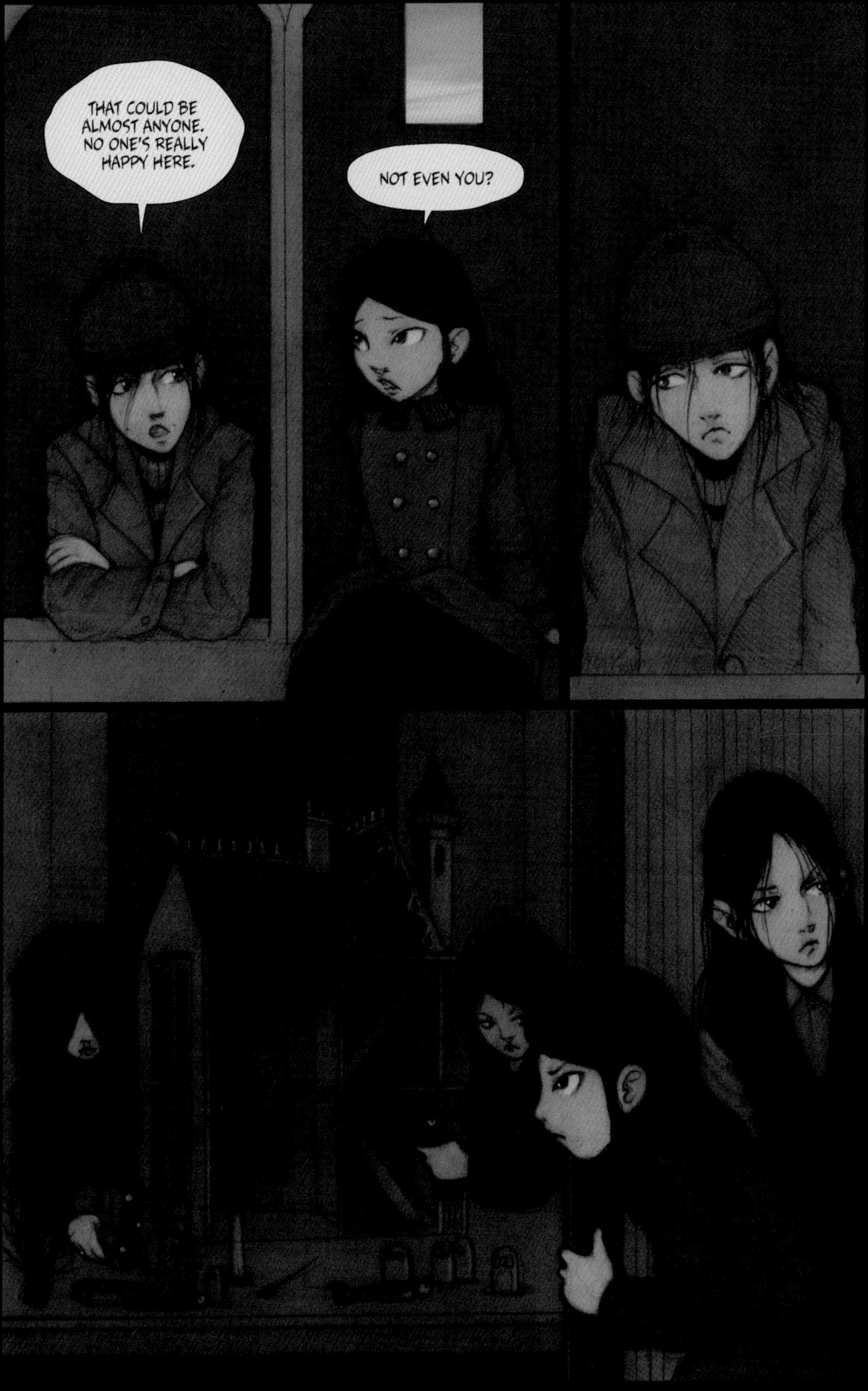
THAT COULD BE ALMOST ANYONE. NO ONE'S REALLY HAPPY HERE.
NOT EVEN YOU?

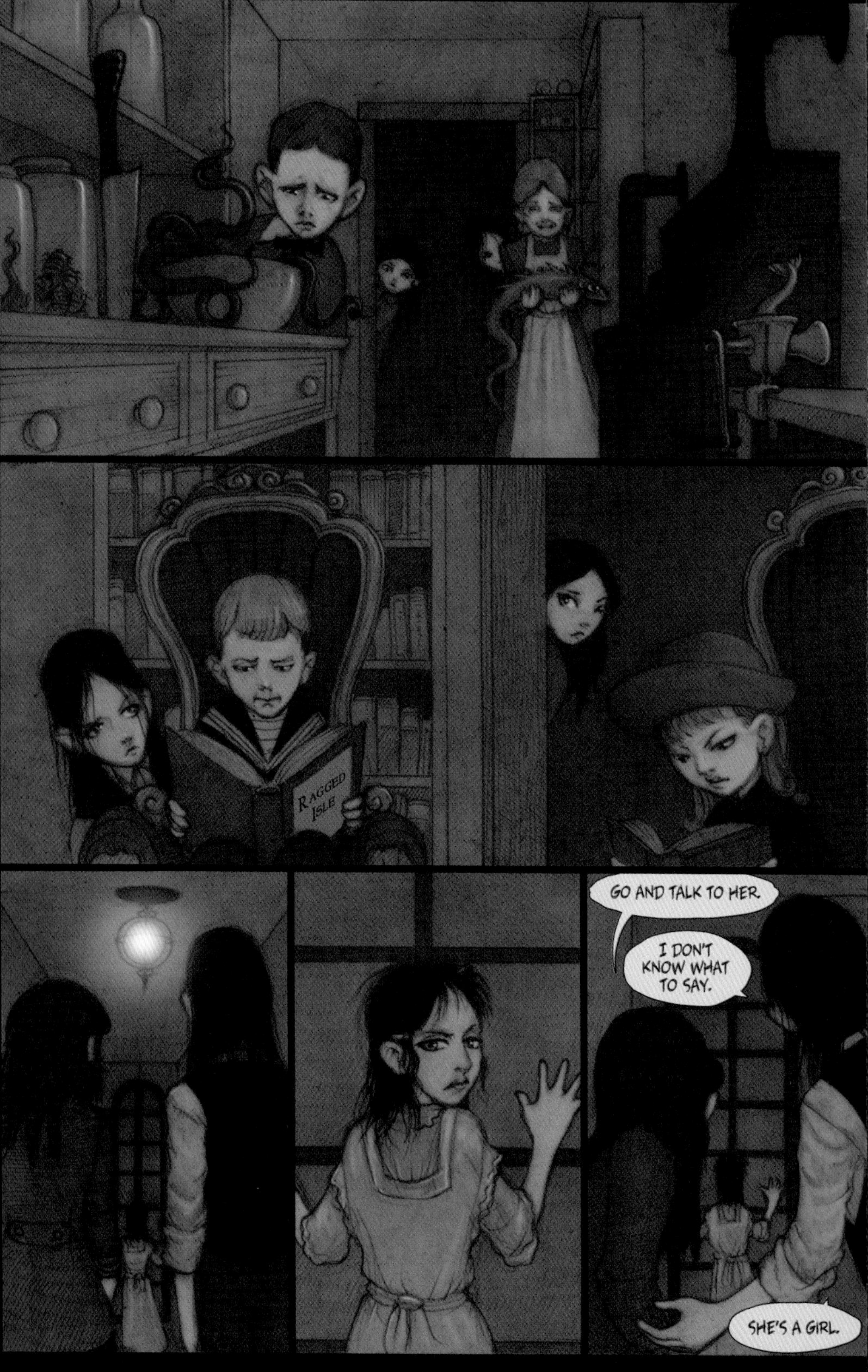
RAGGED ISLE
GO AND TALK TO HER.
I DON'T KNOW WHAT TO SAY.
SHE'S A GIRL.

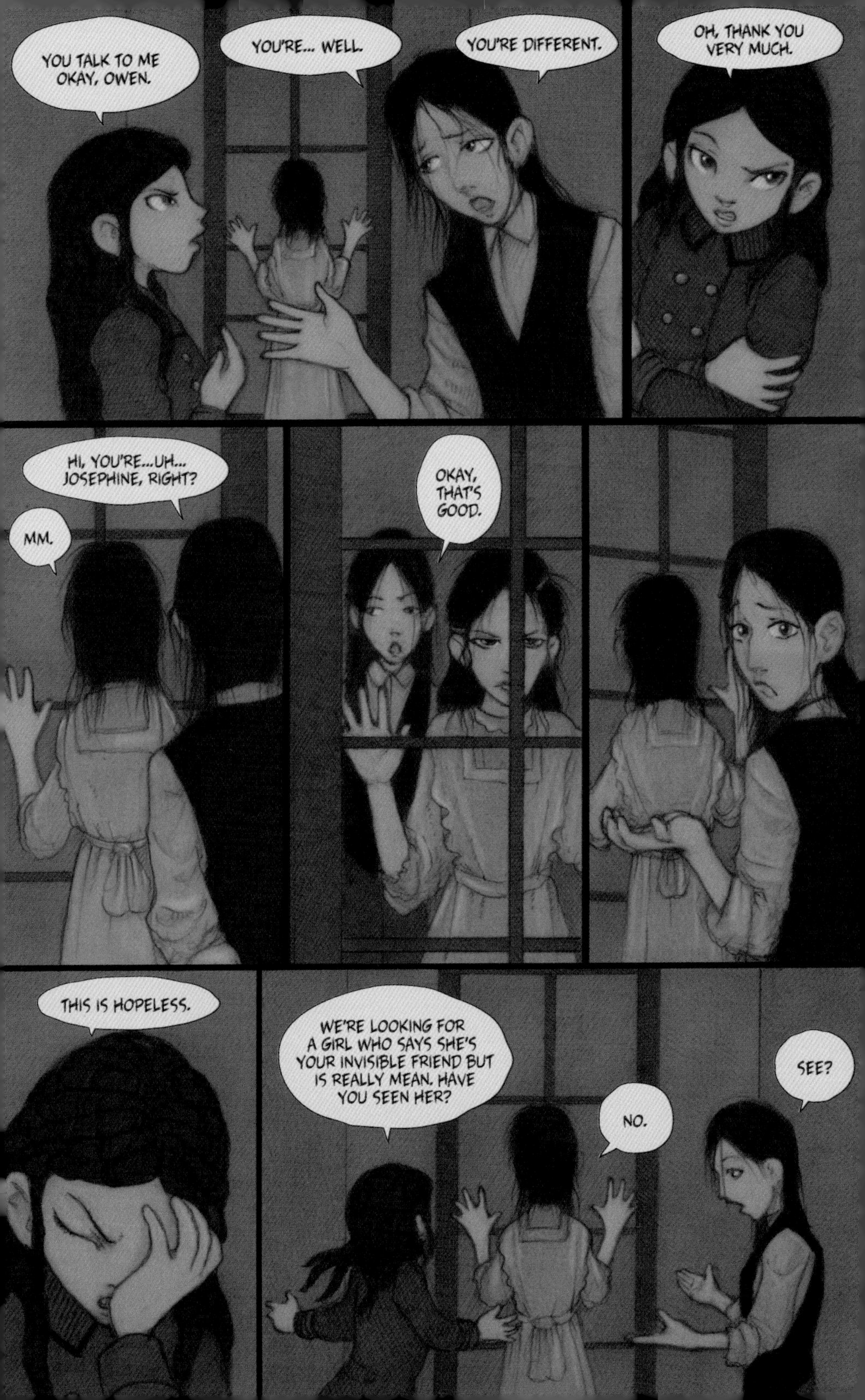
YOU TALK TO ME OKAY, OWEN.
YOU'RE... WELL.
YOU'RE DIFFERENT.
OH, THANK YOU VERY MUCH.
HI, YOU'RE...UH... JOSEPHINE, RIGHT?
MM.
OKAY, THAT'S GOOD.
THIS IS HOPELESS.
WE'RE LOOKING FOR A GIRL WHO SAYS SHE'S YOUR INVISIBLE FRIEND BUT IS REALLY MEAN. HAVE YOU SEEN HER?
NO.
SEE?

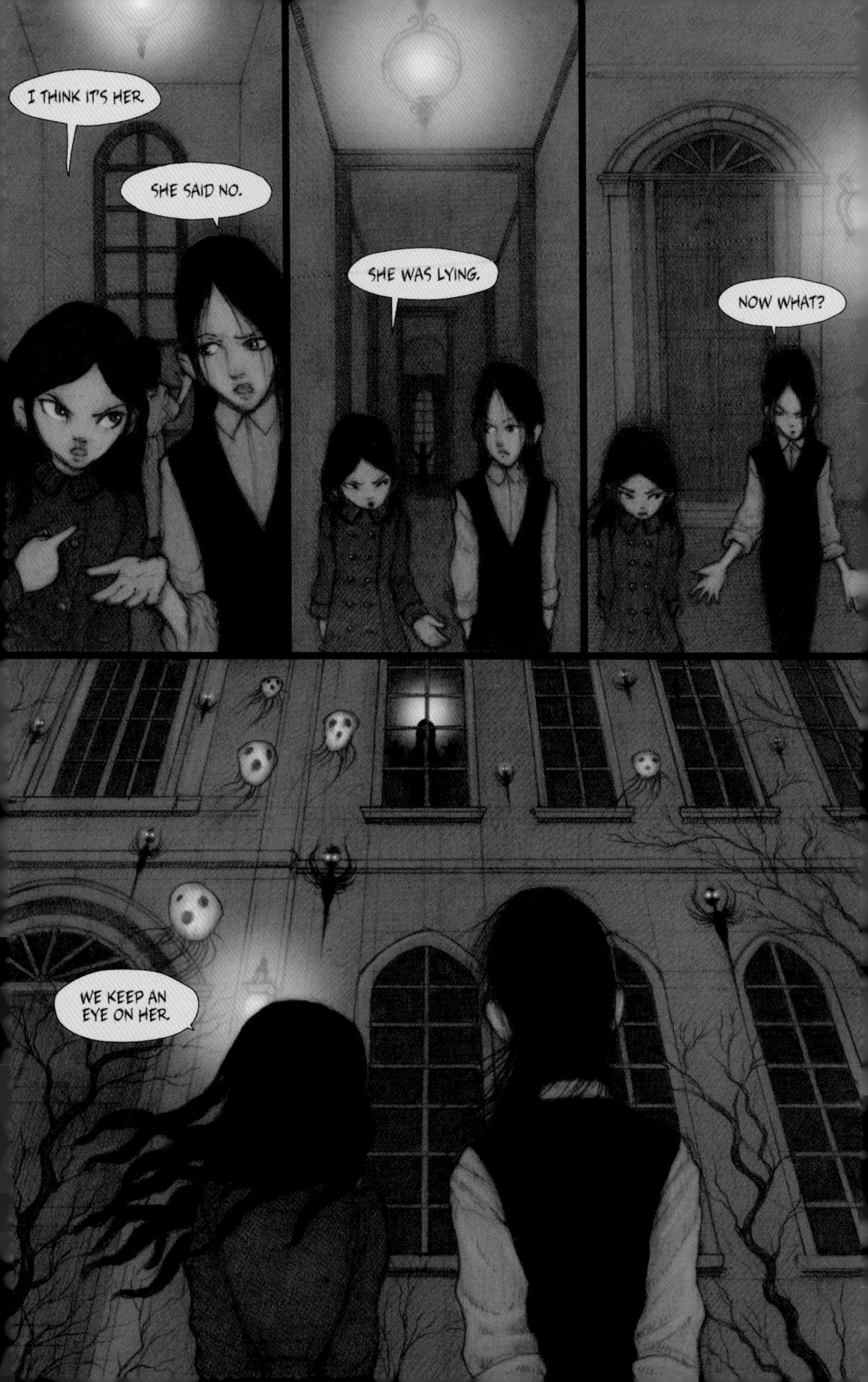
I THINK IT'S HER.
SHE SAID NO.
SHE WAS LYING.
NOW WHAT?
WE KEEP AN EYE ON HER.

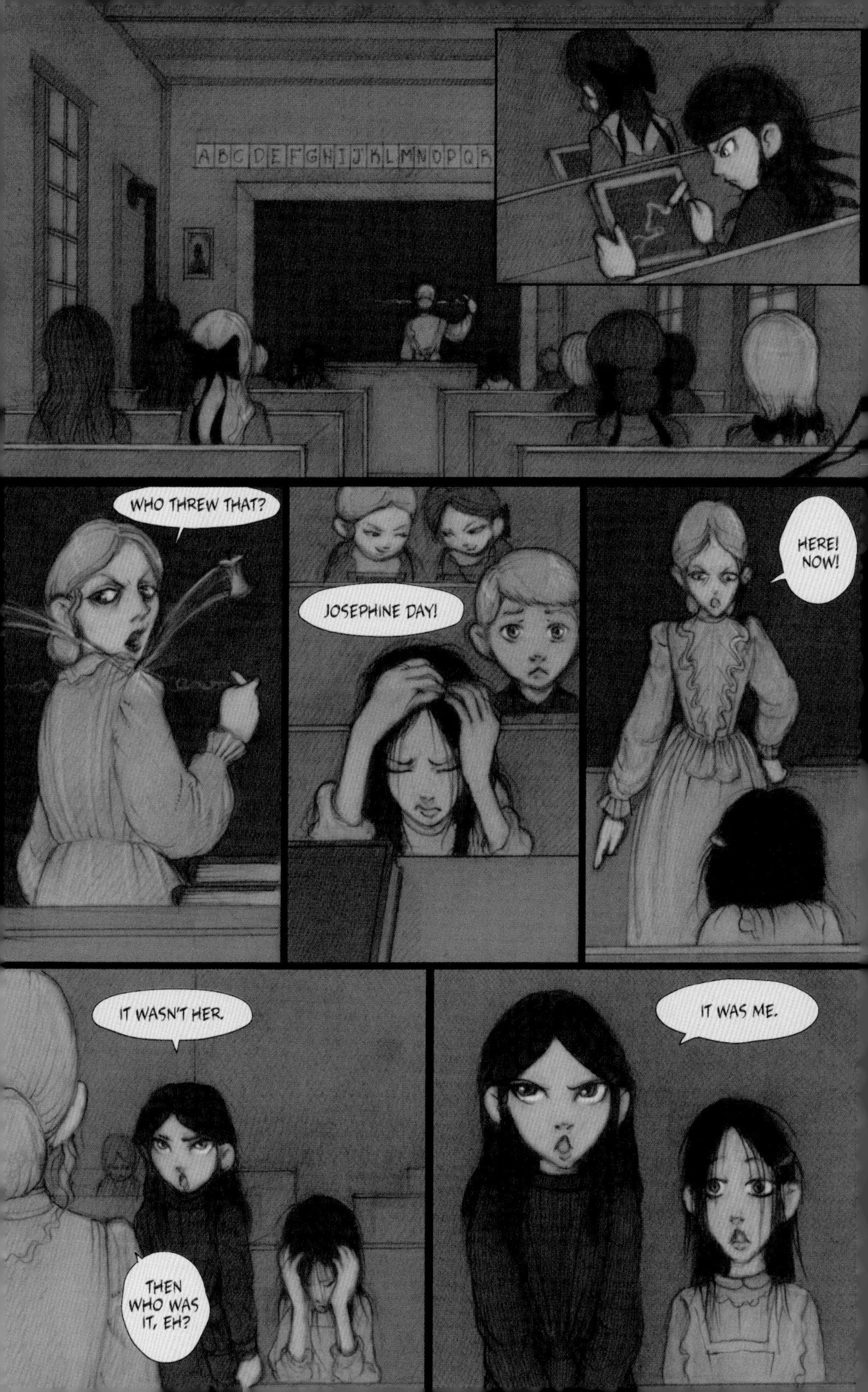
WHO THREW THAT?
JOSEPHINE DAY!
HERE! NOW!
IT WASN'T HER.
THEN WHO WAS IT, EH?
IT WAS ME.

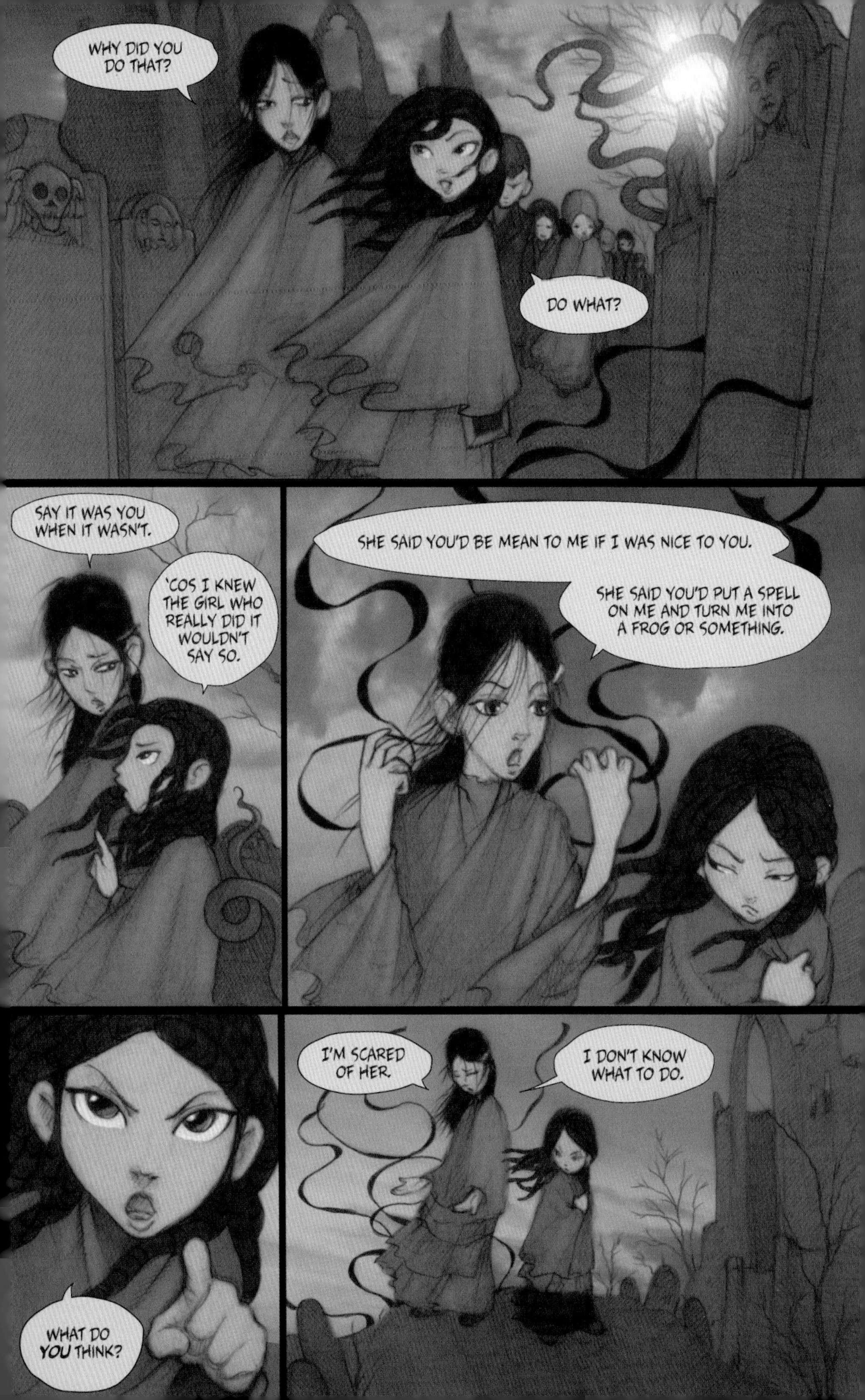
WHY DID YOU DO THAT?
DO WHAT?
SAY IT WAS YOU WHEN IT WASN'T.
'COS I KNEW THE GIRL WHO REALLY DID IT WOULDN'T SAY SO.
SHE SAID YOU'D BE MEAN TO ME IF I WAS NICE TO YOU.
SHE SAID YOU'D PUT A SPELL ON ME AND TURN ME INTO A FROG OR SOMETHING.
WHAT DO **YOU** THINK?
I'M SCARED OF HER.
I DON'T KNOW WHAT TO DO.

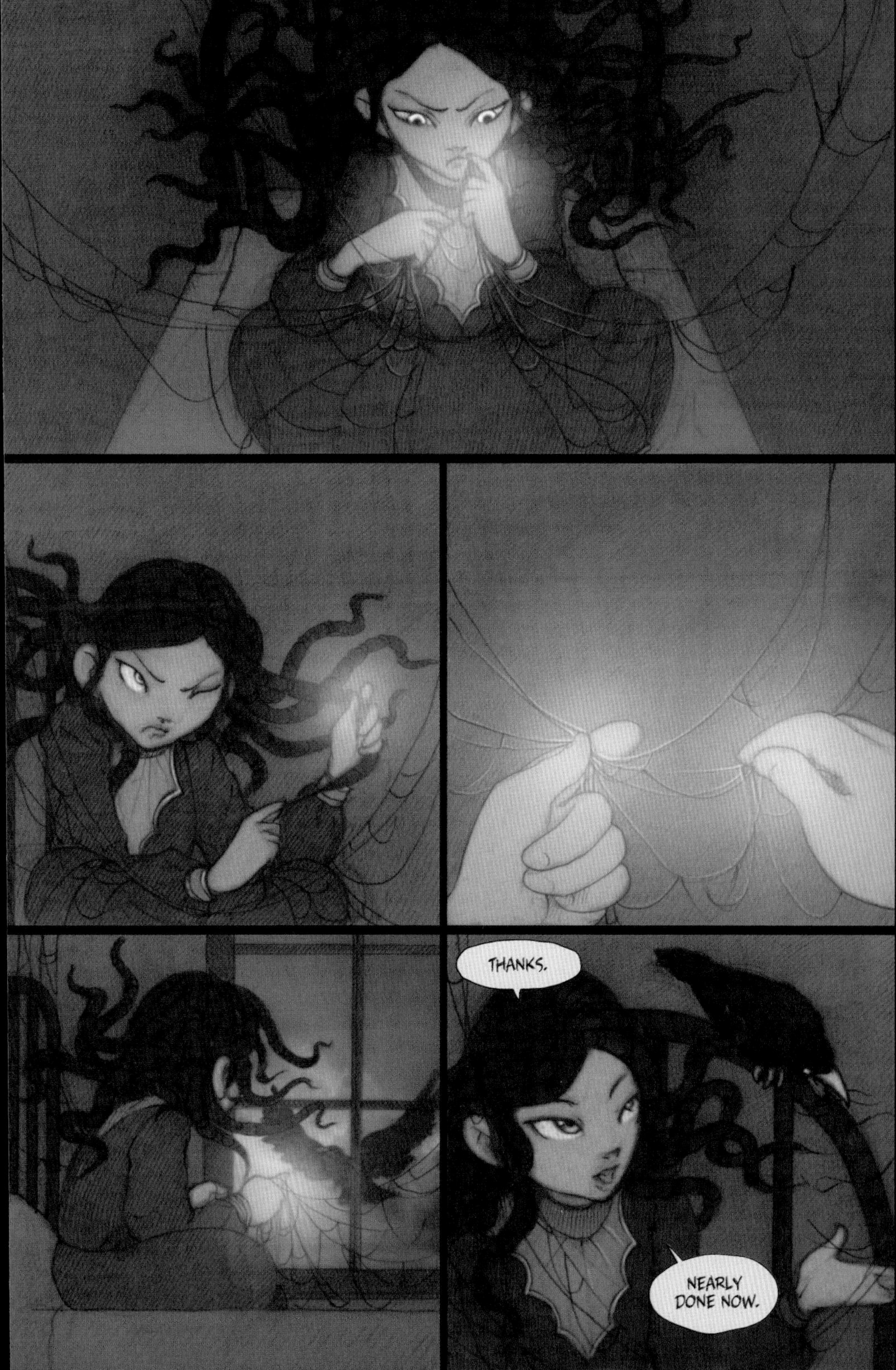
THANKS.
NEARLY DONE NOW.

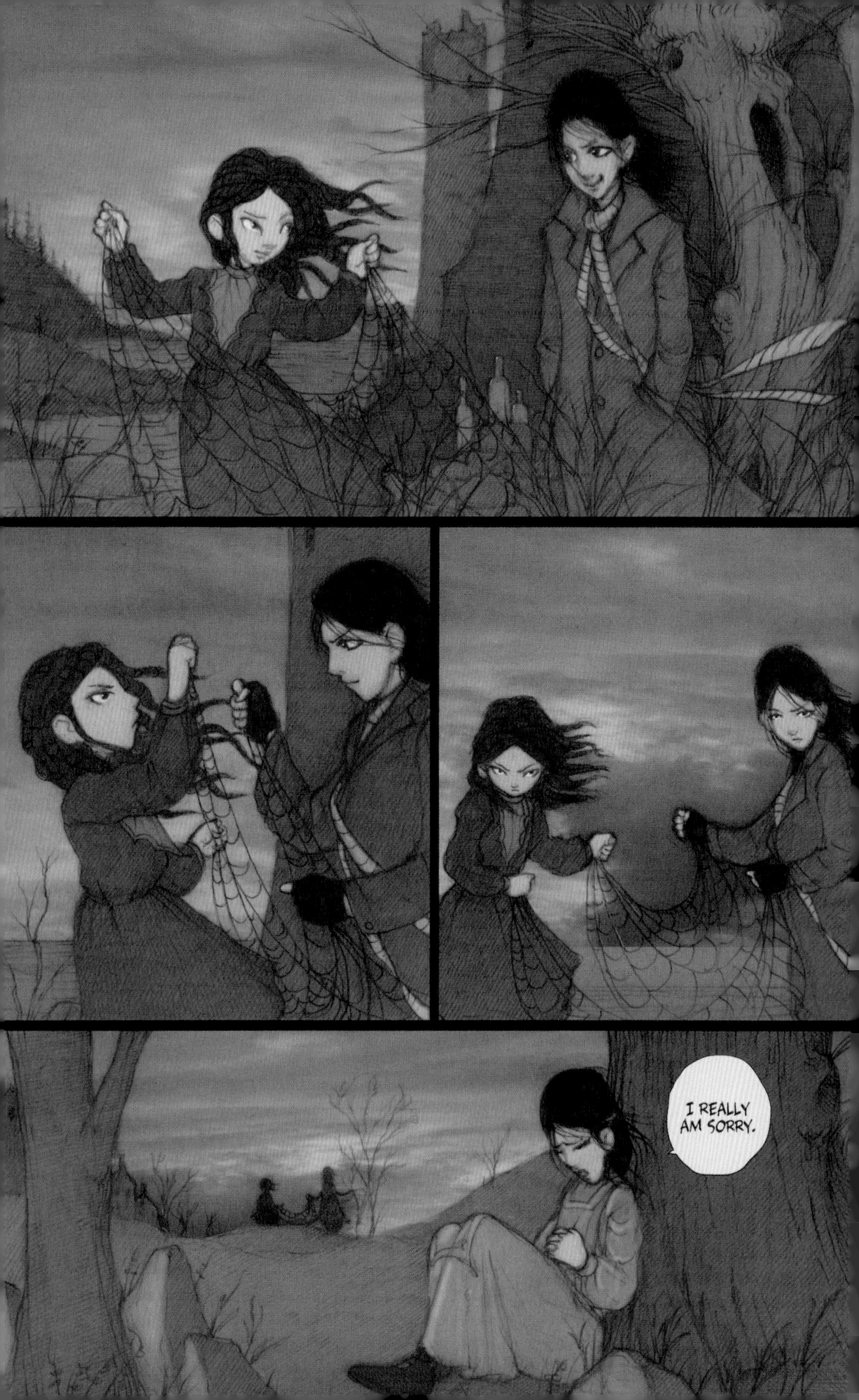
I REALLY AM SORRY.

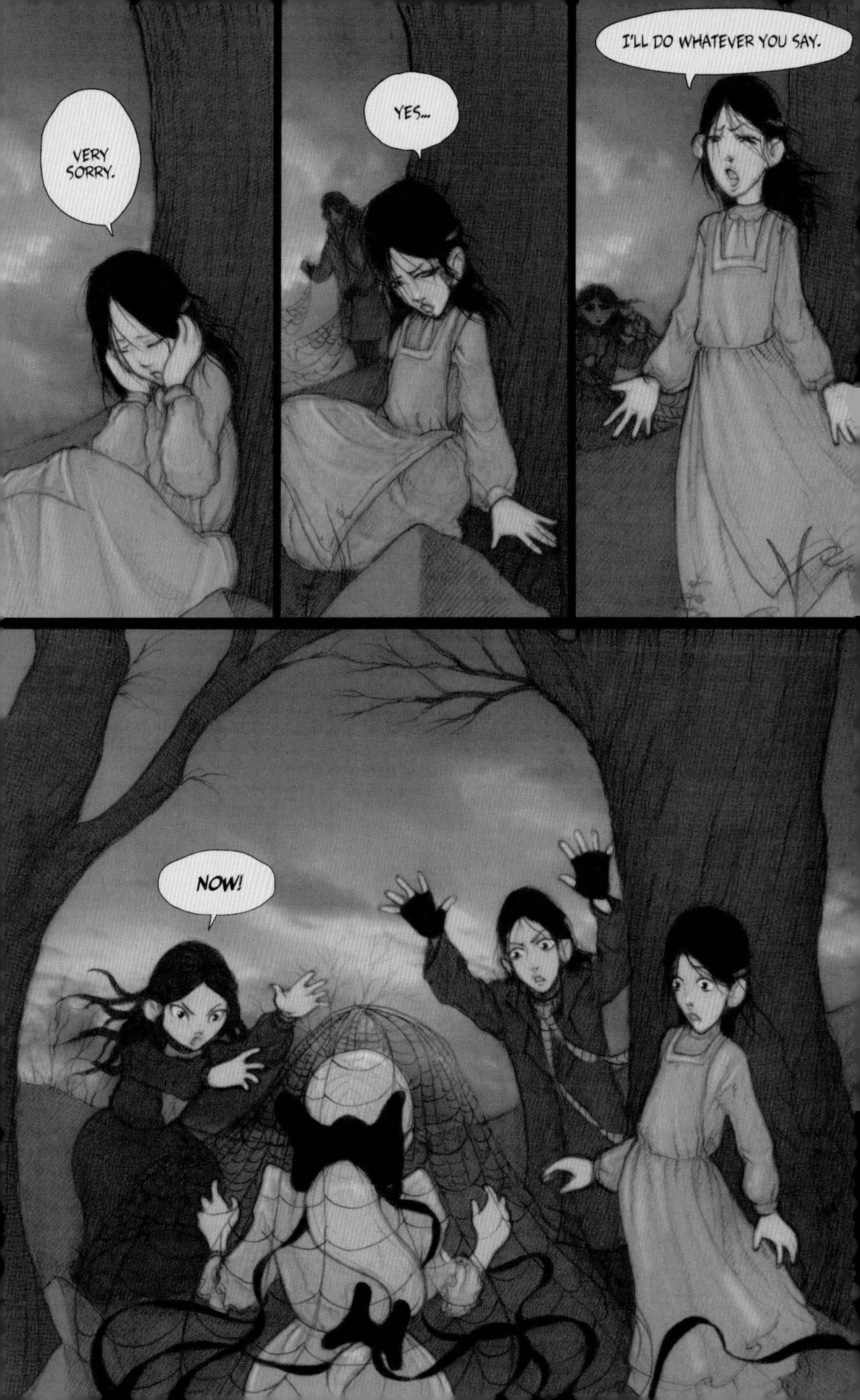
VERY SORRY.
YES...
I'LL DO WHATEVER YOU SAY.
NOW!

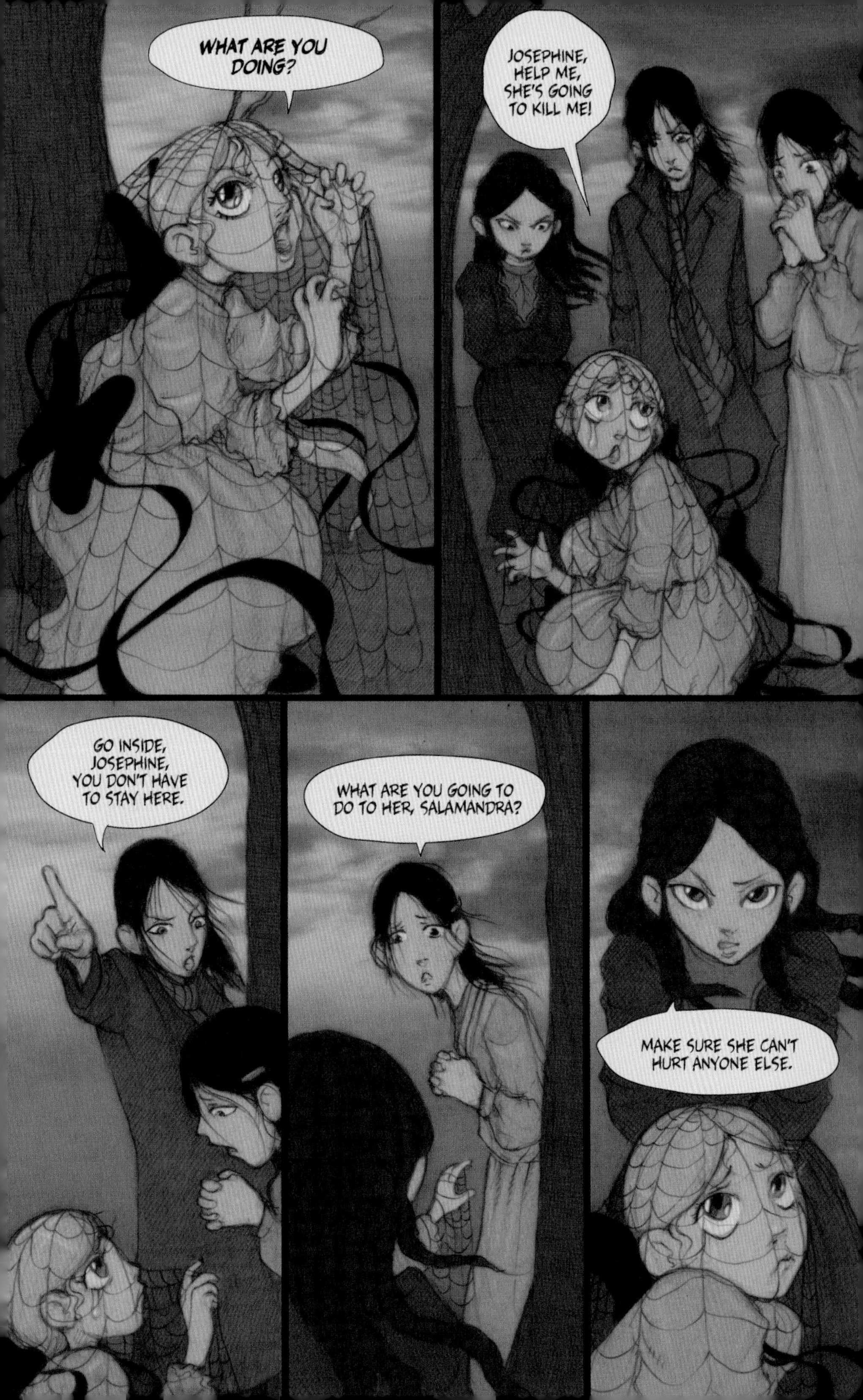
WHAT ARE YOU DOING?
JOSEPHINE, HELP ME, SHE'S GOING TO KILL ME!
GO INSIDE, JOSEPHINE, YOU DON'T HAVE TO STAY HERE.
WHAT ARE YOU GOING TO DO TO HER, SALAMANDRA?
MAKE SURE SHE CAN'T HURT ANYONE ELSE.

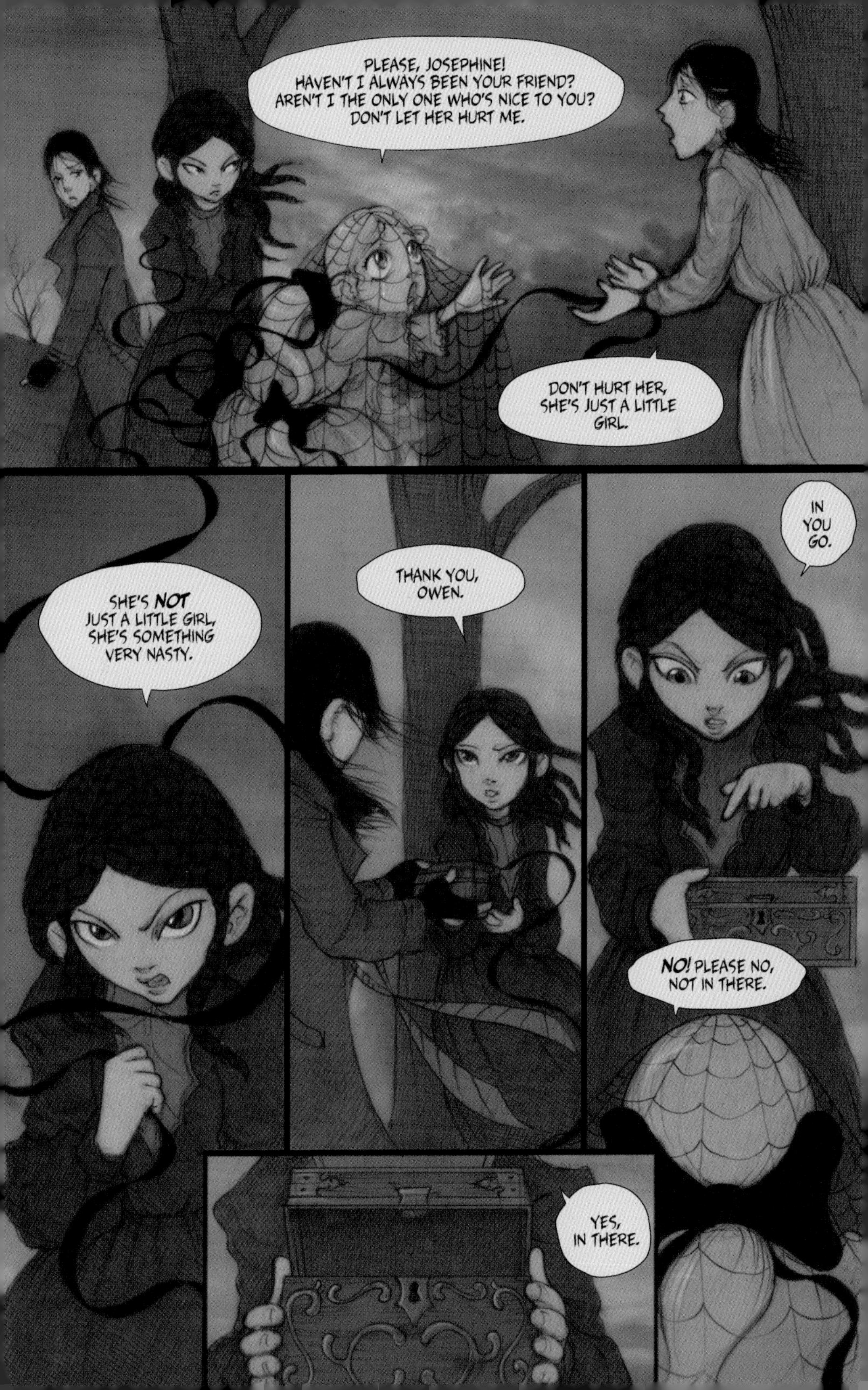
PLEASE, JOSEPHINE! HAVEN'T I ALWAYS BEEN YOUR FRIEND? AREN'T I THE ONLY ONE WHO'S NICE TO YOU? DON'T LET HER HURT ME.
DON'T HURT HER, SHE'S JUST A LITTLE GIRL.
SHE'S **NOT** JUST A LITTLE GIRL, SHE'S SOMETHING VERY NASTY.
THANK YOU, OWEN.
IN YOU GO.
NO! PLEASE NO, NOT IN THERE.
YES, IN THERE.

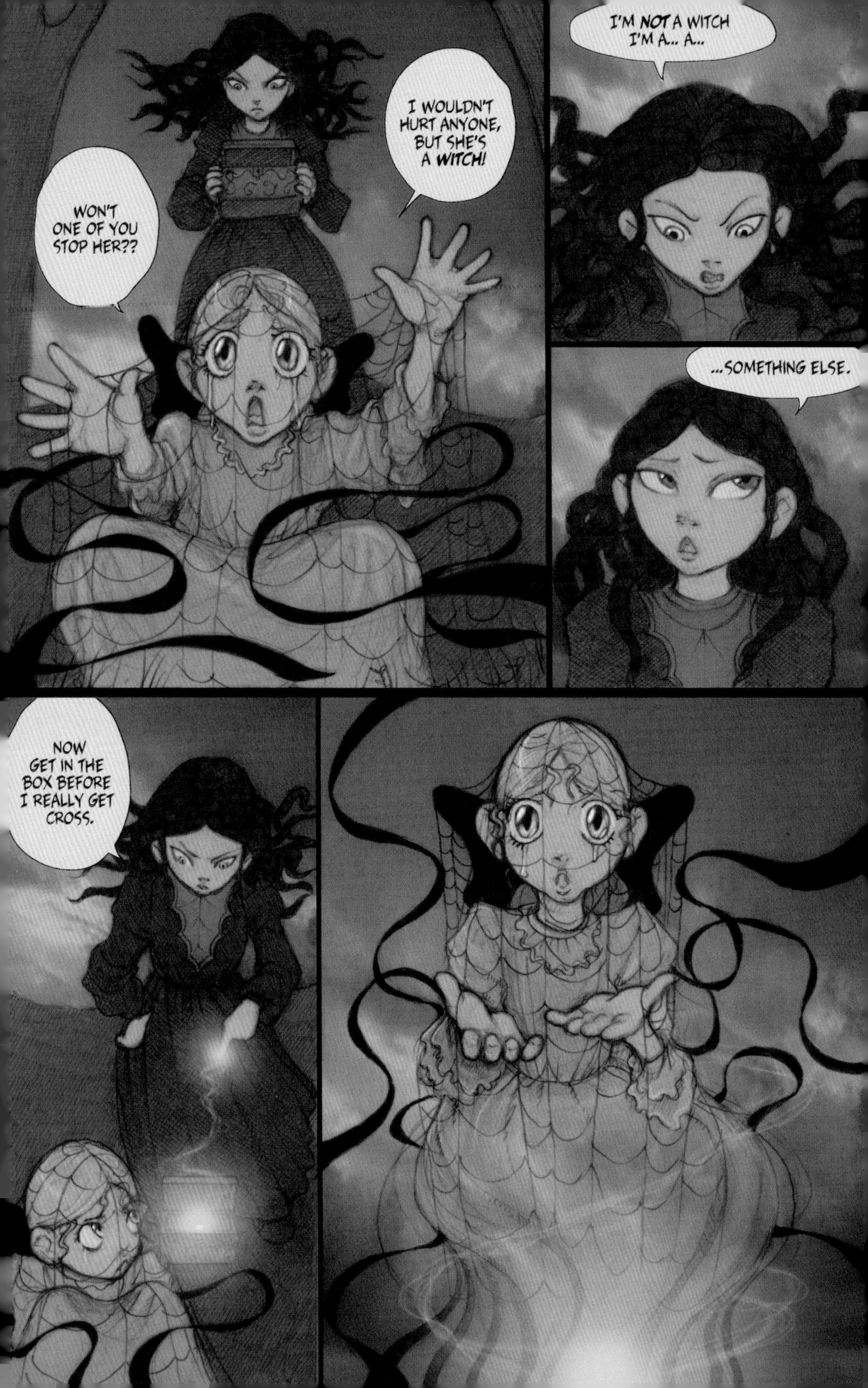
WON'T ONE OF YOU STOP HER??
I WOULDN'T HURT ANYONE, BUT SHE'S A **WITCH**!
I'M **NOT** A WITCH I'M A... A...
...SOMETHING ELSE.
NOW GET IN THE BOX BEFORE I REALLY GET CROSS.

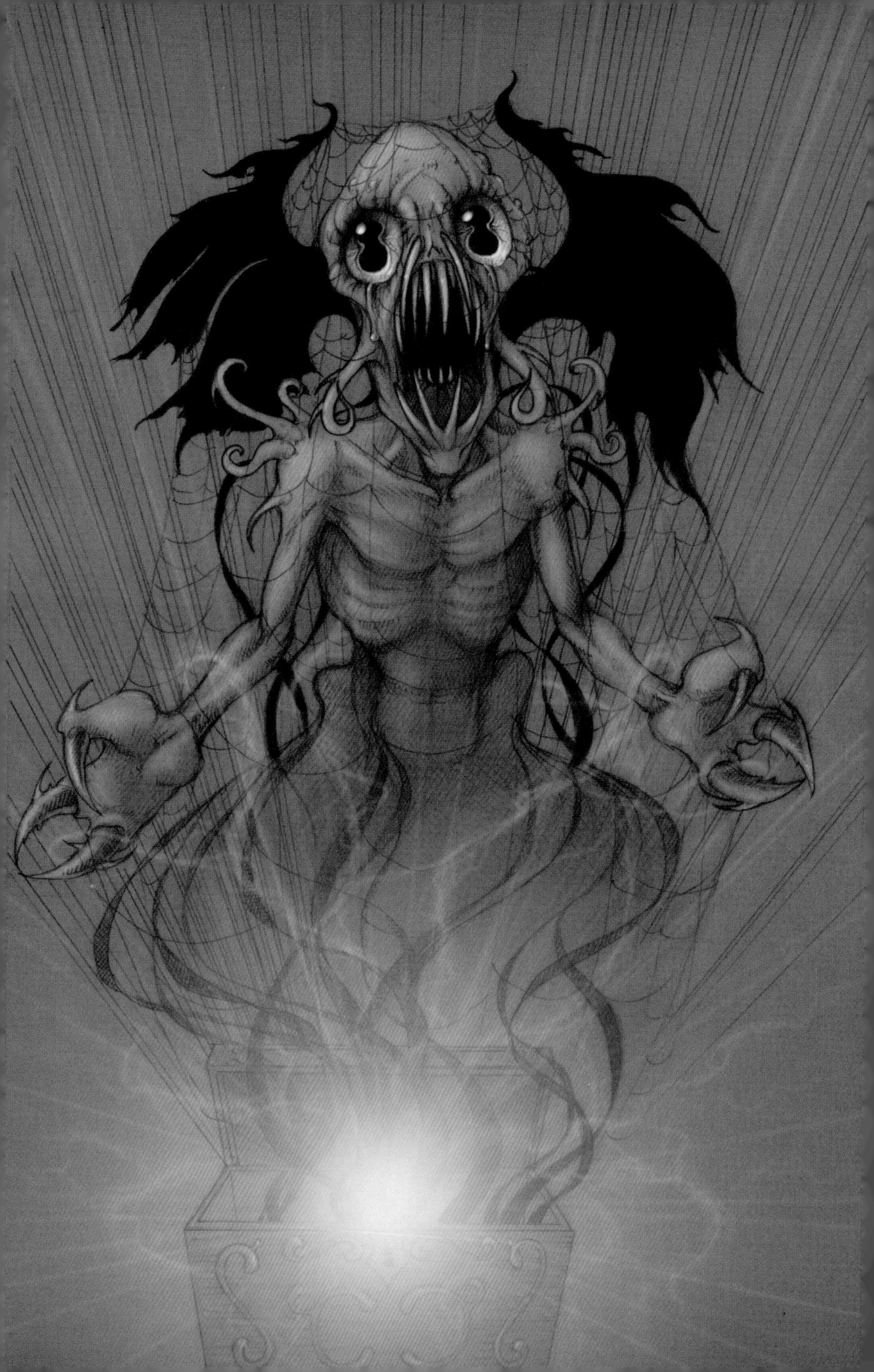

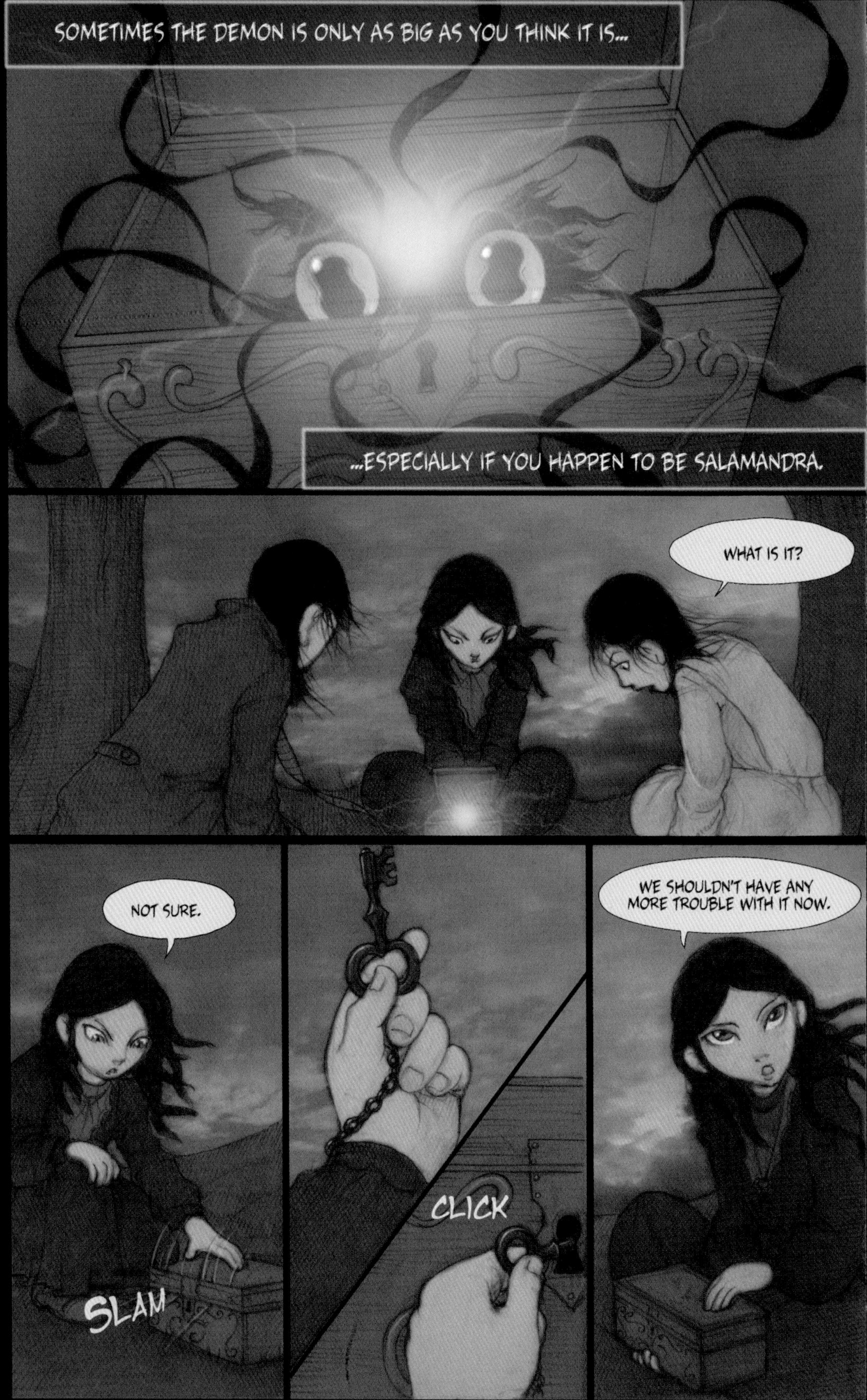
SOMETIMES THE DEMON IS ONLY AS BIG AS YOU THINK IT IS...
...ESPECIALLY IF YOU HAPPEN TO BE SALAMANDRA.
WHAT IS IT?
NOT SURE.
SLAM
CLICK
WE SHOULDN'T HAVE ANY MORE TROUBLE WITH IT NOW.

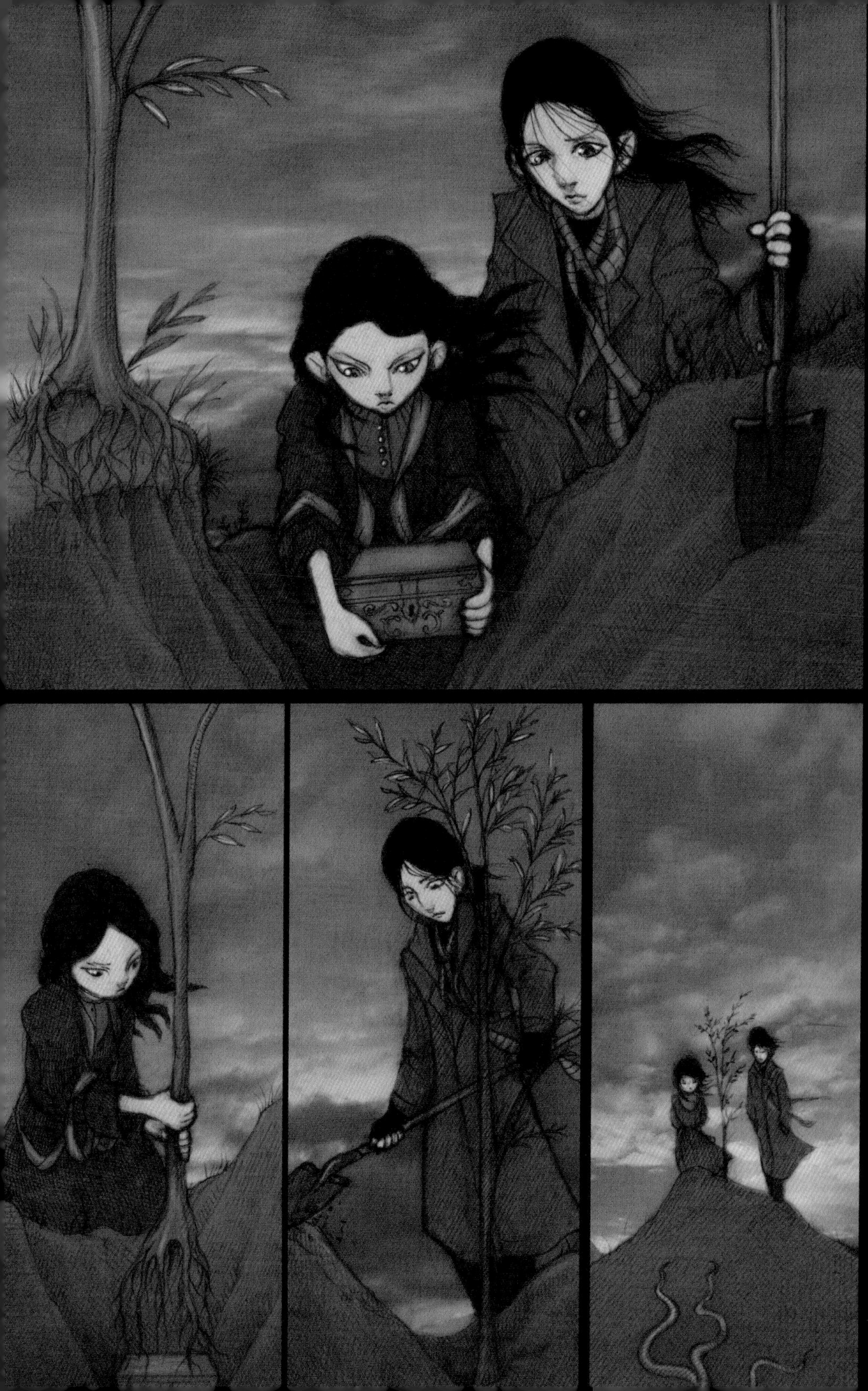

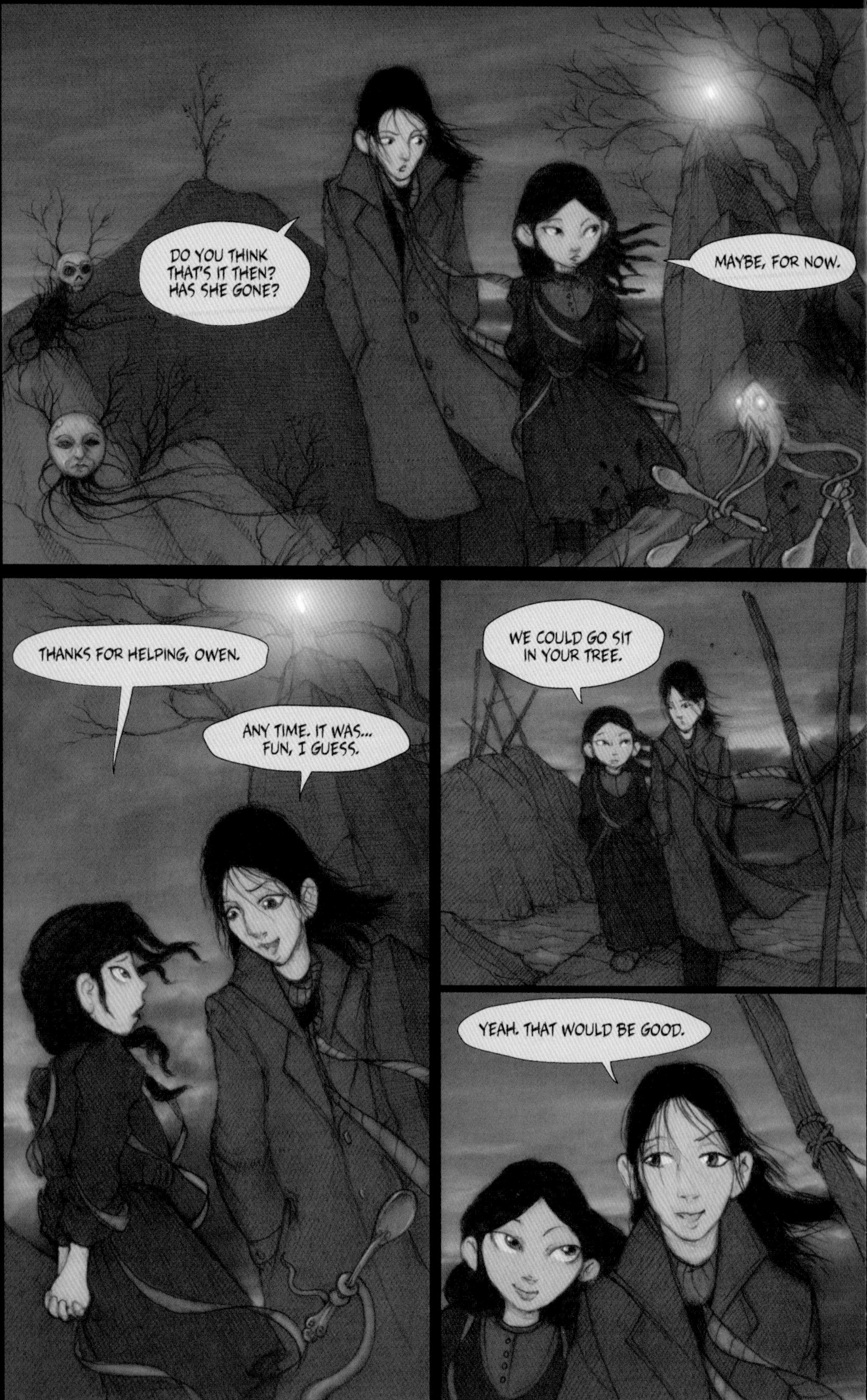
DO YOU THINK THAT'S IT THEN? HAS SHE GONE?
MAYBE, FOR NOW.
THANKS FOR HELPING, OWEN.
ANY TIME. IT WAS... FUN, I GUESS.
WE COULD GO SIT IN YOUR TREE.
YEAH. THAT WOULD BE GOOD.

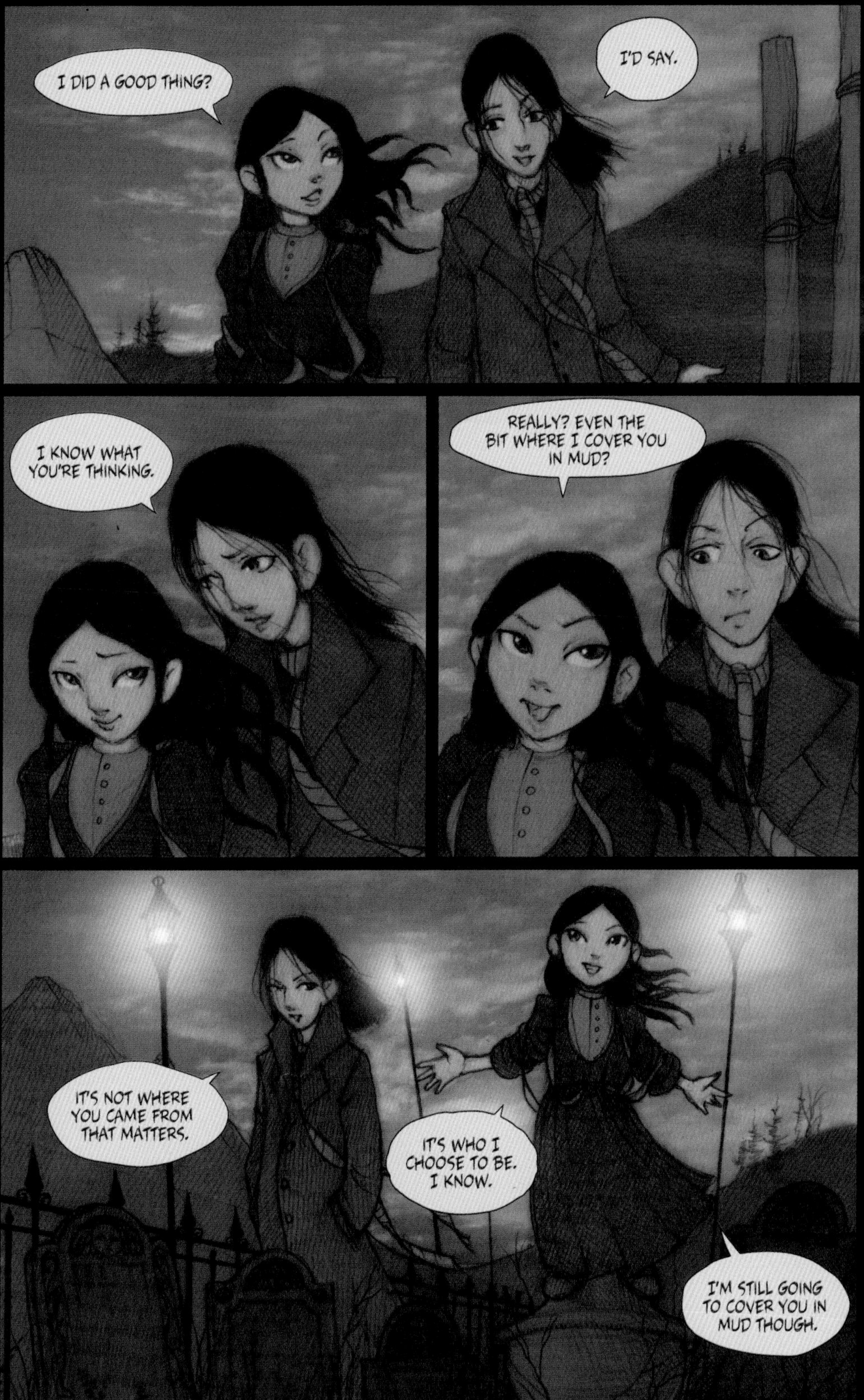
I DID A GOOD THING?
I'D SAY.
I KNOW WHAT YOU'RE THINKING.
REALLY? EVEN THE BIT WHERE I COVER YOU IN MUD?
IT'S NOT WHERE YOU CAME FROM THAT MATTERS.
IT'S WHO I CHOOSE TO BE. I KNOW.
I'M STILL GOING TO COVER YOU IN MUD THOUGH.

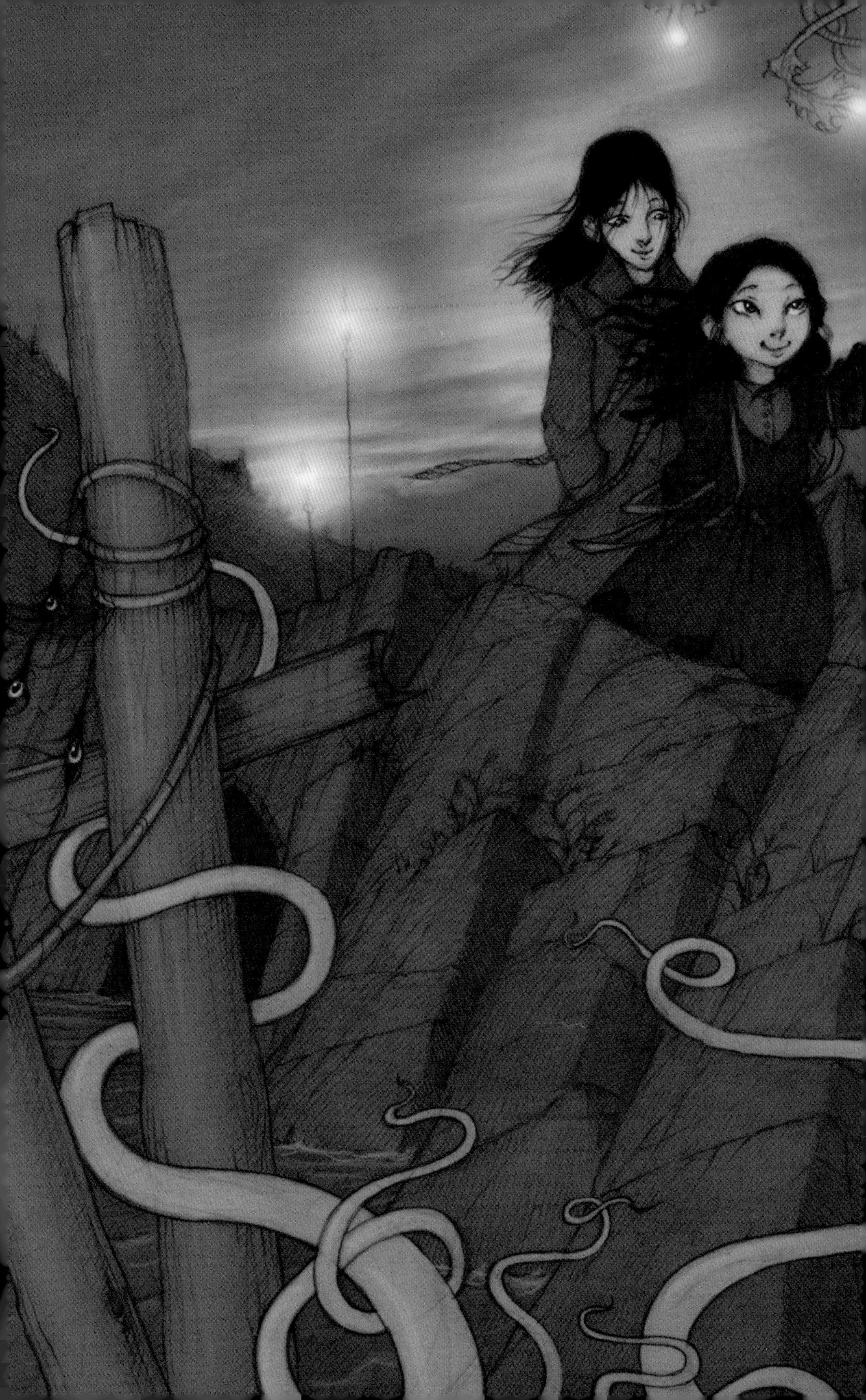

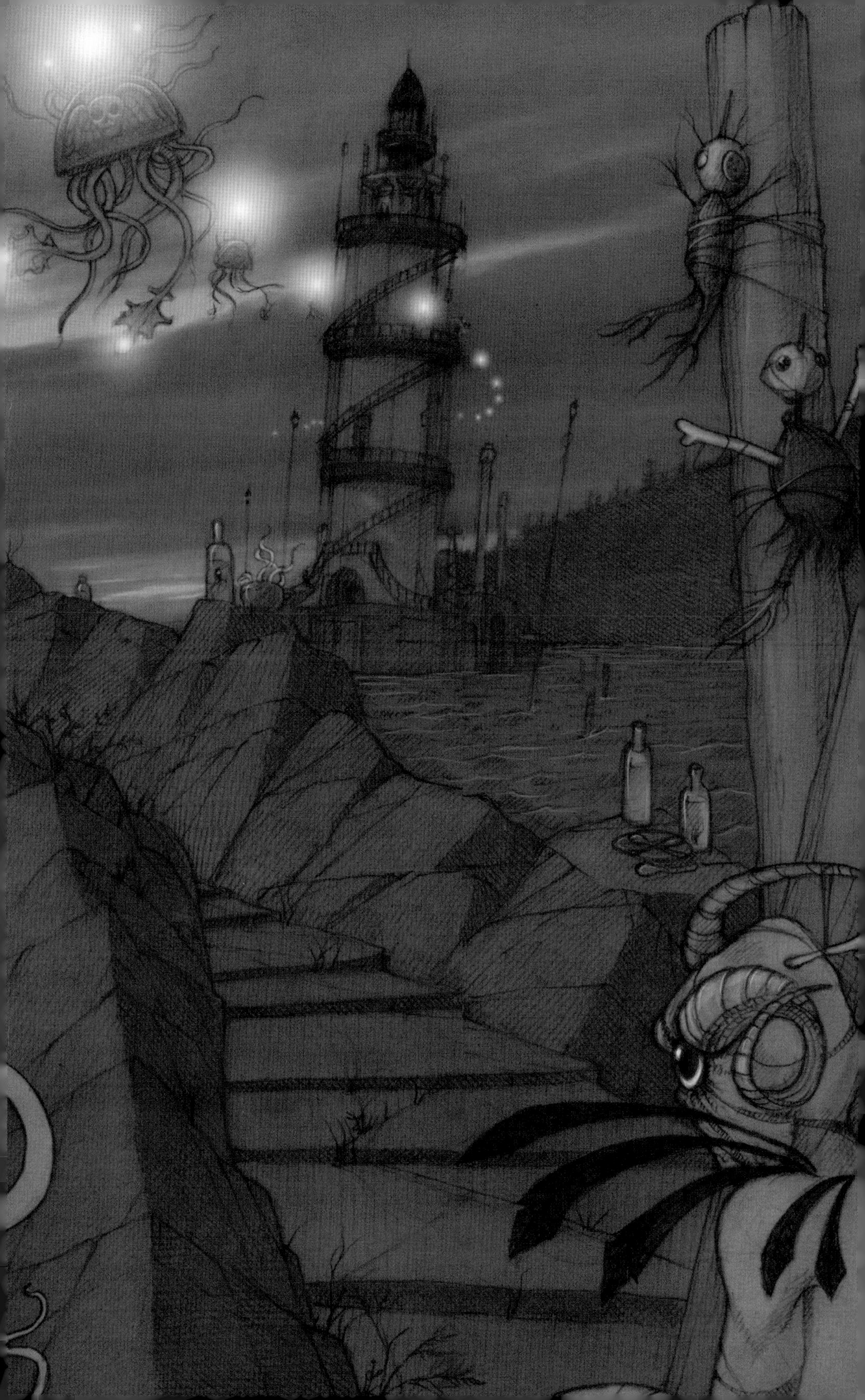

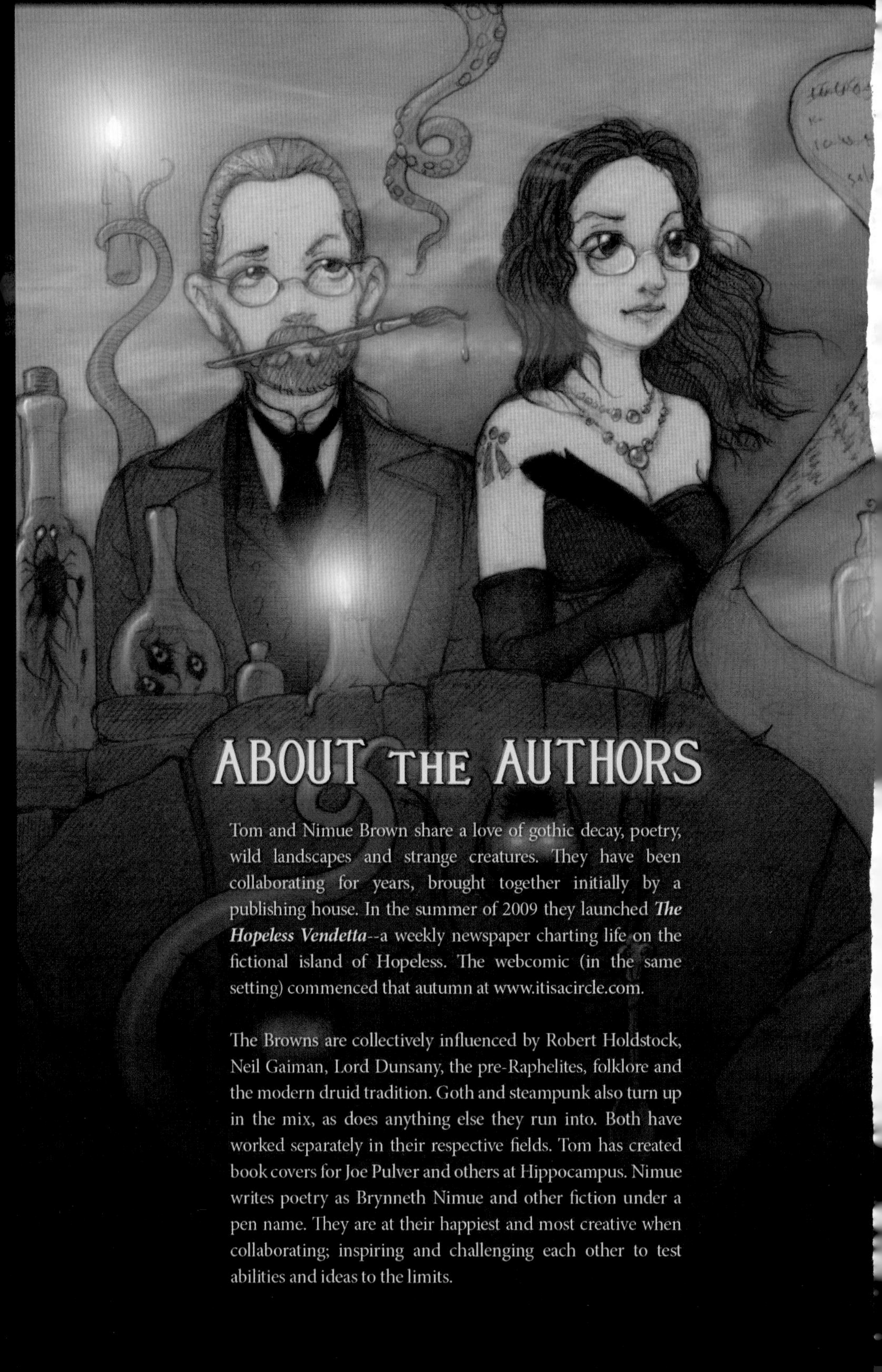

ABOUT THE AUTHORS

Tom and Nimue Brown share a love of gothic decay, poetry, wild landscapes and strange creatures. They have been collaborating for years, brought together initially by a publishing house. In the summer of 2009 they launched ***The Hopeless Vendetta***--a weekly newspaper charting life on the fictional island of Hopeless. The webcomic (in the same setting) commenced that autumn at www.itisacircle.com.

The Browns are collectively influenced by Robert Holdstock, Neil Gaiman, Lord Dunsany, the pre-Raphelites, folklore and the modern druid tradition. Goth and steampunk also turn up in the mix, as does anything else they run into. Both have worked separately in their respective fields. Tom has created book covers for Joe Pulver and others at Hippocampus. Nimue writes poetry as Brynneth Nimue and other fiction under a pen name. They are at their happiest and most creative when collaborating; inspiring and challenging each other to test abilities and ideas to the limits.

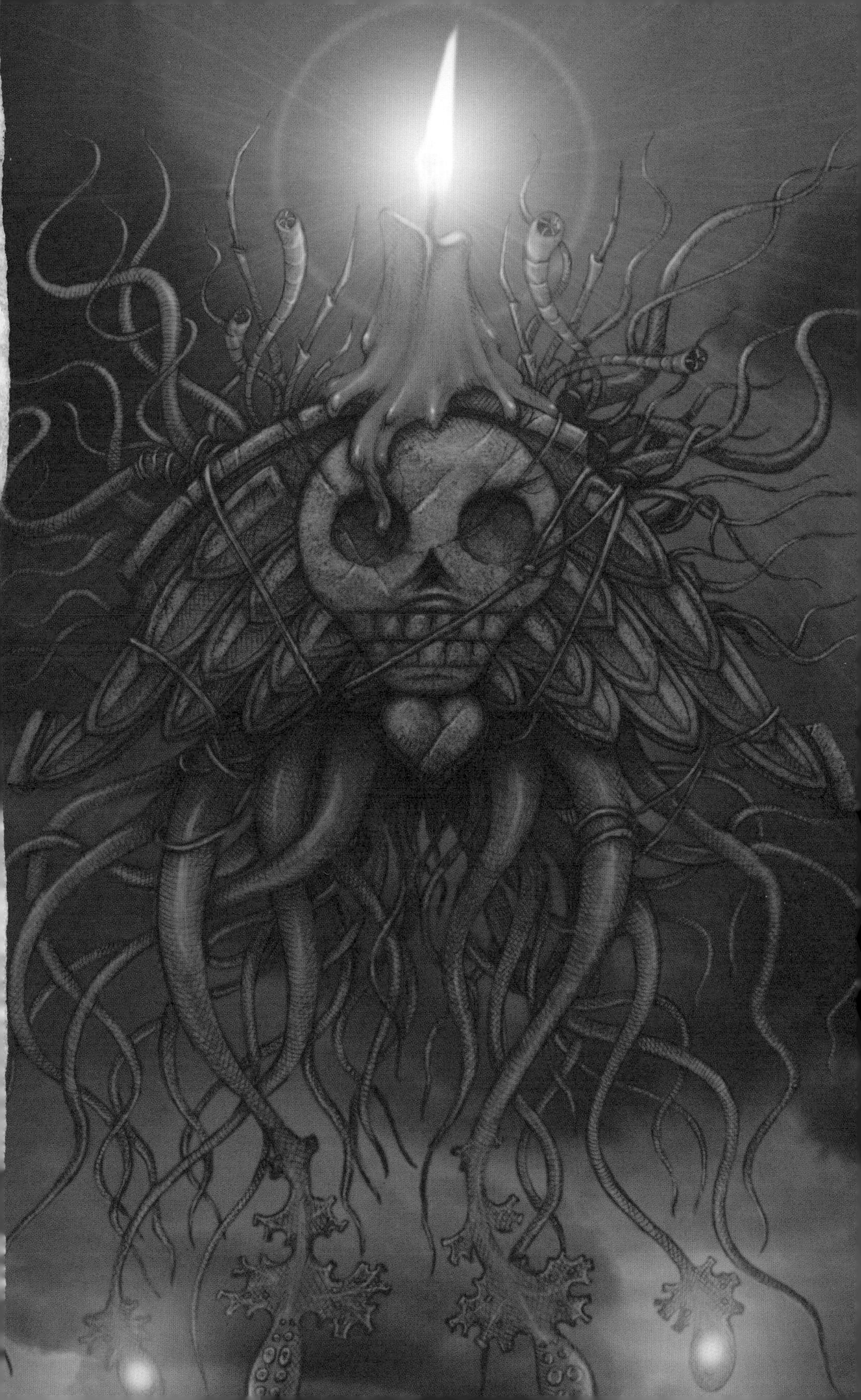

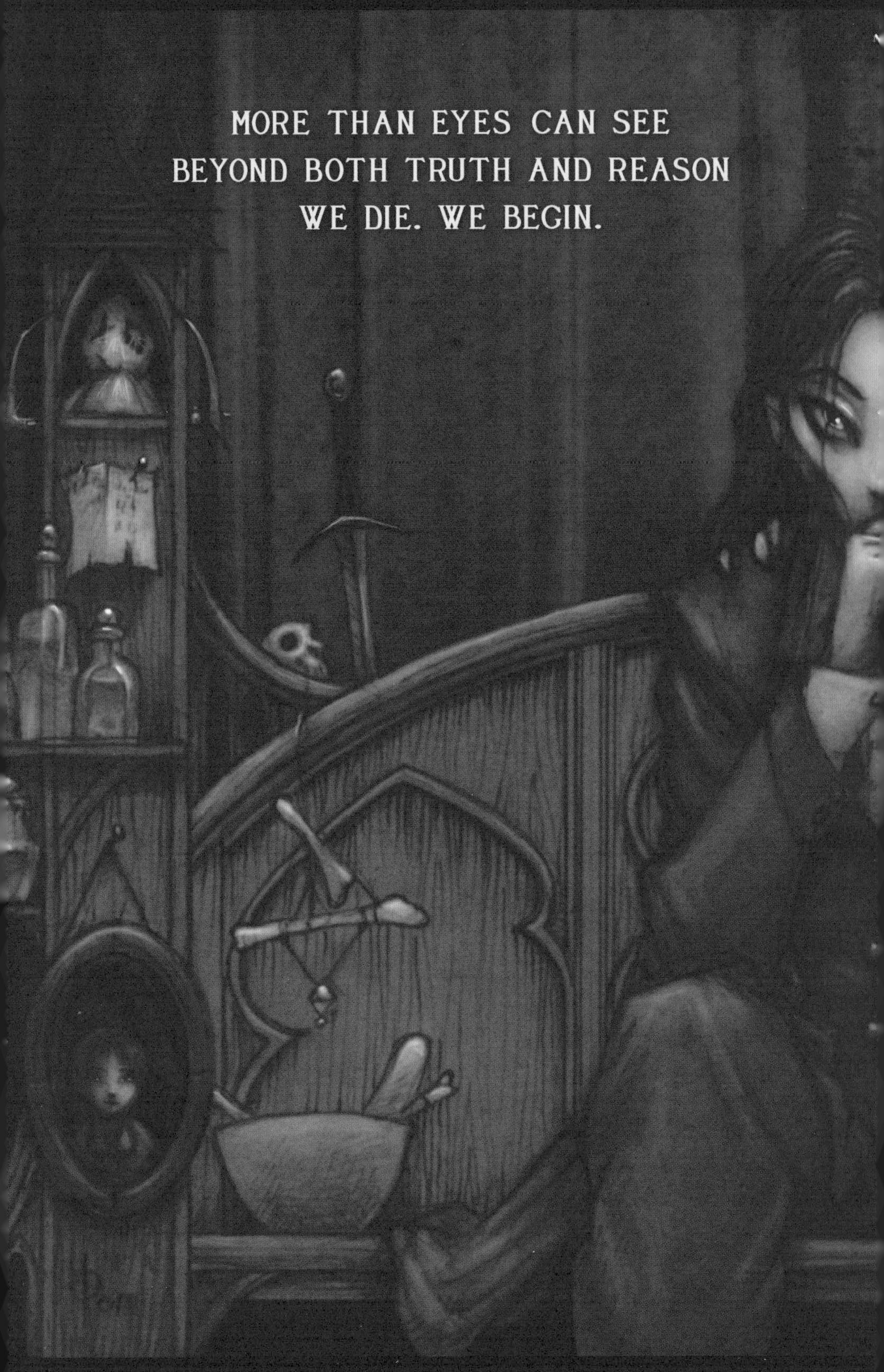
MORE THAN EYES CAN SEE
BEYOND BOTH TRUTH AND REASON
WE DIE. WE BEGIN.